ARMINIUS VAMBERY

faithfully yours

A. Vambéry

ARMINIUS VAMBERY

HIS LIFE AND ADVENTURES

WRITTEN BY HIMSELF

WITH PORTRAIT AND ILLUSTRATIONS

GYAN

Published by

GYAN

Gyan Publishing House
5, Ansari Road
Daryaganj, New Delhi-110002
Phone: 011-47034999, 9811692060
E-mail: books@gyanbooks.com

Distribution Network
gyanbooks.com
India, USA, Canada, UK, Australia, France

ISBN : 978-81-212-3705-5 (PB)
First Published, 1884

2nd Impression 2020

Printed at: Gyan Press, Delhi.

Author: Arminius Vambery

ARMINIUS VAMBÉRY

HIS LIFE AND ADVENTURES

WRITTEN BY HIMSELF

With Portrait and Illustrations

LONDON
T. FISHER UNWIN
26, PATERNOSTER SQUARE
1884

PREFATORY NOTE.

THE following pages contain a strictly personal narrative of my Travels and Adventures in Asia and in Europe. They make no pretence whatever to be a geographical and ethnological description of the actual Central Asia. Upon these points recent works have greatly added to the knowledge we possessed twenty years ago, when I performed my dangerous pilgrimage from Budapest to Samarkand. A *résumé* of the various publications of Russian, English, French and German travellers in this region would have formed a separate book, but these have nothing to do with the variegated adventures of my own career, of which I here propose to give the first complete picture to the English reader.

ARMINIUS VAMBÉRY.

BUDAPEST,
Oct. 1, 1883.

CONTENTS.

I.

EARLY YEARS.

II.

THE FIRST JOURNEY.

III.

LIFE IN STAMBUL.

IV.

FROM TREBIZOND TO ERZERUM.

V.

FROM ERZERUM TO THE PERSIAN FRONTIER.

VI.

FROM THE PERSIAN BORDER TO TEBRIZ.

VII.

IN TEBRIZ.

VIII.

IN ZENDJAN.

IX.

FROM KAZVIN TO TEHERAN.

X.

IN TEHERAN.

XI.

THE SALT DESERT OF DESHTI-KUVIR.

XII.

KUM AND KASHAN.

XIII.

FROM ISFAHAN TO THE SUPPOSED TOMB OF CYRUS.

XIV.

PERSEPOLIS.

XV.

SHIRAZ.

XVI.

PREPARATIONS FOR MY JOURNEY TO CENTRAL ASIA.

XVII.

FROM TEHERAN TO THE LAND OF THE TURKOMANS.

XVIII.

GOMUSHTEPE.

XIX.

FROM GOMUSHTEPE TO THE BORDER OF THE DESERT.

XX.

IN THE DESERT.

XXI.

IN KHIVA.

XXII.

FROM KHIVA TO BOKHARA.

XXIII.

IN BOKHARA.

XXIV.

IN SAMARKAND.

XXV.

FROM SAMARKAND TO HERAT.

XXVI.

IN HERAT AND BEYOND IT.

XXVII.

IN MESHED.

XXVIII.

FROM MESHED TO TEHERAN.

XXIX.

FROM TEHERAN TO TREBIZOND.

XXX.

HOMEWARDS.

XXXI.

IN ENGLAND.

XXXII.

IN PARIS.

XXXIII.

IN HUNGARY.

XXXIV.

MY POLITICAL WRITINGS.

LIST OF ILLUSTRATIONS.

I.

EARLY YEARS.

WHEN my father died in 1832 I was but a few months old. My mother was poor, very poor indeed. By marrying again, however, she fondly hoped she might be enabled to give her helpless and fatherless orphans a better bringing up. But in this expectation she was sadly mistaken. Our stepfather, although a very excellent man, did but very little towards relieving the pressing needs of our small household. In due time, too, our family circle got fresh additions; the number of the little ones who stood in need of food and clothing was increasing. The consequence was that our parents, in their solicitude for the welfare of the smaller children, turned the older ones adrift to seek the best way they could their own livelihood as soon as they were supposed to have attained an age ripe enough to take care of themselves.

My turn came when twelve years old. My mother then thought I had reached a period of my life when I ought to look after myself. Although I had been afflicted since my birth with a lameness from which I began to suffer when three years old, and which compelled me to carry a crutch under my left arm up to the time my mother declared me to be of mature age, I was yet, on the whole, a tolerably hearty and healthy boy. The simple fare, often barely sufficient to still the cravings of hunger, the exceedingly scanty clothing allowed to me, and my want of familiarity with even the meanest comforts of life had, already, at this early stage of my life, hardened my body, and inured it to the most adverse climatic conditions.

I had then been attending school for about three years; and as my teachers were lavish in their praises of my extraordinary memory, enabling me to learn by heart, with great ease, almost anything, even passages in Latin which I did not understand at all, I thought of going on with the pursuit of my studies, in order to become a physician or lawyer,—the two professions which, at that time, were considered in the rural parts of Hungary as the goal of the most exalted ambition of an educated man.

My mother, too, had some such future in view for me, but inexorable poverty stood in the way of all such ambitious schemings. I had to stoop lower, much lower indeed. I was apprenticed to a ladies' dressmaker. When I had got so far as to be able to stitch two pieces of muslin together, a feeling overcame me that Dame Fortune had something better in store for me than stitching away all my life long. I soon left the shop of the ladies' dress artist, and was engaged by the innkeeper of the village to be the private teacher of his only son. I was to initiate him into the mystery of reading, writing and arithmetic. But my duties did not end there; I had to perform, besides, such unusual offices as the cleaning of the boots of the family on Saturday evenings,

PRESSBURG.

[Page 8.

and occasionally waiting on thirsty guests, and handing them a glass of wine or whiskey.

There was, undoubtedly, some slight incongruity between my tender age and the position of a teacher, nor was it easy for one who stood in sore need of instruction himself to impart it to another,—and, indeed, the master of the house did not fail to remind me of this anomaly by a treatment anything but in keeping with the dignity of my position as the mentor of his son.

But I received even worse treatment at the hands of the young master—my pupil. The lad was two years my senior, and on one occasion, when carried away with my pedagogic zeal I had given him a severe reprimand for his rude doings, he, nothing loth, fell on me and would have given me a sound thrashing but for the timely appearance of his mother.

My tutorship proved thus a school of hardship for me; but I bravely persevered until I could carry away with me from the Island of Schütt, where I had spent the first years of my childhood, the large sum of eight florins, which represented my net earnings. With this sum I hastened to St. George, in the vicinity of Pressburg, in order to begin there my studies at the gymnasium.

The money I had brought with me was just sufficient to purchase me the necessary books, and kind and charitable people helped me on in many other ways. Seven different families each gave me one day in the week a free meal, adding to it a big slice of bread for breakfast and another for luncheon. I also got the cast-off clothes of the wealthier schoolboys. By dint of application, and owing, perhaps, to the quick and easy comprehension which was natural to me, I succeeded in passing my examination at the first Latin class, as the second at the head of the class. My whole heart was in my studies; I was soon able to speak Latin with tolerable fluency; my professors remarked me and showed me some favour, which greatly assisted me in my struggles.

I passed, also, at St. George my examination in the second Latin class, successfully. My fondness for roving gave me no rest. I began to long for a change and was particularly desirous of going to Pressburg, where there were schools of a higher grade. I therefore left St. George, although I had my livelihood almost assured there, and the year 1846 saw me, at the age of fourteen, within the walls of the ancient City of Coronation.

There began anew my struggling and striving and desperate exertions to support myself. It became clear to me from the very first that, as buildings became taller and crowds larger, the difficulty of making acquaintances was increasing and the interest of others in my fortunes was diminishing. I remained here, for three years, now in the capacity of a servant, and then teaching she-cooks, chambermaids, and other individuals thirsting for knowledge. Every stone of the pavement of that beautiful little town on the blue Danube, could it but speak, might tell some sad tale of misery which I endured there. But youth is able to bear anything and everything!

I continued my studies, undaunted by want and privations, and was steadily advancing towards the object I had proposed to myself; at the end of the first term of school I was reckoned amongst the best scholars. In recalling these sad days, I never cease to wonder at the never-failing cheerfulness and the high spirits which were my constant companions throughout and helped me through all the adversities of life. My sturdy health aided me in the good fight and did not allow my good-humour to desert me.

In spite of my frugal fare, consisting of bread and

water only, I could boast of the healthiest of complexions, and was the life and soul of all fun and mischief in the schoolroom as well as at play. Every time our school-term drew to its end, I was sure to be among the first to seize my travelling-stick, and launch at random out into the world, limping but always on foot, without a penny in my pocket. In this manner I had already visited Vienna, Prague, and other cities and towns in the Austrian monarchy. Often, when tired as I was marching along the road, I would indulge in a good-humoured parley with the driver of a waggon or carriage that happened to pass me, and get, in return for my pains, a lift in his vehicle for a short distance. At night I usually put up at the houses of the reverend clergy of the place, where my Latin conversation was sure to earn for me some regards and a few kreutzers for my travelling expenses; and by a few happy neatly turned compliments, bestowed upon their housekeepers, I generally succeeded in having my travelling-bag filled with provisions for the next day. Truly, politeness and a cheerful disposition are precious coins current in every country; they stand at a high premium with the young and the old, with men and women; and he who has them at his disposal may very well call himself rich, although his purse be empty.

These rambles were a preparatory school for my wanderings as a dervish in after years, and it was always with a heavy heart that I put my walking-stick into a corner at the end of the vacation. Whether or not it was because I suffered from want and had to struggle hard to eke out a livelihood in town, one thing is certain, I disliked living in cities from my earliest childhood. Upon entering the narrow street with its rows of tall houses, and watching the diminishing sky over my head, my youthful spirits sank within me, and only the hope of standing at the end of the school term again a free man under God's bright heaven communing freely with Nature rendered my stay in town bearable.

In 1847, besides continuing my regular studies at school, I began to devote myself to private studies; for it must be owned that the gymnasiums were rather badly managed in Hungary at that time. In addition to reading the greatest variety of literary productions, on travels, which I all-eagerly devoured, I was learning French. Besides my native language, Hungarian, I had acquired German early in life. At about nearly the same time I had mastered Sclavonian, and as my studies at school had rendered me familiar with Latin and Greek, I found myself, not quite sixteen years old, conversant with so many principal languages that acquiring the idioms kindred to them had become a comparatively easy task for me.

I always took special delight in memorizing. Children have very vague ideas about natural gifts, and when I was able to increase the number of words which I could master in one day from ten to sixty and even to a hundred, my exultation knew no bounds. I must frankly own, however, that I had not at that time the faintest conception as to what the result of these successful exertions, which so flattered my vanity, might be.

Thus it happened that from the private study of French I gradually passed over to the study of the remaining branches of the Latin family. I did the same thing with the Germanic languages, and, beginning with English I soon eagerly extended my studies to Danish and Swedish. I pursued the same method with the Sclavonic dialects, and as I never omitted, in the zeal of learning, to read out loud and to hold conversations with myself in the languages I was learning, I had acquired, in a surprisingly short time, a certain kind of proficiency in all these languages which my youthful conceit made me imagine was perfection itself; and I am afraid I had rather an exalted opinion of myself at that time.

Vanity injures the character of a man in most cases, but it proves at times a very wholesome incentive to exertion. In this instance the conceit which was the result of my undisciplined imagination made me abandon the path of public studies I had entered upon, and induced me to continue my studies by myself. The friendly reader will ask what was the object of this self-education. Indeed I myself did not then know. "*Nulla dies sine linea*" was the maxim ever present in my mind, and even when I was engaged as a private teacher in the country, and was devoting from eight to ten hours daily to teaching, I contrived to make such good use of the remaining time as considerably to improve in my own studies.

The pleasures of general literature had now taken the place of the dry and monotonous memorizing of different languages of former years. I drew to my heart's content from the rich and varied fountain of the mental products of nearly all the European nations. The bards of Albion, the troubadours of Servia, the minstrels of Spain and the inspired poets of Italy; Lomonosoff, Pushkin, Tegnér, Andersen, Oehlenschlaeger, nearly all the muses of the present age and of the past ages beguiled my hours of leisure. I always read out loud, and frequently noted down in writing on the margin of the pages I read my feelings whenever any passage happened to strike my imagination.

Owing to this habit of loud reading and the violent

gestures with which I would often accompany it, the plain people who were about me often thought me wrong in the mind; and upon one occasion this conviction had so grown upon them that I actually lost my position as a teacher, on that account. But what cared I for the small criticisms of these people, so long as my mind was peopled with Tasso's struggle before Jerusalem, Cid's valiant deeds, and Byron's heroes and heroines? Yet, I must confess, no scenes had such a charm for me as those acting in the land of the rising sun, Asia—which then seemed to me so very far away—with her gorgeously brilliant robe, richly covered with pearls and gems, constantly floating before my eyes. How could it be otherwise with one who, in his youth, had read "The Arabian Nights," and who, as in my case, was by birth and education half an Asiatic himself.

I knew Asia as the land of the most fantastic adventures, as the home of the most fabulous successes; and, having led an adventurous life at an age when I was a child still, and being already in pursuit of some great good fortune, my first yearnings after distant lands pointed already to Asia.

In order to be enabled soon to gratify this longing, I thought it necessary to make myself, in the first place, familiar with the languages of Asia; and I began at once with the Turkish language. The Ural-Altaic dialect gave me less trouble than it would have given most Occidental people owing to its affinity with the Magyar language. I found it all the more difficult to master its strange characters without a teacher or any direction. For whole days I went on drawing the letters with a stick on the sand, until I became, at length, familiar with the value of the diacritical points, that is the distinguishing marks indispensable to a correct pronunciation of the letters and words. In this way I steadily improved. I was in want of a dictionary, but I could not afford to pay the high price asked for it, a "Bianchi" costing then nearly forty florins; and as I was compelled to trace the meaning of the single words through the labyrinth of the Turkish text by the aid of a so-called literal translation, "Wickerhauser's Chrestomathy," it did happen to me that after I had got through with the study of a bulky volume, I found out that I had been doing it all in a wrong way, and was obliged to do it all over again. Such bitter disappointments occurred to me more than once in the course of my autodidactic career; but what labour or task will ever restrain the ardour of youth or damp its enthusiasm?

I had now reached my twentieth year, and I was richly rewarded for all the pains I had taken when I was able for the first time to read and understand, without the aid of a dictionary, a short Turkish poem. It was not, indeed, the contents of the Oriental muse, quite inaccessible as yet for me, which kindled my enthusiasm, but rather the fruits, the sweet fruits of my labours, which afforded me such abundant satisfaction, and acted as an incentive spurring me to press forward into the field of Oriental science. All my musings, endeavours, thoughts and feelings tended towards the Land of the East, which was beckoning to me in its halo of splendour. My spirit had been haunting ever so long its fairy fields, and, sooner or later, my body was sure to follow it. For one who had still to struggle for his daily bread, in his European home, it required considerable boldness to think of a journey to the East, a land many hundred miles away. I will not deny that even the boldest flights of youthful enthusiasm, and the all-powerful desire of getting to know strange countries and customs, had to halt at the stumbling-block raised by poverty, and that luring fancy kept dazzling my eyes for many a day before I seriously set to work to carry out my cherished scheme. But a firm resolve with me is almost always like the avalanche which is being precipitated from the lofty summits of the Alps,—beginning with but an insignificant ball of snow set in motion by a favourable breeze, but soon swelling into a tremendous mass which carries before it every impediment, crushing and driving before it with irresistible force everything standing in its way. Such was the impulse which I received through the patronage of Baron Joseph Eötvös, known in Europe as a writer of high merit. This generous countryman of mine was not a man of wealth, but his influence procured me a free passage to the Black Sea. He gave me also a modest obolus and some old clothes. My knapsack, bursting with books, was soon buckled on, and I embarked in a steamer for Galacz, from which place I was to go to Constantinople, the immediate object of my journey.

PESTH—THE STARTING PLACE.

[*Page* 10.

II.

THE FIRST JOURNEY.

WHO can describe the feelings of a young man, barely twenty-two years old, who up to this day had been buffeted about by fortune, finding himself all of a sudden hastening towards the goal of his most cherished wishes, with (say) fifteen Austrian florins in his pocket, and about to enter upon a life full of uncertainty, in a distant region, amongst a strange people, who were rude and savage, and were beginning only then to seek a closer acquaintanceship with the nations of the West? My soul was agitated alternately by feelings of fear and hope, of curiosity and pain. Nobody accompanied me to the landing-place to see me off, nobody was there waiting for me, no warm presence of a friendly hand nor a mother's loving kiss cheered me on in the journey on which I was to start.

I had, thus, reason enough to feel somewhat depressed; nor could I entirely shake off this feeling; but I had no sooner come on deck, and begun to mix with the people, forming the national kaleidoscope one is always sure to meet on a voyage along the Lower Danube, and got an opportunity of conversing in Servian,

Italian, Turkish and other languages of which I had had hitherto only a theoretical knowledge, than every vestige of my former downheartedness gradually vanished. I was now in my element. Add to this that I soon became the object of general admiration owing to the fluency of my conversation in different languages; the crowd being always sure to stand in a sort of awe of every polyglot. They formed a ring around me, trying to guess at my nationality, and received rather sceptically my statement that I had never been abroad.

I was, of course, very much amused at the gaping crowd, but I managed to derive some more solid advantages from the manifestation of the good opinion which my fellow travellers entertained for me; for, when the dinner-bell was rung, and I preferred to remain behind on the deck with a perturbed expression of countenance, some enthusiastic disciple of Mercury was sure to get hold of the so-called youthful prodigy and pay him his meal.

In the absence of such well-disposed stomachic patrons, I would lounge about in the neighbourhood of the kitchen of the ship, the masters of which are for the most part Italians. A few stanzas from Petrarca or Tasso sufficed to attract the attention of the *cuoco* (cook). A conversation in pure Tuscan soon followed, and the upshot was a well-filled plate of maccaroni or risotto, capped by a piece of boiled or roasted meat. "Mille grazie, signore" (a thousand thanks, sir), meant that I would come in the evening, to claim a continuation of the favour shown me. The good Italian would shove his barrett of linen on one side, give a short laugh, and proved by his answer, "Come whenever you like," that the seed of my linguistic experiments had not fallen on a barren soil.

GALACZ.

[Page 18.

My constant good humour and happy disposition were of great help to me in all my straits, and, assisted by my tongue, were the means of procuring for me many a thing upon occasions when the attempts of others would have proved fruitless. In this manner I reached Galacz, a dirty, miserable place at this day even, but at that time much more so. During my voyage on the Lower Danube, the shore on the right hand side, with its Turkish towns and Turkish population, entirely absorbed my attention. To me every turbaned traveller, adorned with a long beard, upon entering the ship became a novel and interesting page meant for my particular study, and at the same time, a never failing object of pleasurable excitement.

When the sun was setting, and the truly faithful sat, or rather knelt down for prayer in the abject attitude peculiar to them on those occasions, I followed with my eyes every one of their movements with the most feverish and breathless attention; watching intensely the very motion of their lips, as they were uttering Arabic words, unintelligible even to them; and not until after they were done did I again breathe freely.

The interest which I so plainly showed could not escape the notice of the fanatic Moslem. We then lived in the era of the Hungarian refugees. Some hundreds of my countrymen made believe that they had been converted to Islam. A popular belief had got abroad that the whole Magyar people would acknowledge Mohammed as their prophet, and whenever a Mohammedan came across a Madjarli, the fire of the missionary was blazing fiercely in his heart.

Such an interest, or a kindred one, must have entered into the friendship shown to me during my voyage to Galacz by some Turks from Widdin, Rustchuk and

Silistria. In this supposition of mine I may possibly be mistaken, and it is quite as likely that their sympathies were excited by the deep national feeling, which then manifested itself everywhere in the Ottoman empire, in favour of the Magyars, who had been defeated by the Russians. This state of affairs, at all events, was of excellent service to me, not only during this passage, but during my entire stay in Turkey.

I was drawn by curiosity towards the half-Asiatic Turks, my fellow travellers, and these very men were the first to introduce me into the Oriental world. I need not say that, after having been with them for a day or two, I improved in my Turkish, to such an extent, that at Galacz I was already able to serve a countryman of mine as an interpreter.

The Oriental, and, I may say, the Mohammedan element was decidedly preponderating amongst the passengers, in whose company I went from Galacz to Constantinople. The reader will not be surprised to learn that I was booked for the cheapest place on the ship, namely, the deck, and that, even for that place, I often paid only half fare. I placed my meagre knapsack near the luggage of the Turks, who were sitting apart from the others, and most of whom were on their pilgrimage to Mecca; I was impatiently looking out to catch a glimpse of the long-hoped-for sea, which I had never seen before.

He who has got his first impressions of the sea, through the reading of Byron's aquatic scenes, Camoen's Lusiade, or Tegnér's Legend of Frithjof, will be overcome by feelings of no common order in finding himself, for the first time in his life, on the boundless watery expanse, especially of the Euxine—gliding along its bosom and being rocked by its waves.

At an hour's distance from the mouths of the Sulina, I gazed, in a reverie, at the awful grandeur of the sea, not in the least disturbed by the deep guttural sounds and savage groans which came from the sea-sick people around me.

Father Poseidon had done no manner of harm to my health. I had rather reason to complain of an unusually keen appetite; the excessive chillness of the evenings, too—we were then in the month of April—cooled my blood more than I thought it desirable. I began to shake with the cold, in spite of a surplus carpet, placed at my disposal for a covering by the kind care of a Turk; and after having feasted my eyes on the bright, star-covered sky for a considerable time, I fell, at length, asleep.

I was suddenly and rudely roused from my dreams towards midnight by peals of thunder and flashes of lightning, accompanied by a violent shower. I had been all day long wishing for a storm; I own my wish was gratified at night in such a thorough manner as fully to satisfy my romantic disposition.

How my heart throbbed upon seeing the ship dance up and down the towering, mountain-like waves, like a nimble gazelle! The creaking of beams, the howling of the wind, with which the shouts of despair from the passengers were mingling, the everlasting appeals to Allah, which resounded everywhere, could not destroy the halo of poetry with which I surrounded a scene, otherwise commonplace enough. Only after getting soaking wet with the chilly rain did I shift my place.

I got up and tried to keep myself warm by taking a walk, but the chaos of legs stretched out, of travelling-bags, bundles, firearms and turbans which were littering the ground rendered the walk well-nigh impracticable. I longingly looked at the open space close by the deck, reserved for the promenading of first-class passengers, where I observed, in the darkness of the night, a man hurrying to and fro. I had at first thoughts of entering into a conversation with him; but, my courage to do so failing me, I hit upon another expedient to attract his attention. I commenced declaiming, in the midst of the violent storm, one of the epic poems I knew by heart. My choice fell on Voltaire's Henriade—

> " Je chante ce héros qui régna sur la France
> Et par droit de conquête et par droit de naissance!" *

And having roared out, with a good will, into the darkness of the night, several verses, I had the satisfaction of seeing the much-envied first class passenger stop, near a crowd of Turks, in a listening attitude; and after a while he joined me and began a conversation with me.

With Voltaire, acting as master of ceremonies, questions about rank and nationality seemed to be out of place. I discovered next morning that the figure, wrapped in the shadows of night, belonged to a gentleman, a Belgian by birth, a diplomat by his calling, who was going to Constantinople in the capacity of a Secretary of Legation. If the gentleman felt some surprise at the rage of declamation prompting a person wet to the skin to recite verses at night, his astonishment increased considerably upon seeing me next morning in broad daylight shabbily attired. He, nevertheless, seemed to have formed no mean opinion of me; he asked me to come and see him in Pera, and promised me his protection to the extent of his power.

We were favoured by the fairest weather from Varna to Constantinople, and nothing more charming could be

* I sing of the hero who reigned in France, by right of conquest and by right of birth.

THE BOSPHORUS.

[Page 17

imagined than this our voyage. The sailing through the most delightful sea road of the world, vulgarly called the Bosphorus, is apt to affect the dullest spirit, and roused—it is needless to say—the utmost enthusiasm in me. But, upon looking about me, and seeing before me the dense forest of masts and flags in the Golden Horn, I fancied I was placed, as it were, in the very centre of the world; and as my fellow passengers were dropping away, one by one, all hurrying in different directions to the shore, a feeling of my forlornness burst upon me. My spirits were damped and I felt anxious and ill at ease.

Of the fifteen florins I had brought with me from Pesth, I had left just enough to pay my fare on the boat which took me to the shore. I now set my foot on Turkish ground, if not with a light heart, certainly with a very light purse, and sauntered pretty recklessly up the narrow street leading to the heights of Pera.

With a spirit less adventurous and at a more sensible age than mine, I should have asked myself: "Where will you sleep to-night, what will you eat—and, altogether, what will you begin to do?" But I never put these questions to myself—I was blind in my enthusiasm. I was quietly stopping to look at some signs, covered with Turkish inscriptions, and was busy deciphering them, when a stranger, a Hungarian, whose curiosity had been roused by the long ribbon which floated from my Hungarian hat, stepped up to me. He inquired in Italian about my nationality and my place of destination, and upon learning that I was a Hungarian he, as a countryman and a political refugee, of course, immediately addressed me in Hungarian, much to the delight of both of us.

Mr. Püspöki had been an honest mechanic in his own country; he was earning a living in Turkey by being, in turn, an officer of the line, a suttler during the Crimean war, an accounting clerk on board of a ship, and, finally, when I met him, a cook. He was occupying a small, poverty-stricken room, on the ground floor, in the dirty quarter of the town which lies in the rear of the walls of the palace of the English Embassy; its modest furniture consisting solely of a mattress, running along the wall, which he shared with me, like a brother.

I shall never forget my first night on this couch. My hospitable countryman had been fast asleep for some time, whilst I, unable to close my eyes, was still pondering over the strange beginning of life in Turkey. I became, all of a sudden, aware that now one, and again the other, of my boots were moving about, by themselves.

"Friend," I said, first in a whisper, and gradually raising my voice, "I think they are carrying away my boots."

He only muttered something unintelligible in reply. I repeated my remark, and the good man finally exclaimed with some ill-humour:

"Do sleep! It is nothing but rats playing."

A very amusing game, indeed, I thought, provided they do not chew up my boots; and I turned to sleep again.

I spent about three days in that miserable hole. I soon extended my acquaintance with my countrymen, and obtained, through them, permission to live in one of the rooms occupied by the "Magyar Club," which was at that time already nearly deserted. At this place I met with fewer frolicsome animals, but the skipping animals were all the more numerous; and one evening, when, suffering from the chilliness of the night, I ventured to ask the secretary of the club to give me something to cover myself with, that worthy gentleman took the tricolour off the flagstaff, and handed it to me, apostrophizing me in the following touching manner :

"Friend! this flag has fired the hearts of many in their heroic flights, it was itself once full of fire ; wrap yourself up in it, dream of glorious battlefields, and maybe it will keep you warm too."

And, oddly enough, I wrapped the old rag around me, shivered yet for a little while, and then fell into a sound sleep.

Several days had passed in this manner. Day by day the circle of my acquaintances was increasing, and all of them were particularly struck with the varied knowledge I exhibited in the matter of languages, and my being able to speak fluently and read easily the language of the country, without having lived in Turkey, was to them a subject of special wonder.

To give instruction in the languages used in the country, with a view to earning my daily bread, suggested itself as the most natural thing. Written advertisements of my desire were distributed, and the first lesson I was to give was, oddly enough, in Danish.

Mr. Hübsch, a noble-minded gentleman of culture, whom I shall always remember with pleasure, had been for some time back in search of a Danish master, and was really glad to meet me ; indeed, he made such rapid progress as to be able, in the course of a few months, to read, under my direction, Andersen's "Spilleman" and "Berlingske Tidninger."

Beginning with this odd lesson, I soon obtained other engagements as a teacher, which I should never have hoped to obtain. The all-promising advertisements did not fail to produce their effects ; and one day, when I happened to be at the book-shop of Mr. S., a young Turk, whose large retinue showed him to be a man of means, came in and inquired after the Madjarli, whose name he had seen in the shop-window, and whom he wished to engage as a "Khodja," or teacher of the French language.

The young Bey was, as I had afterwards occasion to learn, a "Miraskhor," that is, a person who has just come into possession of a rich inheritance, and is trying to acquire the external attributes suitable to his wealth. In Turkey, at that time, these attributes were as follows: (1) a suit of the finest broadcloth, after the latest cut and fashion; (2) tight patent leather shoes; (3) a small, jaunty fez, rakishly worn on one side of the head, and, as a matter of course, gloves, too; (4) an easy, graceful step, accompanied by a fashionable carriage of the arms and hands; and (5) French conversation. European tradesmen had provided him with the first four ingredients for the make-up of a Turkish gentleman, and I was to furnish him with the fifth. I was, accordingly, engaged on the spot as his teacher, the remuneration stipulated for being ten piastres for one hour's lesson daily, besides my expenses of going to his house and returning, as our dandy was living at some distance in Skutari.

This lesson procured me the opportunity of gaining admission for the first time into a genuine Turkish house. I arrived every day punctually at the appointed hour, but generally found my pupil, who had just roused himself from his slumbers, still suffering from the effects of last night's debauch, and scarcely able to lift his heavy eyelids; nor did I discover in him the slightest disposition to acquire the language of the Gauls. It took him an entire month to master the alphabet.

I usually found my pupil in the company of a venerable mollah, who fairly shuddered whenever the sounds of a language of the Giaours reached his ears, for the father of my pupil was a notoriously pious Mussulman, and the walls of the room in which we sat had only re-echoed until now the canting recitals of the Koran, the sacred hymns, and other prayers.

I often heard the mollah muttering in his beard, "This is the way in which the spirit of infidelity is being smuggled into our houses."

I need not say that the instruction I imparted was highly profitable to myself. We did at first some French, but later on we glided from the French lesson into explanatory sketches of European life and European ideas. I told the Bey of our social, political, and scientific institutions, decking them out, as a matter of course, in their brightest colours, for the European, during his first stay in the East, is always looking back with fondness to the West he has just left, and the very things he used to condemn look to him charming at a distance.

My information was almost always received with approval and admiration. Turkey had just seen a good specimen of Europe in her Anglo-French allies who had come to her assistance against the Russians; the Turks were, therefore, eager to learn all the particulars having reference to the Western land, and if the descriptions of these excited now and then their envy, roused them to disapproval or called out their conceit, they were always listened to, and that with pleasure.

At the close of the lesson a well-prepared and abundant breakfast was always brought in, and I must own that from the very first the cooking of the better classes in Constantinople had enlisted my gastronomic partiality. It frequently happened, too, that we started immediately after breakfast for a ride on horseback, my pupil making his calls in my company; in short, I passed a considerable portion of the day in the society of Turks, and I used to return to Pera, that is, to European life, in the evening only.

My permanent stay amongst Turks dates, however, from the time when, at the recommendation of a countryman of mine, I was invited by Hussein Daim Pasha, general of a division, to enter his house as the teacher of his son, Hassan Bey.

I removed my quarters from Pera to the charmingly situated row of houses at Fyndykly; there I got a separate room, and enjoyed for the first time the amenities of Oriental quiet and Turkish comfort. The life in a strictly Mohammedan part of the town, in the vicinity of a mosque, from whose slender minaret the Ezan resounded with gloomy melancholy, affecting my ears with its weirdlike sounds; the grand prospect from my window taking in the sea near by, with its thousand crafts, and the magnificent Beshikash palace; and the dignified and patriarchal air which pervaded the whole house—were all things which had the charm of novelty for me, and which I can never forget.

The figure of the major domo (Vekilkhardj), a graybearded Anatolian, however, has, perhaps, made the deepest impression upon my memory. The good man was particularly indulgent towards me upon all occasions when I happened to sin against the strictly Oriental customs; he took great pains to teach me how to sit decorously, that is, with crossed legs; he taught me to carry my head and to use my hands with propriety, and how I should yawn, sneeze, and so forth. His attention embraced the merest trifles.

"You are, for the first time, in a large city; you have iust entered polite society," he benignly said, "and you must learn everything."

Of course the old man looked upon me as a person

coming from the land of "black infidelity," a land to which, in his opinion, decency, good manners, and morals were utter strangers, and he seemed to think that a stranger hailing from those parts needed to be educated quite as much as a Turkish peasant from the neighbourhood of Kharput and Diarbekir.

The pasha himself, my chief, was a much more interesting personage. It was he who afterwards became known as the leader of the celebrated Kuleili conspiracy, a conspiracy whose object was nothing less than the removal of Sultan Abdul Medjid and of all his grandees; the conspirators flattering themselves with the belief that all the causes of the decay of Turkey would be thereby extirpated, and that, with one stroke, the old and infirm Ottoman empire could be restored to its ancient power.

Hussein Daim Pasha was a Circassian by birth, and had, like so many of his countrymen, brought with him from his mountain home, which was then still free, to the City of the Seven Hills, a strong dose of love of liberty. He had passed his youthful years at the court of Sultan Mahmud, during the turbulent days of the suppression of the Janizaries and the Turco-Egyptian conflict; and he being, as were most of his contemporaries, familiar with the idea of a politic and yet radical change, the thought entered his mind to cure by a miracle the deeply rooted political ills of Turkey.

His close intimacy with the refugees, who were living at that time in Turkey, may have considerably contributed towards making a political enthusiast of him. His imagination was inflamed by what he heard them tell during the long and anxious nights of tent life whilst the siege of Kars was going on. I very well remember, even now, how the eyes of the tall and slenderly built man glistened, how every muscle of his manly face winced, at hearing me relate some of the episodes of the year 1848.

I was an inmate of his house at the time when this notorious conspiracy was being hatched and the plans for its consummation formed. A mollah from Bagdad, by the name of Ahmed Effendi, a man of rare mental gifts, immense reading, ascetic life, and boundless fanaticism was the life and soul of the whole conspiracy. He had taken part in the whole of the Crimean war as a Gazi (a warrior for religion), bareheaded and barefooted, and clad in a garb whose austere simplicity recalled the primitive ages of Islam. His sword never left his lean loins, nor his lance the firm grasp of his clenched fist, either by day or by night, except when he said his prayers, five times a day. Through the snow, in the storm, in the thickest of the fight on the battlefield, during toilsome marches, everywhere could be discovered the ghost-like form of this zealot, his fiery eyes scattering flames, and always at the head of the division, under the command of my chief.

It was quite natural that such a man should please Hussein Daim Pasha. The acquaintance begun in the camp, had here grown into a sort of relationship by consanguinity; for the lean mollah, who was walking about barefoot in Constantinople, had the privilege of crossing even the threshold of the harem, where, under the protection of the sacredness of Turkish family life, unwelcome listeners could be most conveniently got rid of. There was something in the appearance of Ahmed Effendi which terrified me at first, and only, later, upon my allowing myself to be called by my pasha, for the sake of intimacy, Reshid (the brave, the discreet), came this terrible man near me, with some show of friendliness; he probably concluding, from my having adopted this name, that I was very near being converted to Islam. A very false inference! But I did not destroy the hopes of the zealot, gaining thereby his good will, and getting him to give me instruction in Persian.

Ahmed Effendi allowed me even to visit him in his cell in the yard of the mosque. And oh! how interesting were those hours which I spent, sitting at his feet, with other youths who were eager to learn. It seemed as if I had got hold of a fairy key unlocking, to my dazzled eyes in one moment, the whole of Mohammedan Asia.

Ahmed Effendi had an astonishing, almost supernatural memory; he was a thorough Arabic and Persian scholar, and knew a whole series of classics by heart. I had only to begin with a line from Khakani Nizami or Djami, in Spiegel's Persian chrestomathy, and he would at once continue to recite the whole piece to the end. Indeed he would have been able to go on with his declamation for hours.

To this Ahmed Effendi I was indebted, more than to anybody else, for my transformation from a European into an Asiatic. In speaking of my transformation, I trust the friendly reader will not suppose, for one moment, that a more intimate acquaintance with Asiatic modes of thought had led my mind away from the spirit of the West. A thousand times, no! Rather the reverse was the case. The more I studied the civilization of Islam and the views of the nations professing it, the higher rose, in my estimation, the value of western civilization.

III.

LIFE IN STAMBUL.

IN the year 1860, I was, perhaps, the only European who had an easy and uninterrupted access to all classes of Turkish society, and, probably, saw at that time more of genuine Stambul life than any one before me. And, surely, no one will find fault with me, if I recall now, in the midst of my European life, with undisguised pleasure, the generous hospitality I have met with, at the hands of the noblest Turks, in their own houses. The easy affability of persons of high positions in the State, the utter absence of all pride or overbearing superciliousness, are virtues, indeed, which would often be looked for in vain in our civilized West. The stupid pomposity, ridiculous arrogance and pitiable ignorance of certain aristocracies present a miserable picture, when contrasted with the behaviour of the Asiatic grandees, whom it is the custom to sneer at in Europe. The Oriental is particular about nobility of blood only in the matter of his horses and sporting dogs, whereas, with us, the select are boasting of such "animal advantages" that I should like to know in what country of Europe an unknown stranger might succeed, solely by dint of his eagerness to learn, in obtaining access to the most distinguished circles, and gaining their goodwill and protection. With us, to be sure, there is no lack either of protectors and patrons of exalted station, who assist the man of books and art, but in this they never approach the intimacy and close friendship which patrons bestow in the East upon intellectual pursuits. In Europe, the possessors of long pedigrees, the owners of family trees with decayed roots and worm-eaten bark, have frequently assigned to them the leadership in society, but not so in Asia. The Arabs will boast of the heroic deeds and generous actions of their ancestors, but not for their own exaltation, as is the case in many countries of Europe.

In passing over to my literary pursuits, during my stay in Stambul, I will only mention that I published, in 1858, a German-Turkish dictionary, a small volume, of the imperfections and shortcomings of which, I am by no means unaware; but it was the first that had been written, and is, to this day, the only available one which a German traveller, coming to Constantinople, can get. There were two main points which I had principally in view in my studies of Turkish literature. I had, in the first place, found, in the history of the Ottoman Empire, so much that was of interest to the history of my own country, that I felt impelled to make a translation of it. Through these translations, I entered, at an early period, into relations with the Hungarian Academy. The Ottoman historians are wanting, for the most part, in critical judgment, but the laborious and circumstantial completeness of their information frequently proves useful. It may not be generally known that the Turkish Sultans who, at the head of their destructive armies, made inroads into the South-eastern part of Europe, and against whom so many Crusades were preached, were constantly accompanied, at every step they took, by imperial historiographers, and have done more for Clio, the Muse, than many a truly Catholic prince of that time.

I had found, in the second place, in the course of my linguistic researches in the study of Eastern Turkish, a field which had been, at that time, barely cultivated, and devoted to it my full attention. Besides the manuscripts I got hold of in the various libraries, which were of great assistance to me in my studies, I frequented the *Tekkes* (cloisters), inhabited by the Bokhariots, and provided myself, moreover, with a view to attaining to a thorough understanding of these works, with a teacher who was a native of Central Asia. Mollah Khalmurad, as my teacher was called, acquainted me with the customs and modes of thought of Central Asia. I used to hang passionately on his lips when he was relating stories about Bokhara and Samarkand, and told of the Oxus and Taxartes, for he had travelled a great deal in his own country. He had already made two pilgrimages to the holy cities of Arabia, and possessed, to a high degree, the cunning and clearsightedness peculiar to every Asiatic but particularly to the much-travelled Asiatic.

This perspicacity of theirs caused me to tremble for my life more than once during my wanderings as a dervish.

Apart from a scientific, I felt an engrossing national, interest in the study of the Eastern Turkish language, on account of the rich Eastern Turkish vocabulary to be met with in the Magyar language. During my earlier researches, in this connection, I ventured the supposition that this foreign vocabulary may date back to the most ancient dwelling side by side of Osmanlis and Magyars, in Hungary. I observed, however, in Constantinople, and, notably, in my intercourse with Anatolians, that as soon as the home of a Turk lay more to the East, the national characteristics of his language became purer and less adulterated, and that, as a corollary, the analogy to the Magyar language became more frequent and striking. My imagination, however, never indulged me in the hope of finding in the end, in consequence of this increased lingual relationship, a Turanian people, closely allied to the Magyar people. Such an expectation, which has been falsely attributed to me in various quarters, could not, in the first place, have been possibly entertained by any one who was familiar, ever so superficially, with comparative philology; and I should, in the second place, have pleaded guilty to excessive ignorance, had I allowed myself to suppose that there could exist in the interior of Asia, although it had not been at that time thoroughly explored, any people, totally unknown. I therefore repeat that the imputation of having made the discovery of the original seat of the Magyars the object of my journey is utterly unfounded. What I wanted and was looking for solely was the more ancient dialect of the Turkish language, uninfluenced by foreign elements; and as it happened that this dialect could not be learned from books, there was nothing left for me but to travel through those distant regions, and thus acquire practically what I could not acquire theoretically. Yet, I doubt not, for a moment, but that my innate fondness for travel, my insatiable curiosity and my eager pursuit of adventures had as much to do with my resolve as the study of the Djagataic dialect.

Stambul life with all its attractions and interesting phenomena produced a feeling of weariness in me after a while. My frequent visits to Pera, my passing, in less than half an hour, from the innermost recesses of Asiatic life to the turmoil of European stir and bustle, might have continued attractive to me, as giving me an opportunity for the comparative study of the two civilizations. But amongst the very men whom I happened to meet, in this Babel of European nationalities, there were some who fanned the fire within me, and who incited me, that had remained a thorough European in spite of an Orientalizing of several years, to the execution of the boldest feats. And did I require these urgings on—I, who, at the bare mention of the names of Bokhara, Samarkand, and the Oxus, was in a fever of excitement? Certainly not; their encouragement seemed to me only a proof of the practicability of my designs. Indeed, I was quite familiar with the literature of travel of that day, and the only misgivings I felt were on the score of the perils of the undertaking.

I had just been revolving in my mind the plan of a journey through Asia, when I was nominated, quite unexpectedly, corresponding member of the Hungarian Academy. This nomination was to be a reward for my translation of Turkish historical authorities, but it proved an all-powerful incentive, urging me on to the consummation of my plans for the future. Considerable changes had by this time taken place in the political life of Hungary; and when, upon returning in the spring of 1861, after an absence of several years, I went to Pesth, in order to deliver my Academic address, it required but a gentle intimation on the part of the then President of the Academy, Count D., to procure me a travelling stipend of a thousand florins in bank notes, amounting to six hundred florins in silver. At home, of course, there were many sceptics who expressed their doubts as to the success of my undertaking. I was asked how I could accomplish such a long journey, with scanty means and a frail body. These gentlemen were not aware that travelling in Asia required neither legs nor money, but a clever tongue. I paid, however, but slight attention to such comments.

The "Academy" gave me a letter of introduction and recommendation, addressed to all the Sultans, Khans and Begs of Tartary, and drawn up, for the surer enlightenment of the Tartars, in the Latin tongue! A ready gallows or executioner's sword, forsooth, this document meant, if I had produced it anywhere in the desert or along the Oxus. The then government, too, that is, the viceroyalty, were generous enough to furnish me with a passport for my journey to Bokhara. I did not thwart those manifestations of good intentions, and left Pesth, after a stay of three months, for Constantinople, from which place I was to start, in the following spring, on my wanderings through the extensive regions of Central Asia.

My preparations, which took me another six months, had eaten up nearly one half of the six hundred silver florins, and consisted, chiefly, in visits to places, where travellers and pilgrims from Central Asia congregated and could be met with. These people who were, for the most part, poor, I remunerated as well as I could, for every piece of information and for every hour of conversation that I got from them; for I must observe, here, that already, at the outset, I was tolerably well acquainted with the colloquial language of the countries on the Oxus. Indeed, I may add, that many a quarter of a town and region in the distant Mohammedan East was as familiar to me, from hearsay and reading, as is the capital on the Seine to a European who has been a reader of French novels for many years.

Very remarkable and, at times, very amusing was the manner in which my worthy Stambul friends looked upon my preparations for far-off Turkestan. A journey prompted merely by a thirst for knowledge is characterized by the modern Mohammedans as, to say the least, eccentric; for the days of Masudi, Yakut, Ibn Fozlan and Batutah have passed away, ever so long ago. But if any one purposes to undertake a journey through inhospitable, barbarous and dangerous countries, they declare such an enterprise a piece of sheer madness. I can very well recall how these effeminate Effendis shuddered, and the look of unspeakable pity they bestowed upon me, when I was expatiating, with the most intense satisfaction, upon my passage through the deserts. "Allah Akillar" (God lend him reason), was the pious wish they were all muttering. A person who will voluntarily leave the delightful Bosphorus, give up the comfortable life at the house of a Turkish grandee, and resign the charms of sweet repose, must be, to their thinking, a madman.

And, yet, these good people were deeply concerned to smooth my rough path, and to retard the certain destruction before me, as much as lay in their power. Persia was to be the first country on my route, and as a Turkish ambassador, together with his suite, had been residing, for years, at Teheran, and the then plenipotentiary of the Sultan, Haidar Effendi, happened to be a friend of the family of my patron, I received, in addition to the official recommendation of Aali Pasha, a collective letter from all the relations and acquaintances of K. . . Bey, commending unhappy me, in the warmest terms, to his protection. I obtained also firmans, addressed to the authorities on my route through Turkish territory, in all of which I was mentioned as the traveller Reshid Effendi. Of my European descent, of the aims and purposes of my journeyings, not the slightest mention was made in these documents, and all I had to do was to act up to the letter and spirit of their contents; indeed I could do little else if I wished to pass myself off as a genuine Turk and Effendi from Constantinople.

So much for the practical portion of my preparations. As to the mental condition I was in, I need not say that the nearer the moment of my departure approached the stronger became my longing, the more agitated became my mind. What I had dreamt of as a child, mused upon as a youth, and what had haunted my eyes, Fata-Morgana-like, during my wanderings through the literatures of the Occident and Orient, I was to attain at last, and feast upon it my own bodily eyes. When passion thus, like a mighty wave, is rolling in upon us, we turn a deaf ear to the voice of reason and prudence. All I could dread, after all, was bodily want, the fight with the elements and injury to my health; for, at that time, the thought of failure, that is of death, never entered my mind. And now I ask my friendly reader, what vicissitudes, what privations could I undergo, which I had not already been subjected to by the hard fate of my youth? I had been starving up to my eighteenth year, and want of necessary clothing had been the order of the day with me, since my earliest youth. I had learned to know the whims and foibles of mankind, and found that man in the rude Asiatic garb was nearly the same as man in the civilized European dress; yea, I had met at the hands of the former so much more pity and kindness, that the frightful picture of these barbarians, as drawn by our literature, was far from disheartening me. Only one thing might be taken into consideration, with reference to the undertaking I had on hand, that, after having already tasted the sweets of affluence and repose, I was about to venture anew upon a life of misery and struggles. For I had done well, quite well in Constantinople, during these years. I had comfortable quarters and a luxurious fare, and there was even a saddle horse at my disposal, and thus the only thing that may be said in my praise, is that I exchanged all these, of my own free will, for the beggar's staff. But good Heavens! where could we not be led, if spurred on by ambition? And what is our life worth if ambition is not known, does not exist or has been blunted? Wealth, distinction and dignities are gaudy toys which cannot amuse us very long, and of which sound common sense must tire sooner or later. The consciousness, however, of having rendered to mankind in general a service ever so slight, is a truly noble and exalting one; for what is there more glorious than the hope of being able to enrich even by a single letter the book of intellectual life lying open before us? Thus I felt and thus I thought, and in these feelings and thoughts I found the strength to submit to trials and hardships a thousandfold greater than those I had been subjected to hitherto.

Such were the conditions of my life, under which I left the peaceful harbour of Constantinople for my voyage to the Black Sea. Unaccompanied by any friends or parents, I bade farewell to the Golden Horn and to the Bosphorus as to the place where I enjoyed so many agreeable days of useful preparation for my future career. As our good ship turned towards the Asiatic shore, I ventured only to look with a furtive glance towards the West, uncertain whether I should see it again in my life!

IV.

FROM TREBIZOND TO ERZERUM.

THE boom of cannon, sounds of music and shouts of joyous welcome greeted us, as our ship was approaching the harbour of Trebizond. This solemn reception was not intended for me, the future dervish, who was setting out, beggar's staff in hand, to roam through an extensive portion of classic Asia. The ovation was meant for Emir Muhlis Pasha, the newly appointed Governor of Trebizond, who had been our fellow traveller from Constantinople to this place. The people, very likely, indulged in the hope that he would bring in his train a happier state of things than they experienced and relief from past misery, but they were, in all probability, doomed to be disappointed in him, as they had been disappointed in his numerous predecessors before.

Trebizond, the ancient capital of Mithridates, presents a rather fine appearance, when looked at from the sea. Upon closer inspection, the city proves finer, by far, than most of the Turkish sea-towns. Muhlis Pasha, whose acquaintance I had made at Constantinople, proffered me his hospitality, during the whole of my stay in that town. I mounted one of the horses held in readiness on the shore, joined the pasha's retinue, and proceeded with the festive procession towards the governor's palace, lying to the south. Our troops passed, highly pleased, through the thronging crowds. The pasha caused some small silver change to be scattered amongst the populace. There was a great rush and eager scrambling for the coins, and the lucky ones were loud and voluble in the expression of their gratitude. I remained only three days in Trebizond. I employed this short time in the purchase of the necessary travelling requisites, in the hiring of a horse—in short, in supplying myself with everything needful for those adventurous wanderings through Turkey and Persia which I was about to undertake. I resolved to keep up the part of an Effendi as far as Teheran, but thereafter I wished to pass myself off only as a Kiatib, an humble scribe who might appeal to the hospitality of the authorities. My entire luggage consisted of a *khurdjin* (carpet-bag), containing a couple of shirts, a few books, some trifles, two carpets, one to be used as a mattress the other for a covering, a small kettle, tea service and cup. The pasha repeatedly pressed upon me the offer of an escort by two *kavasses* (policemen), not so much as a matter of safety as from considerations of display, customary in these parts. I declined his kind offer with thanks, and in the company of an Armenian *surudji* (an owner and driver of horses), left the Turkish sea-town on the 21st day of May, 1862, wending my way towards the mountains stretching to the east.

The sun had already risen pretty high. I advanced, at a slow pace, along the highway, extending to about an hour's walking distance from the city, and then losing itself in the deep gorge of a valley. My Armenian companion, Hadjator, reminded me that in getting near the valley we should soon lose sight of the sea. I stopped on the height, for a few moments, to give a farewell look to it. However stormy and rough at times, it was just then lying as calm and peaceful before my eyes as the water of a lake. I felt at this moment but faint forebodings of the trials and dangers lying in wait for me; but, faint as they were, they sufficed, as I gazed upon the dark, endlessly-stretching waves of the Euxine, to affect me most deeply. There, at my feet, was Trebizond; I could clearly discern the whole harbour, and as I caught sight of the Austrian ship in which I had come, the flag on the masthead beckoning a farewell to me, a feeling of deep melancholy took possession of my whole being. For six mortal hours on that day I continued, without interruption, my march on horseback. They were a miserable six hours. Although nature was very charming and beautiful all around me, it did not prevent me from feeling extreme weariness in all my limbs. To travel on horseback is in the beginning a rather painful thing, but it is infinitely more so if one is obliged to hire the horse one rides from a surudji. These men employ their animals, chiefly, in the transportation of luggage, and the horses have, in consequence, such a jostling gait that their riders must ache all over upon descending, and they are so indolent, besides, that one must make good use of one's hands and feet to make them move on. Near Köpri I put up at a *khan* (an inn). I had to sleep, nomad fashion, on the ground, but, owing to my excessive fatigue, sleep would not come to my eyes. The place was swarming with horses and mule-drivers, of whom some would scrub their animals, or cook, others sing, and others again chat. It seemed to me as if all this din had been especially got up to disturb my slumbers. I rose into a sitting posture, where I had been lying, and sadly reflected upon the fatigues to come.

After a short nap, I was called by my Armenian. "Bey Effendi," he said, "I think you must feel rested from the fatigues of yesterday's march. Our road to day will be harder; you will not be able to sit comfortably in the saddle in the mountains of Trebizond, and you will therefore do better to walk up, leisurely, to the top, before it gets warmer." I left my couch at once and followed the steep mountain path. I could not help wondering at the mules' toiling up the steep height and reaching the top, with their heavy loads, whilst, to me, on foot, without any incumbrance, the ascent was most painful. On our way we met a long line of overloaded mules, descending amidst the wild screams of their Persian drivers. It is a rare sight to watch them advancing, with the utmost care, without any accident, upon the slippery path cut into the rock, scarcely two spans wide, flanked by the bottomless abyss. And yet it is a very unusual thing for a mule to be precipitated into the abyss yawning along the path. If ever it happens it is in winter. The danger is greatest when two caravans happen to meet face to face. In order to avoid such an encounter, big bells, heard at a great distance, are used by them, warning the caravans to keep out of each other's way.

The continuously steep ascent lasted over four hours. There is hardly a worse road in all Asia; yet this is the only commercial road which connects Armenia with Persia, nay Central Asia with the West. During the summer hundreds of thousands of these animals are traversing this route, going and coming, loaded with the products of Asia and the manufactures of Europe.

I was indebted to my title of Effendi for quieter sleeping quarters at the tolerably crowded Khan at our next station. Before retiring to rest I took the advice of Hadjator, and bathed in salt water those parts of my body which were sore with my riding exertions; the sensation was at first a stinging one, but sitting in the saddle next day was not quite so uncomfortable as before.

Upon reaching the third station, on the 23rd of May, two Armenians joined me. One of them began to speak first French, and then English with me. He was a merchant from Tebriz, who had spent several years in England on matters of business, and was now returning to his native town. We became quite intimate after a while, and his society was all the more agreeable to me as he knew very well the route on which we were to travel together for a considerable time. Three days after that, upon leaving the Khoshab Bunar mountains and descending, we met a Shiraz caravan on our way. I was struck by the shape of the tall hats of the men running into a point. They were gaily stepping alongside of their mules, loaded with the produce of their native country, and I was delighted to hear the songs of Hafiz sung by the leader of the caravan, the youths who were following him joining in chorus every now and then. These were the first Iranian (Persian) words which I heard from the natives themselves. I wished to enter into a conversation with them, but they did not deign to reply. Singing they toiled uphill on the rough road, because, as I was afterwards told by my guide, the animals march more cheerfully at the sound of singing.

V.

FROM ERZERUM TO THE PERSIAN FRONTIER.

I ARRIVED in Erzerum on the 28th of May. In entering this town I was, at once, aware that I was now in the interior of Asia. The houses are here already built in the Eastern fashion; the walls, built of stone or mud, are clumsy and running irregularly in a zigzag line, with windows looking out into the yard rather than the street; secret entrances, and other like things characteristic of Eastern houses.

At Erzerum I was staying at the house of the Circassian, Hussein Daim Pasha, the commanding officer of the place, with whom I had been already acquainted at Constantinople. I had instructed his son in French, and in European sciences. When I told him of my Bokhara plan he was very much surprised, and at first tried to dissuade me from it, but promised me, afterwards, to furnish me with letters of recommendation to some of the prominent Sheikhs of the Turkestan capital. I met amongst the other governmental officers, at Erzerum, some whom I had known in Stambul, and I called upon them at their offices. I shall never forget the appearance of the offices of the Turkish government.

The entrance was nearly barricaded by a promiscuous heap of shoes, sticks, weapons and a troop of dogs lying everywhere about. The interior corresponded with the outside. On a couple of dirty, ragged divans were seated several officials ; in one part of the room a group of women were quarrelling, in another a humorous individual was entertaining the officers, and in another, again, some one gave vent to his complaints, interspersed with oaths.

Evidences of the poverty of the inhabitants of Erzerum meet the eye in whatever direction one may look. The dirt, the squalor and the underground dwellings are unbearable. The smell of their food, which they cook by the fire made of a fuel called *tezek* (cattle dung), is especially loathsome.

I was almost glad when I left this place on the 29th of May, about dusk, in company of my Armenian fellow-traveller. It might have been about midnight when we heard the loud barking of dogs, an indication of the propinquity of human habitations. I rode ahead, over ditches and bushes, towards the lights twinkling from the scattered houses. Everybody in the place was sunk in sleep, and it was only owing to my Effendi way of talking that I succeeded in procuring, for myself and my companion, quarters for the night. The name of the village was Kurudjuk, and the house where we happened to obtain accommodation belonged to the Kizil or chieftain of the place. The dwellings hereabouts consist, usually, of only one room, in which both men and domestic animals live promiscuously together. The cattle are tied on to the crib running along two sides of the spacious room, and the human beings occupy the *saku*, a species of elevated platform. It may be justly said that people, here, are living in stables. One may imagine what an agreeable thing it is to pass the night in the society of from forty to fifty buffaloes, and a couple of calves and a horse. Add to it that there is not a solitary window to this barn. More squalid and miserable dwellings there cannot perhaps be met with in the whole of Asia, than those in the environs of Erzerum. One may then appreciate the feeling of pleasure with which the traveller exchanges the foul air of his night quarters for the sweet morning air of the spring.

After a ride of nearly four hours we reached *Hassan-kale*, a place situated on a promontory. It is fortified against the attacks of the marauding Kurds, living in the country. They hardly dare, it is true, to make a raid upon the villages nowadays, but smaller caravans and the solitary traveller are still exposed to the fury of their marauding propensities. For the sake of safety we had with us two *kavasses* (mounted policemen). I myself had, indeed, nothing to fear from attack, but, out of regard for my Armenian companions, who had about them valuable trinkets which they had brought with them from Europe, I made use, on their behalf, of the firman given to me, as an Effendi, by the governor of Erzerum.

Upon crossing the Araxes river, we arrived ere long at the frontier of Kurdistan proper, whose inhabitants had already enjoyed, in the age of Herodotus, the unenviable reputation of being thieves and robbers of the worst kind. We noticed on our march a lofty rock—and one of our guides told us that the renowned Korouglu had lived on the top of it. He is the most celebrated hero-adventurer of Mohammedan popular poetry; his miraculous feats are told in song, at feasts and on the battlefield, alike by the Turks on the Oxus, the Anatolians near the Mediterranean, and the Roumelians by the waves of the Danube.

As we were passing through a narrow mountain-defile my Armenian companions set to loading their guns and pistols, saying: "We shall meet henceforth no more Osmanlis; only Kurds and Armenians are living here." Letters of recommendation and polite requests have no effect upon the Kurds; if you wish to keep them in awe you must meet them well armed.

At a Kurdistan village, called *Eshek-Eliasz,* we hired two men to accompany us, and we started on our way at the dawn of morning. It was a murky gloomy morning, the tops of the distant mountains were clouded by the fog. We sent the loaded animals ahead, and sat down at the foot of the mountain to make our tea. In the damp and chilly hours of the early dawn tea is a most refreshing beverage, and after having taken a cup or two we remounted our horses in order to overtake our beasts of burden. We overtook them after half an hour's trot, and saw them peaceably advancing along the ridge of the mountain. The rays of the sun had now scattered the fog, and looking about me, admiring the beautiful mountain scenery, I happened to observe that one of our Kurdistan followers was glancing now at the luggage-carriers, now at his companion, betraying great uneasiness. "What is it, what is it?" I asked. Instead of any reply he merely pointed in the direction where the servants of my Armenian companions and a couple of mule drivers were marching on. We looked and saw armed Kurds, on horseback and on foot, rushing in upon us from the right and the left, making straight for the animals laden with precious and valuable goods. "Robbers! Robbers!" shouted the Armenian Karabegoff, who had been in Europe. Quickly seizing his revolver, he rushed forward, followed by his friend and myself, but, although I urged on my horse in every conceivable manner, I was the third and last to arrive upon the scene of action. I still wore, at that time, a brass plate on my fez, in token of my dignity, as an Effendi. The Kurds had scarcely caught sight of me, when they suddenly stopped within a few steps from the badly frightened group of people. "What do you want here?" I asked them in a voice of thunder. An old, one-eyed man, armed with a shield, lance, rifle and sword, now stepped forward, and said: "Bey Effendi our oxen have strayed from us and we have been looking for them all night. Hast thou not met with them somewhere on thy way?"

"And is it customary to look for oxen, armed as thou art?" said I, "Shame on thee! Has thy beard turned grey to be soiled by thieving and robbery? If I did not regard thy old age I should take thee at once before the Kaimakam of Bayazid, thou insolent waylayer!"

My words and the explanations of my Kurd followers caused the band of marauders, consisting of eight men, very soon to understand with whom they had to deal. They are not much afraid of Armenians and Persians as a usual thing, but they do not deem it advisable to attack an officer of the Sultan. I still added a few threats to my former severe reprimands, and we had soon the satisfaction of seeing the robbers disband and quit us. We too continued our march, during which the Armenians never tired of expressing their gratitude to me. If it had not been for me, they said, all the valuables brought with them from London would have fallen into the hands of the Kurds. I especially remarked during the affray, the dismay and pallor of several Persian merchants who had joined us the day before. These men brought me, as we were about to retire to rest, various sweetmeats, as an acknowledgment of my services. I could not help admitting that, in the eyes of the Kurds, the dignity of an Effendi carried considerable weight.

We came in the evening to a village called *Mollah Suleiman*, inhabited, chiefly, by Armenians. At the sight of my Kurdistan followers, our landlord took me aside and said to me in a whisper: "Effendi, thou mayest well deem thyself fortunate for having escaped unhurt. Thy followers are known, far and wide, as the most desperate robbers; they have never before escorted any one across the Dagar mountain but some ill befell him." In an instant the whole adventure became clear to me. These two Kurd fellows were in league with the robbers, and but for my friend's revolver and my Effendi headgear the day might have proved fatal to all of us. Such occurrences are by no means rare in this region. The people and the authorities are well aware of the frequent cases of brigandage; they know who the brigands are; but, nevertheless, everybody is left to his own bravery to defend himself.

Our Armenian host, who had received his fellows in faith and myself with great cordiality, had a sumptuous supper prepared for us; the priest, clergyman and the judge of the village too, came to pay their respects, and there was no end to tales of robbery. In the autumn before, we were told, a caravan, consisting of forty beasts of burden and fifteen men, amongst whom there was an Englishman, was attacked by a robber chief and twelve men. No sooner had the Kurds, with their customary cry of "Lululu!" come upon them, than the Persians and Turks took to their heels, and allowed the brigands to freely rummage in the luggage, without molesting them. They had already driven away a couple of animals, when the Englishman, who had hitherto coolly stood by and watched the doings of the miscreants, raised his revolver without being observed, took deliberate aim at the chief and levelled him to the ground. The Kurds stood for a moment dumbfounded with fright, but they soon recovered and made a simultaneous rush upon the Englishman. The latter, who did not for an instant lose his presence of mind, shot dead another and then again another man, crying out to them fiercely: "Do not come near me or I will kill every one of you." This had its effect, one by one the remaining Kurds slunk away. The family of the dead chief instituted a suit for damages against the Englishman, claiming that the chief had been out hunting, and not robbing, when he was killed. The Turks treated the claim quite seriously, and, in all probability, would have mulcted the brave Englishman in damages but for the intercession of the British Consul.

The rain was pouring down violently when we left our hospitable host next day, and at night we had to put up at an Armenian village, containing about ten houses; for it was too late for us to reach on that day *Diadin*, the next place on our journey. The inhabitants of that village are leading a strange life. Man and beast, food and fuel are all stowed away under one roof, and whilst one part of the inhabitants are sleeping the others mount guard, on the roofs, with their arms in readiness. I asked several of them why they did not ask assistance of the governor of Erzerum, and was told, in reply: "That the governor was himself at the head of the thieves. God alone, and his representative on earth, the Russian Tzar, can help us." And the poor people were certainly right in this.

We forded through the Euphrates river and reached, before long, a monastery, the inmates of which were Armenian friars who were held in high respect by all the inhabitants of the surrounding country, both Christian and Mohammedan. It is a strikingly characteristic feature of all Eastern nations, that with them friars, monks, wizards, and fortune-tellers are indiscriminately, without regard to their religion, the objects of deep veneration. The supernatural, the mysterious excite the humility of the Eastern man, and the Kurds go far away, to distant countries, in pursuit of their predatory ventures, leaving this solitary and unprotected settlement unmolested.

Towards evening we arrived at the border place, Diadin. After considerable inquiry we succeeded in finding the house of the judge, at whose hands we desired to procure accommodations for the night. On looking round there, I saw, sitting in a corner of the barn, an American minister, with his wife and children and his sister. They had been living in Urumia (in Persia) for several years, and were now on their way home, to Philadelphia. Urumia and Philadelphia, what a distance! But the members of the missionary society know no distance.

The Kurdistan Kizil, *i.e.*, chieftain, received me very kindly, and upon my asking him for a night's quarters, he replied: "Effendi, thou art welcome, but I can give thee no accommodation, unless thou desirest to share with a soldier-pasha the only spare room in my house."

"Soldier-pasha, or anybody else in the wide world," I replied. "Just show me into the room. A ride of ten hours will tame a very Satan. Besides, I think, the stranger and I will very well agree together."

The Kurd, holding a small oil-lamp in his hand,

preceded me, and took me to a place looking like a lumber-room. The soldier-pasha was squatting in one corner. In approaching him, to introduce myself, I recognized in the stranger, to my great surprise, General Kolmann, otherwise called Fejzi Pasha, one of my dearest friends. "Well, this is a wonderful meeting," he said, after our greetings were over, and we had settled ourselves, opposite to one another, near the fire. General Kolmann, a distinguished member of the Hungarian emigration, had always befriended me in the most zealous manner, during the whole of my stay in Turkey. He knew of my plans for travelling, and was overjoyed, beyond all measure, to have an opportunity of saying "Good-bye" to me here, at the frontier of Turkey, where he had been detailed by the government to superintend the building of border barracks. We whiled away the time with chatting until late into the night, and it was with a heavy heart that I took leave next morning of my countryman, and of that country to which, for the time being, I belonged.

MOUNT ARARAT.

Page 49.

VI.

FROM THE PERSIAN BORDER TO TEBRIZ.

KIZIL-DIZE is the name of the first village on Persian soil. Leaving it we came to the base of *Ararat.* Mount Ararat, whose tapering head is covered with snow even in summer, was at that season clad in its wintry garb to more than half its height. The inhabitants of the surrounding country all insist that the remains of Noah's Ark may still be seen on its top, and many a *vartabet* (priest), rich in grace, boasts of having seen with his own eyes, the precious relics of the holy Ark in the waters, clear as crystal, of a lake on the top of the mountain. Others, again, produce chips from the remains of the Ark and recommend it highly against pain in the stomach, sore eyes and other maladies; and woe to him who would dare to cast the slightest doubt upon the existence, to this day, of at least two planks and a couple of masts of Noah's Ark on mount Ararat. During my travels in Asia I came across four other places, of which sacred tradition tells that Noah's Ark had rested there, and at least four other places, again, where people have discovered the unmistakable traces of the scriptural Paradise.

After we crossed the Turco-Persian border line the country became visibly more and more beautiful, as if Nature meant to support the haughty presumptuousness of the Persians. The most modest and reserved of my Persian fellow-travellers kept on saying during the whole journey, "Iran is a land very different from thine, Effendi! Look out, thou shalt see wonders." The faces of the Persians beamed with indescribable joy from the moment they had set their eyes upon the first Persian village, for the poor fellows had a great deal to suffer, all the way from Erzerum, in the numerous Armenian villages. According to the rigid Shi-ite law, not only is the Christian impure, but he defiles everything he touches, and the pious Shi-ite will rather starve than eat of any food a Christian had come in contact with.

We slept for the first time on Persian soil, in *Ovadjik*. Here, in Iran, I thought it advisable to part with my dignity of Effendi, for in the country of the Shi-ites, everything that approaches, in the least, the Sunnite faith of the Turks, is hated and despised, although both sects are professors of Islam.

We started early in the morning, on the fifth of June, and as our way was to lead us, on that day, through the *Karaayne* mountains, which did not enjoy the best reputation for safety, my Armenian companions thought it proper to provide themselves with the escort of a small number of mounted armed men. Fortunately nothing unpleasant happened. We came to *Karaayne* early in the afternoon, and I was delighted to hear issuing, from the house opposite to our quarters, sounds of music, the report of firearms, and shouts of merriment. They were celebrating a wedding, and, upon my question, if the wedding folks would have any objection to my going over and looking at them, I was taken there, at once, by the son of my host. A numerous troop of groomsmen had just arrived when we entered, in order to conduct the bride from the paternal house to her husband. They gave notice of their arrival outside by the report of firearms, then entered, wrapped a red-coloured veil round the bride, led her out into the street, and two of the groomsmen assisted her to mount her horse. Although her wide dress, falling down in many folds, impeded her movements, she sat quite firmly in the saddle. The bride was then surrounded by the women, singing in chorus a very curious song, the burden of which, repeated at the end of each stanza, was: "Let friend remain friend, and the enemy turn blind, O Allah!" At last, the procession started for the house of the bridegroom. I, too, mixed with the crowd, accompanying them, and was afterwards invited to take a prominent seat at the table. Wedding gifts were collected of the guests during the meal. The marriage rites agreed in every particular with those used by the Turcomans.

We had proceeded about two hours on the road leading from Karaayne to *Tchuruk*, our nearest station, when we were startled by a peculiar kind of barking and howling, coming from the depths of the mountains, before us. We had just reached an eminence on the road. Our little company of travellers halted at once, and our Persian escort, bending their eyes anxiously upon the entrance of the deep road, prepared their arms for action. The howling grew louder and louder, and suddenly a magnificent stag burst upon our sight, hotly pursued by two wolves. The Persians, who are very fond of the chase, were electrified by this sight, and two of them springing forward advanced in a run towards the animal—one of the two, although running, took such excellent aim at it, that upon his firing the beautiful deer fell lifeless to the ground. The wolves were scared by the shooting and ran away. One of the wolves, however, as soon as everything became quiet again, either pushed by hunger, or feeling sore at the loss of his prey, soon reappeared to our great surprise. The hunters allowed him to approach, unmolested, within a few paces from the lifeless stag, and then fired at him, killing him on the spot. Every member of our small company was delighted with the adventure. We dismounted, stripped off the skin of the deer, cut him up and set to work at once to roast the best parts on the spit, leaving the rest of the carcass and the wolf behind us.

The first place of note the traveller from the west comes to, in Persia, is called *Khoy*. I was particularly struck by its bazaar. The life and commotion in it was marked by that primitive quaintness and splendour of ancient times which are, to a great extent, wanting in the Stambul bazaars, owing to the influence of the Europeans. Any one who has witnessed in Khoy, during the hours of the forenoon, the stir and bustle in the cool and narrow streets, watched the gesticulations of buyers and sellers, seen the variety of splendid fabrics and arms, and the food offered for sale, and observed the behaviour of the thronging and screaming crowd, must own that in the matter of Oriental characteristics, at least, the bazaar of Constantinople is inferior to that of Khoy.

The first impression was a truly bewildering and bewitching one, I could hardly tear myself away from the strange spectacle ; the peculiar sounds, the strange din and noise, the seething life everywhere, were things I had never witnessed before. As I was entering a place, topped by a cupola, where about thirty braziers were striking away, with a will, each at a kettle or pan, I was struck with astonishment upon seeing that, in the midst of this infernal din, there were, in an unoccupied portion of the building, two schools in full blast. There sat the schoolmaster—amongst the children who were ranged round him in the shape of a half moon—armed with a long stick probably in order to enable him to reach the children sitting on the hindmost forms. I went quite near them and listened with the utmost attention, but could not catch a solitary word, although both teacher and pupils were screaming at the top of their lungs. The exertion told on them, too, for with their inflated red faces and starting veins they looked like so many infuriated turkeys. They pretend, nevertheless, that an improper stress laid upon any Arabic word in the Koran, by any children, is immediately observed and duly rebuked by the master.

I was surprised, even more agreeably, by the neat little caravansary which we entered. The traveller meets everywhere in Arabia and Turkey with dirty khans only; but here, in Persia, where, from ancient times, much care has been bestowed upon the comfort and facilities of intercourse, the caravansaries will be found to be inns which—I am speaking, of course, of Eastern pretensions—leave nothing to be desired. These inns stand mostly in the due centre of the bazaar, and generally form a square building, each side of which is divided off into a certain number of cells. A half circular opening, doing service both as a door and window, leads to a terrace-like elevation running round the building. Beneath it are placed the stables, so that a traveller, living on the first floor, can be ostler to his own horse, on the ground floor. This terrace is from four to six feet high, and leads to what is in reality the yard, in the centre of which there is a well, often surrounded by a small flower-garden. The cells offer a cool and pleasant retreat during the day, and a place of safety, for travellers, during the night. The *dalundar* (door-keeper), who is stationed at the cupola-shaped entrance-door, is charged with maintaining order. This person is quick in discerning the rank and station of a traveller, by his horse and saddle-gear, and he provides him with corresponding accommodation. Sentinels are stationed on the flat roofs during the night, who are scaring away with their monotonous cries all evil-doers, and it is a rare thing for theft or robbery to be committed at the caravansaries.

We left Khoy towards evening, on the 8th of June, for fear of being interrupted in our journey, on account of the feast of *Kuram Bairam* (the month of merry-making after the fast), and stopped at the village of *Hadji Aga,* inhabited altogether by *Seids*, that is, descendants of the prophet. These men are the most pretentious men in all Persia in their pride of descent, but they are especially arrogant in their behaviour towards strangers, and indeed one must have Job's patience to bear their impertinences meekly. No matter how rich they are, they will beg wherever they see a chance of getting something. Indeed they do not ask for any alms, but they impose a tax, due to them as the descendants of the head of Islam. They commit capital crimes, under the plea of sanctity, and the people rarely dare to call them to account. The authorities seem to be less indulgent, for I was told that the governor of Tebriz, to the horror of the whole world, condemned a Seid who had committed robbery to death by fire. The Mollahs fell to protesting, but the governor gave them the follow-reply: "If he is a true Seid he will not be touched by the flames," and caused the culprit to be cast into the blazing pile.

VII.

IN TEBRIZ.

TEBRIZ is a town of remote antiquity, and is said to have been built by the wife of Harun el Rashid. But of the ancient greatness and splendour in which Tebriz was said to have once vied with the city of Raghes, very little is now to be seen. Its commerce, however, is quite as flourishing to-day as it was reputed to have been in ancient times. The grand life of the bazaar had surprised me already at Khoy, but compared to that of Tebriz, it was only a picture in miniature. Here the din and noise, the stir and bustle, the pushing and elbowing, the stifling crowds are magnified a hundred-fold. At the recommendation of several persons I put up at the Emir Caravansary, which, however, it took me over an hour to find. Not being used to this deafening noise, and to pushing through such dense crowds of people and mules without number, which seemed perilous to both life and limb, I was apprehensive lest I might at any moment ride over somebody with my horse. In recalling how the dervishes were dancing onward ahead of me through this dire confusion, uttering their unearthly screams, brandishing high, and casting up, into the air their sharp axes, seizing them again by their handles upon coming down, I wonder, to this day, how I ever got safely to the Emir Caravansary.

My Armenian companions ordered a modest cell for me, and, as they had already reached their place of destination, they parted with the promise of returning the next day and installing themselves as my guides through their native city. I sat down at the door of my narrow little room and remained there until late in the evening, partly to take some rest after my previous fatigues, partly to watch the life stirring about me. Very soon, true to the custom of their country, a curious crowd gathered around me; by some I was taken to be a merchant and was offered goods by them, by others a money changer and was asked if I had any Imperiales or Kopeks which I wished to exchange; others, again, offered me their services, judging me by my attire to be a member of the embassy of Teheran. It is wearisome work for a newly arrived stranger at a caravansary, this being catechised from all sides.

I passed two entire weeks in Tebriz; I desired to rest after the fatigues of my long journey, making, at the same time, excellent use of my leisure in studying the peculiarities of the Shi-ite sect, a study which revealed to me a great deal that was novel and interesting. I did so with all the more pleasure as my uninterrupted stay, for many years, among all the Sunnite circles, my perfect knowledge of their modes of life, customs, and dispositions, had especially fitted me for instituting relevant comparisons.

I had been often told that the Shi-ites were the Protestants of Islam, and their superior intelligence and industry led me to at one time share this supposition.

I was therefore quite astonished to find, on the very day of my arrival, wherever I turned, instances of a fanaticism far more savage, and of a sanctimoniousness far more glaring, than I had ever met with in Turkey. First of all I was disagreeably impressed with the reserve and spirit of exclusiveness shown by the Persians towards Europeans. They are commanded by their law, for instance, in case the hem of a European's garment but happens to touch the dress of a Persian, that the Persian immediately becomes *nedjiz*, that is unclean, and must forthwith resort to a bath to regain his purity. My faith in their cleanliness, of which they were so fond of boasting, very soon received a rude shock, in witnessing the following scene. In the centre of the yard of the caravansary, as everywhere else, is placed a basin full of water, originally intended for the performance of ritual lavations, but, as I was watching their proceedings at the basin, I saw that whilst at one side of the reservoir some were washing their dirty things, others placing half-tanned skins into the same water for soaking, and a third was cleansing his baby, there were standing men on the opposite side of the basin, gravely performing their religious washings with the identical water, and one of them, who must have been very thirsty indeed, crouched down and eagerly drank of the dark green fluid. I could not repress at the sight a manifestation of loathing. A Persian, standing near, immediately confronted me and reproved me for my ignorance. He asked me if I did not know that according to the *Sheriat* (the holy law) a quantity of water, in excess of a hundred and twenty pints, turns blind, that is, it cannot become soiled or unclean.

In mentioning their fanaticism I cannot omit citing

a remarkable instance of it in the person of one of their wonderful dervishes. This man happened to pass just then through Tebriz, and was an object of general admiration at the bazaar. He was thoroughly convinced that the divinity of the Caliphate, after the death of Mohammed, ought, by right, to have devolved upon Ali, Mohammed's son-in-law, and not upon Abubekr, the prophet's brother-in-law. Acting upon this conviction, he had solemnly vowed, more than thirty years before, that he would never employ his organs of speech otherwise but in uttering, everlastingly, the name of his favourite, *Ali! Ali!* He thus wished to signify to the world that he was the most devoted partisan of that Ali who had been defunct more than a thousand years. In his own home, speaking with his wife, children and friends, no other word but "Ali!" ever passed his lips. If he wanted food or drink, or anything else, he expressed his wants still by repeating "Ali!" Begging or buying at the bazaar it was always "Ali!" Treated ill or generously, he would still harp on his monotonous "Ali!" Latterly his zeal assumed such tremendous proportions that, like a madman, he would race, the whole day, up and down the streets of the town, throwing his stick high up into the air, and shriek out, all the while, at the top of his voice, "Ali!" This dervish was venerated by everybody as a saint, and received everywhere with great distinction. The wealthiest man of a town presented him once with a magnificent steed, saddle, bridle and all. He immediately vaulted into the saddle and sped along the streets uttering his customary fierce cry. The colour of his dress was either white or green, and the staff he carried corresponded in colour with the dress he wore. When he came to the front of the Emir Caravansary, he stopped and lifted his voice, midst the frightful din of the bazaar, with such tremendous power, shouting "Ali! Ali!" that the veins on his head and neck started out like strings.

After passing a few days at Tebriz, it dawned upon me that this, indeed, was genuine Eastern life, and that distant Stambul, the gaudily painted curtain of the Eastern world, presented but a tame and lifeless and somewhat Europified picture of the Orient. True, after the first excitement at the great variety of wonderful sights was over, my mind immediately reverted to the sweets of Western life, and right glad was I, therefore, to meet, at the caravansary, with two Swiss gentlemen of culture, Mr. Würth and Mr. Hanhardt. They at once insisted upon my moving my quarters to their lodgings, but I declined with thanks, availing myself, however, at times, of their cordial invitation to take my meals with them. Through them I became acquainted with other Europeans residing here, and it was to me a source of great delight to change about, and after having passed with Europeans a considerable time discussing Western ideas and conversing in a Western tongue, all of a sudden to become an Effendi again in some Persian society. My fancy was tickled by this almost theatrical transition from the East to the West and back again; I used to indulge in this pastime with great pleasure while in Stambul.

The Persian world rather wondered at my intimacy with the Europeans, but refrained from making any comments upon it to me, knowing that the Sunnites, to whom I was supposed to belong, were far less rigorous than the Shi-ites in their intercourse with persons differing from them in faith. If my European friends communicated to me their views of certain local institutions and customs, I did not accept them unconditionally; I looked at them, again, in the light shed upon them by the observations and feelings of the natives on the subject. Should some kind reader wish to rebuke me for my seeming double-facedness, I have only to say that I shall meekly submit to it, but that, at the same time, I am indebted to the acting of this double part for the satisfaction I had in obtaining a proper insight into native life, and being able to gather many and varied experiences about the nations of the East, from the Bosphorus to Samarkand.

It was here, in the Caravansary Emir, that I met with a rather curious adventure, which I must relate. One afternoon, whilst the heat was rather unbearably strong, I sat at the door of my cell, and engaged myself, as is usual with dervishes, in delivering my linen of certain animals which intrude upon the poor traveller in the East in spite of all his efforts after cleanliness. Two Englishmen, whom I recognized by their Indian hats, and who were strolling in the caravansary, stopped suddenly before me, and after admiring for a while my patient and untasteful occupation, the younger one said to the older, "Look at the hunting zeal of this fellow!" I raised my eyes and said in English, "Will you join, sir?" Amazed, nay bewildered, one of them immediately asked me, "How did you learn English, and what countryman are you?" From reasons formerly explained, I abstained from a further conversation, and notwithstanding all the exertions, I did not utter another English word, nay, withdrew altogether to the interior of my cell.

Years passed, and after returning to Europe I happened to be at an evening party in the house of an English nobleman at Whitehall. Whilst at dinner I recognized in one of the guests present my interlocutor of Tebriz, but unsure of my discovery I did not address him. After dinner, however, the lady of the house asked me to relate something of my perilous adventures, and seeking courage, I asked her to introduce me to the man in whom I supposed a former acquaintance. "Oh, that is Lord R——," said the lady. "Well, I don't know his name, but I have seen him," was my answer. Lord R—— received me politely, but denied the fact of a former acquaintance. Upon my saying, "My lord, you have been to Tebriz, and you do not remember the dervish who addressed you in English?" The extraordinary surprise of Lord R—— was indescribable, he recognized me at once, and related the whole adventure to the highly amused company.

The days I spent in Tebriz passed quickly and pleasantly owing to my intercourse being partly with Europeans and not being exclusively confined to Asiatics. While I was there, an interesting festival took place, to which I succeeded in obtaining admission. The solemn investiture of the recently nominated Veli Ahd (heir apparent to the throne) gave me an opportunity of gazing upon the pageant and pomp of the Orient in all its splendour. Muzaffar-ed-din Mirza, the son of the king, now nine years old, but who, according to the custom of the country, had been elected, in his childhood, successor to the throne, was to be publicly invested with the Khalat, the royal parade robe. The whole town was on the alert. The festival lasted several days, and when, on its first day, I entered through the gate of the Ala Konak (the royal residence), which was surrounded by a dense crowd of people, into the interior court, my curiosity rose to the highest pitch. What a strange contrast of squalor and splendour, of pomp and misery!

There, in the covered hall, opposite the gate, were seated the grandees of the land, and amongst them the prince with the principal officers of his household. Every face wore a solemnly grave expression, and the bearing of their manly forms, wrapped in flowing garments, the dignified motion of their arms, the proud carriage of their heads, everything indicated that they were well versed in the art of exhibiting a public pageant. Around the interior of the court were ranged two lines of *serbasses* (soldiers), sad-looking fellows, in European uniforms and with Persian fur caps on their heads, looking as uncomfortable and awkward as possible in their foreign clothes. The most comical things about them were their cravats, some tied in front, others at the back, and others again anywhere between those two points.

One of the sides of the garden was entirely occupied by loaves of sugar and various Persian cakes and sweetmeats, which it is the custom to place upon huge wooden platters, and without which any festive occasion in Persia would be considered incomplete.

In the centre rose the throne, upon which the young boy-prince, looking feeble and pale, took his seat, surrounded by his splendid retinue. When he was seated, the loud booming of cannon was heard, the military band struck up a martial march, and immediately afterwards appeared the royal envoy bearing the robe of honour, which he placed upon the shoulders of the young prince in token of his new dignity. The envoy then produced the insignia of the diamond order of Shir-ú-Khurshid, fastened it upon the breast of the princely heir apparent, concluding the ceremony by suddenly removing a costly carpet which had concealed the portrait of the king, painted in oil upon canvas. At this moment the whole company rose to their feet; the young prince rushed forward and imprinted a kiss upon the portrait, which was then immediately covered up again with the carpet. Upon the prince returning to his seat from the ceremony of osculation, the deafening roar of cannon and the swelling sounds of music were heard again. A high priest came forward and invoked a blessing upon the prince, the royal order was loudly proclaimed, and finally a young poet stepped forward, and, taking a seat opposite to the prince, recited to his glorification a *Kascide* (glorifying song). The proceedings of the young poet were quite new to me, and struck me even more than the bombastic tenor of his poetical effusion. He compared the prince to a tender rose, to the brilliant sun, and finally to a precious pearl fished out of the sea of the royal family, and destined to become now the most precious ornament in the crown of Iran. Then he called him a powerful hero, who with a single blow of his sword destroys whole armies, at whose glance the mountains tremble, and the flame of whose eyes makes the rivers run dry.

The prince then joined the great lords, who were in the background, and the sweetmeats were removed from the enormous platters and divided amongst the guests present, the master of ceremonies expressing to each of them, besides, his thanks for their appearance. And, now, the pageant was over.

These festivities were followed by the reception of Cerutti, the Italian ambassador, who, at the head of an embassy consisting of twenty-five members, was passing through Tebriz, on his way to Teheran. Their arrival caused a great ferment both amongst the members of the native government and the European colony. The former, the Persian officials with the viceregent Serdar-

Aziz-Khan, at their head, were delighted to have an opportunity afforded them to indulge in their passionate fondness for display, and the latter were gratified to set their eyes upon the representatives of the new Italian kingdom. I joined the latter in order to be present at the reception. In the early morning of a sultry day in June we rode out of the town, a distance of about two hours, to meet them, and when we came up to them they were just changing their dresses. They wished to appear before the Persians in full parade, and it took considerable time for twenty-five Europeans, diplomatists, military men, merchants, and men of science, to accomplish the task of donning their best attire. It was not far from noon, the heat being intolerable, when these gentleman entered the gates of the town, in their highly ornamental uniforms and costumes, their breasts resplendent with the insignia of the various orders, in plumed helmets and magnificent swords. Of course the sight was to us Europeans a very attractive one, but wishing to hear the opinion of the natives, I left my company and mixed with the crowd. During the whole procession I heard nothing but ironical remarks, the Persians looking upon things considered by us splendid, as ridiculous. According to their notions, our short coats, fitting the body, are the most indecorous things, without any taste, and everything plain, tightfitting, and unassuming in dress looks to them mean and insignificant. Their idea of the beautiful in dress consists in what is ample, flowing in rich folds and showy. Their prudery and mock modesty make them regard as indecent any mode of dressing which sharply defines the limbs and outlines of the human body, whilst Europeans affect that style, and thereby rouse the displeasure of the Asiatics. They also criticise the stiff carriage of the Europeans on horseback, and in this they are not far from wrong, for the European with his protruding chest looks like a caricature besides one who sits with easy grace, yet proudly, on his steed.

The Embassy, on the day of their arrival, were worked very hard indeed. For two hours they were dragged through the town, in every possible direction, in order to gratify the curiosity of the populace. When they got at last to the place assigned to them for their residence, they were far from being allowed to rest. For three whole days they were besieged by a host of polite visitors, each of them attended by a troop of servants who were to bring back to their master's house, in return, the ampler and more valuable presents which they expected to receive from the Embassy.

The roads leading from Tebriz into the interior of Persia were fairly swarming with caravans and troops of travellers. I, therefore, deemed the roads sufficiently safe, and resolved to continue alone my journey to the capital of the country, accompanied only by a *tcharvador*, a man who lets horses and animals of burden for hire. I hired from him a rather sorry-looking nag, corresponding to the modest sum I paid for its use, placed my scanty baggage on it, and said good-bye to Tebriz.

VIII.

IN ZENDJAN.

TWO days after leaving Tebriz, I arrived at a village called *Turkmantchay*, and passed the night there. This village is celebrated for being the place where the Treaty of Peace, which put an end to the Perso-Russian war of 1826–28, was concluded. Nothing particular happened on my way from here to *Miane*, except a slight intermezzo, occurring during my noon's rest at a solitary caravansary. I had been asked before by Shi-ites, here and there, in my capacity of a Sunnite, to give them some kind of *nuskha* (talisman). A Shi-ite Seid came to me there on the same errand, and I readily granted his request by writing one or two passages of the Koran on a slip of paper. He was not satisfied with this, but begged of me, in addition, tobacco for his pipe, some of the strong kind my friends in Tebriz had presented me with. "Seid," I said, "I give it to thee willingly, but thou art used to the mild tobacco of Kurdistan, and I am afraid this will make thee sick." As he kept on insisting, I was obliged to let him have some. He filled his pipe, lighted it, but hardly had he taken a few puffs at it when he was seized by a violent attack of dizziness, became dreadfully pale and had a fit of vomiting. The Seid rushed, screaming, into the yard and shouted: "Help, help, Shi-ites; the Sunnite has poisoned me." I ran after him as fast as I could, and when I overtook him I found him lying on his back surrounded by a small group of Persians. If my eloquence had not been equal to the task of persuading the bystanders of my innocence, I should have fared badly.

While yet at a distance of several hours from *Zendjan* I was joined by a Persian man, who, judging by his appearance, seemed to belong to the learned class. He addressed me, to my surprise, at once as Effendi, although I had never set my eyes on him before. He was very talkative, like most Persians, and discoursed about a thousand things in the course of half an hour. He introduced himself to me as a physician who was just returning from his visits to his patients in the neighbourhood. Very soon he was overtaken by his servant leading a mule so heavily laden that it well-nigh sank beneath the weight of its load. The poor beast was carrying the fees collected in kind by the physician, such as dried fruit, corn and so forth. This loquacious disciple of Æsculap dwelt, during the whole time, upon the miraculous cures he had accomplished, and gave vent to his unbounded astonishment at the impudence of the Frengis (Europeans) who dared to appear as physicians in the home of *Ali Ben Sina* (Avicenna). He unceasingly dilated upon the efficacy of his amulets and talismans, and how he had driven devils out of his patients, made the dumb speak, the blind see and the deaf hear. When we reached the town my head fairly ached with the man's incessant flow of speech.

Along the road leading to the caravansary I observed a great many black flags hoisted upon tall poles. We were in the first ten days of the month of Moharrem, during which period the Islamite world abstains from every kind of merry-making. But the Shi-ites begin the doleful feast one month sooner; everybody arrays himself in mourning, fasts, and employs his time in the recital of elegies and in visiting the *Tazies*. The black flags marked the places where the performances were to take place. At that time, a celebrated singer was everywhere spoken of, who had won great distinction in the part of *Ali Ekber*, and who was to perform on that very day in the Tazie of the governor. I was burning with impatience to witness a Tazie, and I had hardly arrived at the caravansary when I determined to start at once. I joined the populace, and was carried by the stream of people into the court of the governor. There in the centre stood an elevated platform, a little above two yards high, around which, upon poles of considerable height, were suspended tiger and panther skins, black flags, shields of steel and skin, and bare swords, interspersed with here and there a lamp, to light up the evening performance. This was the stage. The women were seated on the right side of the court, and the men were gathering on the opposite side. The governor himself (who had the Tazie performed) and his family, surrounded by the prominent men of the town, looked at the spectacle from the second story. Everything was wrapped in deep mourning, every face wore an expression of indescribable sadness and dejection.

The Tazie represents the tragic history of Hussein, of which a short outline will be here in place. After the death of Mohammed, he having designated no one as his successor, the faithful divided into two camps. The larger portion thought Abubekr, the oldest companion and follower of the Prophet, most worthy of the succession, whilst the minority endeavoured to place Ali upon the throne, guided by the strength of those words uttered by Mohammed: "Even as I am lord, so is Ali lord, too." But Ali's party was vanquished. After Abubekr came Osman, and the latter was succeeded by Omar. Ali's partisans, however, did not despair of their cause; they made several attempts to seat him on the throne, and after the death of Omar, Ali actually became Caliph. His reign was of short duration; his enemies, at whose head the Prophet's widow herself stood, had him assassinated. His sad vicissitudes, cruel sufferings and tragic end only increased the number of his followers; he was mourned as a martyr and almost deified. He had nine wives, but of these mention is made only of Fatima, the Prophet's most beloved daughter, who bore Ali two sons, Hassan and Hussein. The right of succession was claimed by Hussein. The latter, upon one occasion, was going from Mecca to the town of Kuffa, at the invitation of its inhabitants, who were his partisans. He was accompanied by those of his followers who expatriated themselves from Mecca. On the banks of the Tigris, in the middle of the desert, they were suddenly attacked by hostile bands, sent against them by Yezid, and every one of them cruelly massacred. This catastrophe is commemorated, in Persia, by numberless mournful and plaintive songs and theatrical exhibitions, called *Tazies*.

Just before the Tazie commenced, a ragged and, from excessive indulgence in opium, rather rickety-looking dervish stepped upon the platform, crying: "Ya Muminin!" (Oh! you true believers), and in an instant the utmost stillness prevailed. He now engaged in a long prayer, lauding the perfections and brave deeds of the Shi-ite great, and then enumerating in exaggerated language the sins and wickedness of the Sunnites, and in mentioning the names of some distinguished Sunnite men, he exclaimed, with a fury bordering on madness: "Brethren, ought we not to curse them, ought we not to call down damnation upon their heads? I tell you, a curse upon the three dogs, the three usurpers, Abubekr, Omar and Osman!" There he paused, waiting for the effect of his words on the assembled multitude. The whole multitude expressed their approval of his curses and anathemas by loud cries of "Bishbad, bishbad!" (More even than that, more even than that!) The dervish went on cursing Ayesha, the Prophet's wife, Moavie, Yezid and all the distinguished foes to Shi-itism, pausing at the name of each, and the audience roared out every time "Bishbad!" A speech by the same person, glorifying the Shah, the present Ulemas of Persia and the Governor, followed the cursing, at the end of which he descended from the platform and hurried amongst the audience to gather in a substantial reward for the zeal he had shown. This was the prologue. Shortly afterwards several persons clad in ample flowing robes made their appearance on the stage, singing elegies now in solos, now in chorus, in order to move the hearts of the hearers and prepare their minds for the coming play. Imam Hussein comes now upon the stage; he is on his way to Kuffa, in the very heart of the desert, and accompanied by his family and a small band of faithful followers. They are all horribly suffering from want of water, and Hussein is endeavouring to assuage the woes of his family, caused by their tantalizing thirst, by words of comfort and encouragement. Meanwhile a throne is rising in the background, the throne of Yezid,

Hussein's enemy, seated upon which is Yezid herself, in all the pride of pomp, distributing orders of the most cruel nature against Hussein and his friends amongst her mailed and warlike followers. Ali Ekber, the youngest child of Hussein, is so moved at the sight of the sad plight in which his parents and sisters and brothers are, that he determines to fetch them water from the Tigris, although he well knows that the enemy is lurking everywhere. His parents and their friends dissuade him from this enterprise, in the tenderest language, their voices attuned to the emotions of love and anxiety for his safety. There was something really affecting in the beseeching tones of the weeping mother and in the prayers of the father, and the sobs of Hussein and his little band could hardly be heard on account of the sympathizing howling round about. The women, in particular, wept so bitterly that I could catch, at rare intervals, only here and there a word of the beautiful and deeply affecting dialogue.

But Ali Ekber remains firm in his resolve; his mother swoons away but soon recovers; she wishes to see her son become a hero and utters prayers for his safety. His own father girds on his sword, and he mounts his steed on the spot, and rides around the stage a couple of times. He is immediately pursued by one of Yezid's band, a powerful warrior, who, in pursuit, is not sparing of the most violent outbreaks against the persecuted youth. The struggle grows heated, the scene interesting, and the interest more and more intense. The brave youth is at last overtaken, blow falls after blow, and Ali Ekber's blood is flowing from numerous wounds. Groans and shrieks of despair from Ali Ekber's family and followers, who, watching the event of the fight with bated breath, perceive the awful finale. He sinks to the ground and is carried, half dead, to the front of the stage. At this moment, when father, mother, sisters and brothers with loud wailings precipitate themselves upon the yawning wounds of the unhappy youth, shedding into them their tears instead of balm, the moaning, groaning and shrieks of spectators rise to the highest pitch. Women beat their breasts, and everybody, as a mark of sorrow, strews dust and chopped straw, instead of ashes, upon his head. The spectators are indeed so carried away with the play, that I doubt if there be anywhere in Europe a tragedian capable of producing a similar effect upon his audience. At the sight of his dying son, Hussein's wrath knows no bounds, and vowing vengeance, he, too, vaults into the saddle, but is hotly pressed by Shamr, one of Yezid's knights, and killed. His dead body is brought forward, and at the sight of it the multitude break out afresh into never-ending lamentations and weeping. They place him beside his son, and they are covered with black mourning shawls. At last a general massacre ensues, and every member of Hussein's family is killed. There they all lie stark dead, stretched out on the floor, and the pious spectators are so filled with holy horror that they dare not lift their eyes to look at the appalling spectacle on the stage—the performers leave the stage, and there is an end to the tragedy.

The other piece which followed represented a biblical scene—Abraham being about to sacrifice his son Isaac. This, too, was acted with considerable fidelity. After the old patriarch has patiently listened to God's command to the end, he seizes his child, kisses him, hugs him to his breast and finally ties him and lays him upon the altar. He then draws his sword, places the edge of his sword upon the child's bare throat, and just as he is about to cut the boy's throat, an angel of the Lord appears with two lambs. Isaac starts up from the altar and Abraham kills, in his place, the two lambs, which afford afterwards a succulent supper to the comedians. I was particularly struck with the grave demeanour and cleverness of the child-performers. There were some amongst them not above six years old, who knew their parts, amounting to a couple of hundred lines, perfectly well by heart. Their mimic acting and gestures were quite unexceptionable, too. The parts are always sung by the performers, and there were some actors who sang, especially the mournful parts, with such true expression and skill that the most delicate ear and the severest artistic sensibility would be gratified in hearing them.

Such and similar are the subjects of the Tazie. The performance and its getting up, of course, vary very much, according to the person at whose expense it takes place. The finest Tazies I saw were those performed at the court of Teheran, to which, however, usually, no strangers, except the members of the Turkish Embassy, are invited. As their guest I had an opportunity to go and see it with them, and the splendour displayed there is something not easily to be forgotten. All the actors were wrapped in shawls of the most costly quality; their arms were studded with genuine diamonds and precious stones, and the handles of their swords were either gilded or made of solid silver. The acting and the scenery were perfect; one could almost imagine Yezid, in person, to be before one's eyes. There is one thing, however, which detracts a great deal from the illusion of the representation; the female parts must be assumed by men, as the law of Islam rigidly forbids women to appear in public places.

IX.

FROM KAZVIN TO TEHERAN.

MY next place of destination was *Kazvin*, once the capital of Iran. There is not at present, however, a trace left of its ancient grandeur. The finely cultivated and luxuriant gardens in the suburbs were objects of great interest to me, and I lost so much time in their observation that it was already late at night when I entered the caravansary. I set down my luggage and immediately went off to purchase the necessary articles of food, but found, to my great surprise, all the shops closed. After half an hour's fruitless search I was compelled to retire to my cell hungry and worn-out with the fatigues of a whole day's travelling. In my vain attempts to procure some food I invariably received the same answer: "To-morrow will be the anniversary day of Hussein's death; the Shi-ites are good Mussulmans, and much too devout to carry on their business on the day on which Hussein and the other saints suffered so much." There was nothing left to me but to have recourse to begging; but the scanty alms one can obtain from the close-fisted Persian are by no means sufficient to satisfy the tremendous appetite of a traveller. On the following morning I succeeded in buying, under the seal of the profoundest secrecy, of a man who was not a shopkeeper, some bread and boiled rice. I hastened back to the caravansary and persuaded my travelling companion to leave at once. As we were advancing through the bazaar, towards the gate of the town, we were met by a funeral and atoning procession,—such as on this day may be seen everywhere in Persia, in pursuance of an ancient custom,—trying to excite the devotion of Believers by their frightful yelling and barbarous fanaticism. No imagination is equal to the task of picturing the wild antics in which those who participate in these processions indulge. One is taking a mad leap, another is striking his chest until blood issues from his mouth, a third is cutting up his body with a sharp knife, in order to make an impression upon the crowd by his flowing blood. I withdrew into a corner of the bazaar, waiting until the maddened crowd, with whose yells the whole neighbourhood resounded, had passed. My companion informed me that Kazvin —devout Kazvin, as he called it—distinguished itself on this day amongst all other towns in Persia by the death of at least two persons, out of devotion for Hussein. I readily believed him, for the scenes which transpire here on the tenth day of Moharrem vividly recall the self-mutilations of the Indians, inspired by religious fanaticism, or that scene in Egypt when on the day of Bairam men lie down upon the ground, in front of the mosque, to be trampled upon by the hoofs of the chief priest's well-fed horse.

The heat of the day compelled us to travel by night, and we were favoured in having just then full moon. The only objection I had was the extreme stillness of the night; I found it unsociable; for although we met now and then with solitary travellers and smaller caravans, returning from Teheran, yet we never had any one to join us, and were obliged to jog on by ourselves. On the third night after our departure from Kazvin, as we were riding in a flat country, I heard, about night, voices in the distance, and soon after the steadily approaching clatter of horses' hoofs. Placing my firearms before me on the saddle head, I bent forward in order to be able to see and observe better. Three horsemen brandishing aloft their arms came swooping down upon us. Holding my pistols ready for firing, I called out to them: "Get out of the way, or I will shoot you down." Either the strange sound of the foreign dialect, or our costume, so unlike that of the Persians, frightened them away and they took to their heels; but although my companion looked upon the occurrence as a joke, I could not help feeling uneasy, and had some comfort, on the evening of the following day, in the certainty that Teheran would be our next station.

I had brought with me several letters of recommendation from prominent Effendis and Pashas in Constantinople, introducing me to Haider Effendi, the then Turkish Ambassador in Persia. I was spoken of in these, for the most part, as an eccentric person who, tired of the idyllic repose of a quiet life in Constantinople, had set out to look for distraction in the wilds of Persia. Some laid special stress upon my being led to the East by the queer idea of studying the Eastern Turkish language; in one word, they did everything to satisfy Haider Effendi that I was in no way connected with politics, but a mere dreamer, worthy of his patronage. Haider Effendi had, besides, the reputation of being an affable, kind and straightforward man, and I felt convinced of a friendly reception at the Turkish Embassy, where I intended putting up.

I was thinking of this as I came up to the banks of a small brook called *Keretch.* I found there a large crowd of travellers, some preparing for their ablutions, others engaged in prayer on the banks. It was a cool summer's morning, a sure indication of excessive heat during the day. My curiosity to see the capital of Iran gave me no rest. I quickly washed myself in the clear water of the brook, and, greatly to the disgust of my companion, who wished to rest here for another half-hour, immediately mounted my horse, and started in the direction of the capital. I repeatedly asked, "Where is Teheran?" for I saw no indication of it. My companion's stolid answer always remained the same: "There," he said, pointing with his finger onward. In vain I exerted my sight, I could not discover the city. At last the gray mass of fog which hovered over it caught my eyes, and there was Teheran spread along the sloping base of a mountain. We were but half an hour's distance from it. The fog soon gave way to the rising sun. I got a glimpse first of roofs covered with green glazed tiles, then of gilded cupolas, and at last the panorama of the whole town unrolled before my eyes—I was at the gate of the seat of government of the "King of Kings," as the Shah calls himself.

I had now been serving an apprenticeship of two months to the art of travelling, and but for having got thinner, darker and considerably speckled in the face, I had every reason to be satisfied with the state of my health, which had successfully resisted so far the by no means slight fatigues of Asiatic caravan travelling on miserable nags.

X.

IN TEHERAN.

THE wall upon which Teheran and its inhabitants rely for their protection is built of mud, but it is nevertheless talked about by the Persians, with their usual exaggeration, as an impregnable wall of solid rock. I rode into the capital of Iran through a narrow gate in this wall, and had to push my way through the throng of pedestrians, horsemen and laden mules that were crossing the narrow, irregular and crooked streets. After protracted inquiry I succeeded in finding the palace of the Turkish Embassy, but it was empty; its occupants were gone. The soldiers mounting guard informed me that the entire *personnel* of the Embassy, following the fashion of the upper classes here, were living in the country, in a village called *Djizer*, at the foot of the neighbouring mountains, where the air was cooler and more bearable than that of the capital.

I was rather pleased with this news, for one day's experience was sufficient to convince me that Teheran was almost uninhabitable during the summer months, owing to the intolerable heat and a stifled atmosphere choked with noxious miasmas. The new-comer feels immediately the effects of these miasmas, for I could hardly eat anything on the day of my arrival. Towards evening the air became somewhat cooler, and as I had parted with my fellow-traveller from Tebriz, and consequently with my nag, too, I was obliged to hire an ass, in order to accomplish my trip to *Djizer*, which was about two hours' distance off. It was late in the evening when I arrived. The members of the Embassy were just then taking their supper beneath a tent of silk, in the garden. I was received by them with a cordiality exceeding my most sanguine expectations, and immediately invited to join them at their meal. Haider Effendi and his secretaries, the latter of whom had known me slightly in Constantinople, looked at me as if I had dropped from the sky; and if everybody in Persia, even the Persians themselves, are pleased to listen to accounts about Constantinople, one can easily imagine with what eagerness I was listened to by Turks, and especially by people from Constantinople. There was no end to all sorts of questions and inquiries. I had to tell them about the government of the new Sultan, and a thousand other things, and spoke, of course, as in duty bound, of the heavenly beauties of the Bosphorus, until it was midnight. When I told them of the journey I contemplated, the kind-hearted Osmanlis only stared at me. They could not conceive how a sensible man should wish to go to Central Asia, a region spoken of, even in Persia, as the dreadful desert and the dwelling-place of all that is most savage and barbarous. The ambassador in chief was foremost in condemning my plan as eccentric. "First of all," he said, "stay with us for a couple of months, and then we will talk about your travels in Central Asia. Take first a good look at Persia, and it will be time enough afterwards to proceed on your journey." He evidently thought that I should gladly renounce, in the meantime, my adventurous schemes.

In order that I might fully recover from the fatigues of the journey, the good Osmanlis surrounded me with every imaginable comfort. I was put into a tent by myself and provided with a horse and a servant; in short, I was transferred from a poor traveller into a great lord. I was thus placed in a position to study at my leisure Teheran, the capital of Iran.

The first thing the stranger is struck with is the utter want of cleanliness in the streets, as well as in the interior of the houses. The Persian covers the large unfurnished halls—what we should term drawing-rooms—of his house with costly carpets, and decorates its walls with rich ornaments, but the kitchen, the room he lives in and the pantry are most shamefully neglected by him. It is the same with his dress. A person who will spend from fifty to a hundred gold pieces for his outer garments is rarely the owner of more than two or three shirts. Soap is looked upon as an article of luxury, being hardly ever used, and I have met with Khans of high social standing and refinement who made use of their servants' pocket-handkerchiefs. The henna-painting, however, is that which renders every Persian grandee particularly loathsome, in spite of his outward splendour and rich dress. Henna is a yellow powder obtained from a plant called *Lawsonia inermis*, which, by being dissolved in water, furnishes a red dye of brick-colour. With this henna they dye their fine black beards and their very eyes red, the colour of bricks. Persons of standing also dye with henna their finger-nails and hands. The coat of paint hides the dirt; and a gentleman or lady, having made use of it, can afford to do without washing for several days.

Knives, forks and spoons are things unknown in Persia. It is utterly repulsive to the European to see the master of the house pulling to pieces, with his fingers, a boiled chicken, and giving each guest a piece of it, or having a cup of sherbet passed round, in which a dozen men have already steeped their henna-dyed moustaches.

Persian refinement is confined only to gestures, speech and conversational manner. But in these they excel all the Eastern nations—perhaps the nations of the West, too—and these elegant manners are, of course, to be found in their highest perfection at the capital. Volumes could be filled with the strict laws laid down for visits and return visits, and the proprieties of correspondence and conversation. Each Persian wishes to surpass the other in expressions of politeness and delicacy, which seem the more absurd the more we happen to know of the private lives of the Persians.

At every turn in the street the eye meets shocking contrasts of splendour and misery. At one end of the street may be seen a swarm of half-naked dervishes and beggars loitering about, whilst a Khan on horseback, followed by a numerous retinue, appears at the other end. Forty to sixty servants, armed with long staves, are ranged on each side of the Khan, who, on his richly caparisoned horse, looks very pompous indeed, and keeps his head continually wagging with an air of great importance. You might suppose their lord to be at least a high officer of state, judging by the noisy conduct and impudent behaviour of his followers towards every one they meet. Far from it! Often he is but a poor Khan, weighted down with debts, who has been in the capital ante-chambering and begging for some office for months past. His very men are not paid by him; they are a set of starvelings who follow him in the hope of his obtaining some office, and meanwhile try to add to the splendour of his appearance in public. Nothing but deception and delusion!

The Persians exhibit in the presence of their sovereign the most abject humility; but I have often heard expressions, and witnessed acts of disrespect towards him as soon as they were out of his sight. As an instance of their cringing manner may be cited the reply given by a courtier who was asked by the Shah to draw nearer to him. "Sire," he answered, covering up his eyes with his hand, "spare me, I dare not approach nearer to thy person; the glory of thy magnificent splendour dazzles my eyes." They do not, on the other hand, pay the slightest attention to their sovereign's commands, requests or threats, and the more distant the place or province is from the capital the more surely are commands and threats ignored. The courtiers highest in his confidence, the servants and officers standing nearest to his person, those whom his generosity has enriched, are the very men to spread the vilest rumours about him. These slanders find their way amongst the people; poets compose lampoons about them, and these are declaimed in all the alleys and byways of the kingdom.

The easy and comfortable life at the Embassy was very pleasant to me for a week or so, but the desire for stirring about again very soon got hold of me. I had often walked to see the ancient ruins of Raghes, which are but half an hour's distance from Teheran, and their frequent sight excited in my mind an irresistible longing to visit and examine the rich and abundant memorials yet extant, which bear witness to the splendour and former glories of ancient Iran. As the most interesting monuments of that era were most frequently to be found in the south, in the environs of Shiraz, I could not resist the temptation of making an excursion into the province of Fars.

Up to Shiraz! was the burden of all my thoughts. The first thing, however, which suggested itself in this connection, was the question in what capacity, and under the guise of what nationality, I was to travel? The solution of this problem gave me a great deal of thought. I made my *début* in Teheran as an Osmanli; as such I had been introduced to the Persian authorities, and it would have therefore seemed odd if I had suddenly turned European and proceeded on my way in that character. The name of Sunnite grates more harshly on the ears of a Shi-ite Persian than that of a Frengi (European); and although one could move pretty freely under the protecting wings of the Turkish Embassy in the capital, yet once outside the town, and especially in Shi-ite southern Persia, famous for its fanaticism, even that powerful protection would be of little avail. It is but seldom that an Osmanli strays to Southern Persia, where the Sunnites, without exception, are hated and despised. I therefore knew beforehand that travelling as an Osmanli, although it might not expose me to any real danger, would certainly cause me a great deal of unpleasantness. But such trifles could not deter me, the future dervish. Besides, my curiosity was excited to know how Ali's zealous followers would treat a Dissenter of their own faith. Uninfluenced by the arguments to the contrary of my well-wishers at the Embassy, I remained fixed in my purpose, and in a few days I was ready to join a smaller sort of caravan about to start for Shiraz.

XI.

THE SALT DESERT OF DESHTI-KUVIR.

I LEFT Teheran on the 2nd of September, 1862, by the gate of *Shah Abdul-Azim*, dressed in the costume of a Sunnite dervish from Bagdad, my *entari* (nether garment) reaching down to my heels, a red girdle round my waist, a striped black *mashlak* (a waterproof coat) on my back, and on my head a neat *keffie*,* both useful and ornamental. As it was usual to close the gates of Teheran after sunset, our little caravan had fixed upon a caravansary outside the town for our place of meeting. The travellers composing the caravan, became, for the most part, first acquainted with each other there. The caravan consisted of about thirty laden mules, a couple of horsemen, mollahs, pilgrims returning from Meshed, merchants, mechanics and my insignificant self. It was two hours after midnight when we started and proceeded along the wide path leading to Shah Abdul-Azim, a place which is held in high esteem by the Teheran people as a resort for pilgrims. I walked there

* An Arab headgear, consisting of a large handkerchief of silk with yellow stripes.

frequently during my stay in Teheran. The place is full of life and noise during the day, especially in the afternoon hours. There can be seen at all times a troop of gaudily dressed women of the better classes, sitting on horseback man fashion, prominent mirzahs and khans with numerous followers, and now and then a European coach, used generally by the court only. Of course at the time of night that we passed through it a dead silence was brooding over it. The moon shed an almost day-like light upon the mountain range stretching to the left and upon the gilded cupola beneath which the earthly remains of Shah Abdul-Azim reposed. After we had been riding in silence for two hours, some of the members of our caravan began to thaw into a social mood, and interrupted the monotony of our march by conversation and lively sallies.

I selected for my companion a young Seid from Bagdad, who was about to make a starring tour, as a *rawzekhan* (singer of sacred songs), through Southern Persia. Properly speaking only such persons are called rawzekhans who sing Tazies, *i.e.*, elegies in honour of Hussein, of great renown in Persia. These men are the most fanatic Shi-ites, and it may cause some surprise that we became more intimately acquainted. But the Seid, as an inhabitant of Bagdad, and a subject of the Sublime Porte, was willing enough to cultivate the acquaintance of an Effendi. He introduced me to the other members of the caravan, and being a jovial fellow, who would easily pass from his funeral songs to a livelier and more worldly tune, he very soon became a favourite with the whole company, and I, too, indirectly, profited by his popularity.

I at first scrupulously avoided all religious discussions, as I wished to ingratiate myself with my fellow-travellers, although it was by no means easy to do so; the Persians being very fond of arguing, and willingly entering into a discussion with Christians, Ghebers, and especially with Sunnites. The night was a magnificent one, and in Persia these moonlit nights are simply entrancing. The clear, transparent air, the graceful outline of the mountains, the darkling ruins, the spectre-like shadows of the advancing caravan, and, above all, the wonders of the starry vault above us, do not fail to produce an unutterable impression upon the imagination of a traveller coming from the far West to the East. Our road, however, was the worst imaginable; we had to make our way over fragments and boulders of rock, and cross ditches, ravines and the beds of rivers run dry. The difficulties of the road affected me but little; I abandoned myself entirely to the safe gait of my trusty asinine quadruped, and watched with intense interest every movement of the Seid, who contemplated the star-covered sky, and had some story to tell about each star. Every star had a legend of its own, an influence good or baneful, and I listened to his wonderful accounts with a soul full of faith. The constellation of the Great Bear was already inclining towards the margin of the western sky when we reached the height of *Karizek*, upon whose downward slopes *Kenaregird*, the village which was to be our first station, was lying. I cast one more glance at the beautiful moonlit landscape before descending, and as we went down on the other side of the mountain, the soft light of the moon slowly paled at the approach of the dawning day. As soon as the morning star appears to the eye it is the custom, for the whole caravan, to hail the coming day. The most zealous person in the company engages in the recital of the Ezan, a task which quite naturally fell this time to the lot of our Seid. The ablutions are performed in the twilight of the dawn of morning, and before the first rays of the sun touch the crest of the mountains, the caravan stops and morning prayers are engaged in.

The animals stand quietly with their heads bent low, whilst the men, with their faces turned towards the East, are kneeling, in a line, side by side, with such a penitent and remorseful expression on their countenances, as may be witnessed only with Mohammedans. When the rays of the sun reach the devout faithful, they lift up their voices and chant the melodious prayer beginning with the words Allah Ekber (*i.e.*, God is the greatest). After sunrise it is customary for the caravan to march on for a longer or shorter space of time, according as it happens to start earlier or later the night before, or as the next station is nearer or farther off. When we turned into our station the rays of the sun shot down mercilessly on our heads. We put up at the spacious caravansary, near the village of Kenaregird. The meaning of its name is, "Border of Sand," for to the east of it extends the salt desert of *Deshti-Kuvir*. This desert must be an awful place, for during all my wanderings through Persia I never met with a native who had travelled over that portion of it lying between Kenaregird and *Tebbes*. A Persian talking about the desert of Deshti-Kuvir is always ready to frighten his listeners with a batch of tales of horror, in each of which devils and evil spirits conspicuously figure. The favourite legend which is most often repeated, is the story of *Shamr*, Hussein's murderer and the mortal enemy of every Shi-ite Persian, to whom the desolation of this region is attributed. Flying from his own remorse, he took refuge here, and the once flourishing country suddenly became a sterile desert. The salt lakes and the bottomless morasses are caused by the drops of sweat rolling down his body in the agony of his sufferings. The most dreadful place of all is *Kebir Kuh*, where Shamr is dwelling to this day. Woe to the poor traveller who allows himself to be lured to this region by the deceptive light of the ignis fatuus! Such and similar stories I was regaled with by my fellow-travellers in connection with the salt desert of Persia. As soon as we arrived at the caravansary every one of us hastened to seek a shelter in the shade, and we were all of us soon comfortably settled. In a few instants the city of travellers presented the appearance of a lively and stirring settlement. Whilst the animals were crunching their dry barley straw, the Persians looked to the preparation of their meals. Those who were better off got their servants to rub their backs and shoulders and to pull their limbs until they cracked, this somewhat singular pastime being evidently intended to restore elasticity to the body. After a short rest we breakfasted, and then immediately retired to rest again. The caravan recuperates from the fatigues of the journey during the heat of the day, and continues its way at the dusk of evening. The animals follow the example of their masters. Towards evening men and cattle are on their feet again, and whilst the animals are being scrubbed and attended to, the men prepare their *pilar* (a dish composed of meat and rice). The supper is eaten about an hour before starting. The dervish fares better than any one else, for no sooner does the caravan arrive than he, without a care, seeks his rest, and when the savory steam of the kettle announces the approach of the evening meal, he seizes his *keshkul* (a vessel made of the shell of the cocoanut), and goes the rounds of the various groups, shouting out lustily "Ya hu, Ya hakk!" He gets a few slices from every one, mixes the heterogeneous contributions, and swallows it all with a good appetite. "He carries with him nothing," say the people of the East; "he does not cook, yet he eats; his kitchen is provided by God."

We had to cross the desert in its entire length to get to our next station. The silence of the night becomes, in this wilderness, doubly oppressive, and as far as the eye of the traveller can reach he will find no spot to repose it upon. Only here and there may be seen piled up columns of sand, driven about by the wind, and gliding from place to place like so many dark spectres. I did not wonder that these shifting shadows were taken by timid and credulous souls for evil spirits pursued by furies. My companion seemed to belong to the superstitious class, for wrapping his cloak tightly round him, he kept close to the densest part of the caravan, and would not, for the world, so much as glance at the wilderness stretching to the east.

It was about midnight when we heard the sound of bells, and upon my inquiry as to the meaning of this, I was told that a larger caravan, which had left an hour earlier than we did, was in front of us. We accelerated our march in order to overtake it, but had hardly come within a hundred paces from it when an intolerable stench, as if of dead bodies, filled the air. The Persians were aware of the cause of this poisonous stench and hurried silently on; but it went on increasing the further we advanced. I could not restrain my curiosity any longer, but turning to my nearest neighbour, I asked again what this meant, but he curtly replied, betraying, however, great anxiety: "Hurry up, hurry up! this is the caravan of the dead." This information was sufficient to make me urge my wearied beast forward to greater speed, and after a while I reached, together with my companions, the caravan. It consisted of about forty animals, horses and mules, under the leadership of three Arabs. The backs of the animals were laden with coffins, and we made every effort to avoid the dread procession. In passing near one of the horsemen who had charge of the caravan I caught sight of a face, which was frightful to look at; the eyes and nose were concealed by some wraps, and the rest of his lividly pale face looked ghastly by the light of the moon. Undaunted by the sickening atmosphere, I rode up to his side and inquired about the particulars of his errand. The Arab informed me that he had been now ten days on the way, and that twenty more would pass in taking the dead bodies to Kerbela, the place where, out of devotion for Hussein, the pious wish to sleep their eternal sleep. This custom prevails all over Persia; and every person who can afford it, even if he live in distant Khorassan, makes arrangements to have his remains carried to Kerbela, in order that they may be interred in the soil wherein the beloved Imam Hussein is reposing. It takes sometimes two months before the dead body can reach its place of destination. One mule is frequently laden with four coffins, and whilst their conveyance during the winter is comparatively harmless, it is of deadly effect, to beast and man alike, in the heat of July in Persia.

At some distance from the caravan of the dead, I glanced back at the strange funeral procession. The animals with their sad burden of coffins hung their heads, seemingly trying to bury their nostrils in their breasts, whilst the horsemen keeping at a good distance from them, were urging them on with loud cries to greater speed. It was a spectacle which seen anywhere could not fail to produce a profound impression of terror, but seen in the very centre of the desert, at the dead hour of the night, in the ghastly illumination of the moon, it could not fail to strike the most intrepid soul with awe and terror.

XII.

KUM AND KASHAN.

THE members of the little caravan had now been travelling together for three days, and this short time was amply sufficient to establish the friendliest feelings of good fellowship amongst them. Of course, no one entertained the faintest suspicion of my being one of those Europeans, the barest touch of whom renders a Shi-ite unclean, and with whom to eat out of the same plate is a capital sin. In their eyes I was the Effendi from Constantinople, the guest of the Turkish Embassy, who instigated by a desire to travel was about to visit imperial Isfahan and Shiraz, the paradise-like. I rapidly made friends with most of the company, although some of the most obdurate Shi-ites could not refrain, at times, from casting in my teeth, the manifold wrong-doings of the Sunnites. One man in particular, a shoemaker, whose tall green turban denoted his descent from Ali, annoyed me with his everlasting reiterations of the sinful usurpations of the three Caliphs. The quieter members of the company would try to soothe his ruffled spirits on such occasions, and turn the conversation into calmer channels; but my man very soon came back to the charge, and waxing warm with his favourite topic, he would take hold of the horse's bridle and talk with as much animation about the case of succession mooted a trifle of twelve hundred years ago, as though the whole affair had happened but yesterday.

Kum, with its green cupolas, loomed up before our eyes on the fourth day of our march. It is the sacred city of the Persian female world, for here, in the company of 444 saints, repose in eternal sleep the remains of Fatima, a sister to Imam (Saint) Riza, who, longing to see her brother, undertook for that purpose a journey from Bagdad to Meshed, but, on her way, was attacked by sickness in Kum, and died there. Kum, like Kerbela, is a favourite place of burial for Persian women, who cause their remains to be brought to this place from all parts of the country. But the town of Kum enjoys the less enviable distinction of being known as the abode of numerous evil-doers, owing to its having the privilege of sanctuary; and he who is lucky enough to escape the hands of the executioner, and to find a refuge within its sacred walls, is safe from all molestation.

Every member of our caravan was eager to visit Kum, some wanting to take part in the penitential processions as pilgrims, others to make purchases and to attend to their affairs. At a considerable distance from Kum, the environs, like those of all places of resort for pilgrims, are dotted by small heaps of stones, which are raised by the hands of pious pilgrims, amidst the chanting of sacred psalms. Here and there a bush can be seen, too, decorated with the gaudiest kind of rags which are hanging on it. Every one is anxious to leave some mark of his devotion in the neighbourhood;

according to their inclinations, some resort to stones, others to rags in the accomplishment of their devotional duties. It is said that in former times another custom prevailed by which travellers might pay their tribute of respect—every passer-by would drive a nail into some tree on the road. I, too, dismounted and hung upon a bush a red silk tassel from my keffie. What a wonderful collection of fabrics from all parts of the world! On these bushes are represented the costly handiwork of India and Cashmere, the manufactures of England and America, and the humble frieze and coarse linen of the nomadic Turkoman, Arab and Kurdistan tribes. Now and then the eye is caught by a magnificent shawl suspended on the branches of a bush, exciting no doubt the cupidity of more than one pious pilgrim passing by; but it is perfectly safe, as no one would dare to touch it, it being considered the blackest act of sacrilege to remove any of these tokens of piety.

Before reaching the town we had to pass a cemetery of extraordinary dimensions, almost two English miles in length. My fellow-travellers, however, perceiving my astonishment at the extent of the burial ground, assured me that in point of size it could not be compared to that of Kerbek. We were in Kum at last; our caravan put up at the caravansary in the centre of the bazaar, and I learned with pleasure that we were to take a two days' rest here.

As pious pilgrims we allowed ourselves but little time for rest, and shortly after our arrival, having washed and brushed our clothes, we repaired to the holy tomb. No European before me ever saw the interior of this sanctuary, for there is no power on earth to procure admission to it for a Frengi.

Innumerable Seids, entrusted with the custody of the

tomb of their "first ancestress," are camping in the outer courtyard, planted with trees. A chapel with a richly gilded cupola rises in the centre of the inner court. Twelve marble steps lead up to the door. The pilgrims remove their shoes at the first of these steps; their arms or sticks are taken away from them, and not until they have kissed the marble threshold are they permitted to enter. The beholder is struck with the extraordinary splendour of the interior of the chapel. The coffin, enclosed by a strong trellised bar of solid silver, remains always covered with a costly carpet. From the enclosure are suspended tablets containing prayers, which the faithful either read themselves, or have read to them by one of the numerous Seids who are loitering about. Any amount of shouting, singing, weeping, and moaning, and vociferous begging of the Seids is going on in the chapel; but this infernal din does not interfere with the devotions of a great number of pious pilgrims, who, leaning their foreheads against the cold bars of the enclosure, gaze with fixed eyes upon the coffin, and mutter their silent prayers. I particularly admired the many valuable and precious objects, ornaments of pearls and diamonds, arms inlaid with gold, which were laid down upon the tomb of St. Fatima as sacrificial gift-offerings. My Bagdad costume offended the eye of many a person in the fanatic Shi-ite crowd, but, thanks to the kindness of my fellow-travellers, I experienced no annoyance whatever. From the tomb of Fatima the pilgrims frequently go to the tombs of some of the great ones of the earth; and I followed my companions to the tomb of Feth Ali Shah and his two sons, who for some reason or other stood in particularly high favour with the devout. The tomb was of the purest alabaster, and the portraits of the departed ones were very cleverly carved into it on the outside. After having thus accomplished our pious devotions, we felt at liberty to wander back to the town and look at its remarkable sights.

Here, as elsewhere, the first thing to look at was the bazaar. We were just then in the season of ripe fruit, and the whole bazaar was filled with the water-melons, which are so celebrated throughout all Persia. The water-melon is, during the autumnal months, the almost exclusive food of one portion of the people of Iran, and its juice is frequently used in case of sickness for its medicinal properties. The Kum bazaar is remarkable not only for the abundance and delicacy of its water-melons, but also for its earthenware, one variety of which in particular, a long-necked pitcher, manufactured from potter's clay taken from the soil of the sacred city, is highly valued in trade. As I was making my rounds in the bazaar, examining everything, I happened to stop before a muslin dyer's shop. The Persian tradesman was industriously engaged in stamping and printing the rude stuff spread out before him, by means of stencils, which had been previously dipped in a blue dye, pressing them down with all his strength; and as he observed me looking at his doings, he turned upon me angrily, and evidently taking me for a Frengi, exclaimed: "We shall get rid of your expensive cotton fabrics, and will by and by know all your tricks of trade; and when the Persians will be able to do without Frengistan manufacture, I know you will all come begging to us."

We left Kum on the third day after our arrival there, and passing through several smaller places, where nothing worthy of note could be seen, we came to *Kashan*, after a fatiguing march of two days. My

Persian fellow-travellers, long before we arrived in Kashan, were praising up, in the most extravagant style, as usual, the beauty and attractions of that town. For my part, the only thing of note I saw there was the bazaar of the braziers, where the celebrated kettles of Kashan are being manufactured. About eighty braziers' shops are standing close to each other in a line, and in each of them muscular arms are hammering away the whole blessed day. The brass wares manufactured here are considered to be without rivals in point of solid workmanship and elegance. Those highly polished bricks, which retain the brilliancy of their shining colours for centuries, are said to have been invented in this town. Formerly they were called bricks of Kashan, but now they are known only by the name of Kashi, and serve as the chief ornaments in all architectural monuments throughout Central Asia. The inhabitants had also a great deal to tell about a dangerous species of scorpion, which made Kashan their home, but from motives of hospitality never hurt a stranger. I never came across any of these scorpions, but I had a great deal to suffer from a no less annoying tribe of animals, the *lutis* (strolling comedians), who attack every stranger coming to Kashan, and from whose clutches nothing can save you except a ransom in the shape of some gift. About ten of them stood there looking out for me as I was entering the caravansary, and immediately made a rush upon me, some producing hideous ear-splitting music with their fifes, drums and trumpets, others showing off a dancing bear; and one of them, seating himself opposite to me, engaged in a declamation, at the top of his voice, of a panegyrical poem, in my honour, in which, to my utter astonishment, I heard my name mentioned. Of course, he had managed to ferret out my name from my companions. I bore the infliction for a little while patiently enough, listening to this charivari of sounds, but finally retired. But it was not an easy thing, by any means, to effect my retreat, for I was followed, on the spot, by one of the artists, evidently the chief of the strolling company, insisting upon some remuneration; and although I argued with him that I was but a beggar myself, he would not listen to reason, but bravely stood his place until I had given him something.

Leaving Kashan we had to proceed along a narrow mountain pass, flanked by gigantic rocks and mountains of strange and fantastic shapes. The moon shed a light almost as clear as that of the day, and the wonderful tints in which the landscape before me was clothed seemed to vary and change at every step we took. When we arrived beneath the great Bend, as is called the large water-basin cut by Shah Abbas the Great into the solid rock, in order to convey the waters produced by the snow melting on the mountains to the sterile plain not far off, the scene before us was startling in its rare and exceeding beauty. Although it was late in autumn, the oval-shaped basin, formed by the enclosed valley, was brimful of water, and the waterfall rushing down the rocky wall from a height of fifty feet looked in the moon-lit night, to borrow a Persian phrase, like a river of diamonds. The deep roar of the waterfall is heard far off in the stilly night, and the tired traveller coming from the desert and quenching his thirst at the limpid waters of the basin, would not exchange the refreshing and crystal-like fluid for all the costly wines in the world.

The road from *Kuhrud* goes uphill for a time, and then inclines with a rather abrupt slope towards the plain lying on the other side of the mountain, where our next station was to be. The mornings had grown rather chilly and the travellers used to dismount on the way and pick up stray sticks of *buta*, a species of gumwood growing in bushes, which burns very well in its green state, but blazes with a loud crackling sound when dry. It is usual to raise a large pile of these sticks and then kindle it; the travellers range themselves round the blazing fire and afterwards resume their journey. We were standing for the second time, on the same morning, around this sort of fire when we were suddenly startled by the sound of voices, in the rear, mingling with savage exclamations, as if people were quarrelling, and upon listening attentively we heard two reports from firearms, and the loud yelling of some person badly hurt. The whole caravan was thoroughly alarmed, and, running in the direction whence the report of the fire-arm had proceeded, found there lying on the ground one of our companions, with a shattered arm. The affray had happened in this way. Several horsemen who were conveying the annual taxes from Shiraz to Teheran had come up with a couple of Jewish shopkeepers, whom they first insulted, and afterwards, passing from insult to injury, were about to lay violent hands upon. One of our company, a Persian, happening to be present, had pity on the poor Jews, stood up in their defence and took the impudent fellows from Shiraz rather roughly to task for their unbecoming conduct. One of the horsemen, a hotheaded young fellow, became so enraged at this interference, that he lifted his rifle and shot at the Jews. He afterwards pretended that the whole thing had been a joke, that he intended only to frighten one of the Jews by sending a bullet through his tall fur cap, but that unluckily he missed his aim and hit, instead, the Persian's arm. The incident so exasperated the whole caravan that our men at once started in pursuit of the culprit, who had meanwhile turned his horse's head and galloped away for his life, at a break-neck speed, but he was finally overtaken, dreadfully beaten, spit at amid loud curses, securely tied and brought back to the caravansary. Both the Shiraz man, who was bruised all over, and our wounded companion being unable to proceed either on foot or on horseback, they were placed side by side each in a basket, upon the back of a mule, and in the course of half an hour they were chatting away in the friendliest manner. They tied up each other's wounds, consoled one another, and went so far in their newborn friendship as to kiss each other; for according to the Eastern way of thinking neither of them was to be held responsible for what had happened. Fate had willed it so, and in its decrees every one must acquiesce.

In a village, called *Murtchekhar*, the judge of that place, evidently desirous of currying favour with the governor of Shiraz, attempted to liberate him, but the caravan stoutly refused to give him up, and only delivered him over, later, into the hands of justice, at Isfahan.

On the 13th of September I saw Isfahan, the former capital of Shah Abbas, through the thin mist of the morning. Whenever a Persian, and, especially a native of Isfahan, sets his eyes, after an absence of some time, upon his native town he is sure to exclaim: "Isfahan is half the world, but for Lahore," meaning thereby that Isfahan is, after Lahore, the largest city in the world. The citizens determine the extent of their city, by stating, with Oriental exaggeration, that it would take the boldest horseman two full days to make the circuit of its walls. And indeed the appearance of the city, with its extensive gardens, avenues of trees, and cupolas is really an imposing one. But in the East things look beautiful only on the surface, and shine only at a distance, and I was therefore but little disappointed when upon entering the town I met with the same labyrinth of crooked, narrow streets, the same miserable huts, dirt and extensive mud puddles in the roads, that I had before occasion to observe in Teheran and other towns of Persia.

XIII.

FROM ISFAHAN TO THE SUPPOSED TOMB OF CYRUS.

THE bazaar here, as in other cities, attracted my attention, it being the centre of every Eastern town. For hours one can wander through these lofty and covered streets, branching off in every direction and leading to every part of the town, and a stranger, unless conducted by a practical cicerone, may very easily lose his way. The sight of this bazaar must have been a truly magnificent one while the town was in a flourishing condition, but now it is almost deserted, and in the many splendid and spacious shops only stray watermelon sellers still linger.

A road leads from the bazaar to the celebrated *Meidani Shah* (the Shah's chief public square). This is an immense square, enclosed on every side by shops, which were in olden times the marts for the most costly articles of luxury, but are now crumbling into dust. I then visited the mosque of Lutf Ali, the gates of which are said to have been covered in ancient times with silver. From the balcony of this building the view is a splendid one, and I enjoyed a truly impressive sight.

There lay stretched out before me the immense square of Meidani Shah, and in my imagination I conjured up the ancient splendour of the city and repeopled the square with surging crowds. I fancied I saw the great Shah Abbas review from this very balcony thousands of his warriors who had gathered from every part of Asia to pay homage to their powerful king; the Persians who had inherited the horsemanship of the Parthians, the Turkomans on their swift Arab steeds, the Afghans, the Georgians, the Indians, the Armenians—these savage and stalwart forms of antiquity, they all used to gather here. And to-day it is a sad and forlorn desert, the silence of the grave brooding over it. One corner of the square serves twice a week as a market-place for dealers in asses, and occasionally, on a holiday, a green turbaned procession headed by the chief priest may be seen passing through it.

I had an opportunity of getting acquainted with all classes of the inhabitants of Isfahan at the house of the Imam Djuma, *i.e.*, the high priest. He was the most influential priest in Persia, and at the capital he went by the name of *Aga Buzurg* (great lord). Indeed he was the real Pope of the Shi-ite sect, and the letters of recommendation, brought with me from Teheran, procured me admission to his house. I was very cordially received by him and invited to call on him on the evening of the following day. Aga Buzurg is one of those Seids whose descent from the house of Ali is least doubted, and very proud he is of his origin. The company I met there treated me as Shi-ites generally treat their Sunnite guest—they could not refrain from occasionally launching out in satirical and biting remarks. The master of the house only made a few condemnatory remarks, blaming the government of Constantinople for its friendship with the European Powers. But he did not omit to praise the tolerance of the Sultan towards the Shi-ites, who could now journey, unmolested, to Mecca and Medina, without being exposed to the annoyances and outrages they had formerly to submit to. To avoid familiarity and for the purpose of preserving his dignity, he was very chary of his words, and retired very soon after supper was over.

I found the middle classes of Isfahan to be remarkably cultivated. There were shoemakers, tailors and shop-keepers who knew hundreds of verses of their best poets by heart, and were quite familiar with the masterpieces in the literature of their country. They are, as a rule, very intelligent, poetic, and quick at a telling retort. Malcolm, the excellent English writer on Persia, relates the story how, at the time when most of the high offices in the Persian towns were filled by relatives of the Vezir Hadji Ibrahim, a merchant who was unable to pay his taxes was summoned to the presence of a brother of Hadji Ibrahim, the governor of Isfahan, and upon entering was addressed by the latter, in an angry tone of voice, as follows:

"If thou art not able to pay like the others, begone, get thee gone!"

"Where shall I go?" asked the merchant.

"Go to Shiraz or Kashan."

"Oh, sir, then it would be going from the frying-pan into the fire, for thy cousin is governing in one place, and thy uncle in the other."

"Then go to the king and make complaint."

"This would not help me much, either, for there again thy brother is prime minister."

"Then go to h——," thundered at him the irate governor.

"Oh, sir, it is not so very long that thy sainted father, the pious Hadji, is dead," retorted the witty Persian.

The governor thereupon burst out laughing, and said: "Since thou findest it so hard to be reconciled to my relatives, I will pay thy debts for thee."

I occupied in Isfahan the same lodgings as my fellow-traveller, the singer of elegies. He found here ample opportunity to practise his art, and exhibited his performances several times during the day, at the bazaar and in the courtyards of the mosques. He yelled, bellowed, wept, indulged in the most heart-rending lamentations, and could, at his pleasure, set going "the fruitful river in the eye" and shed a shower of veritable tears. But on returning home, after the day's hard work was over, the spirit of tragedy deserted him at once, and he gave way to the merriest and most rollicking humour. I went, in his company, amongst people of every kind and rather mixed societies, but he was a man commanding respect everywhere. He would at first sing a sacred song or two and then pass over to worldly ones; and although he wore a green turban in token of his descent from the family of the Prophet, he drank like a trooper.

The inhabitants of Isfahan are very proud of their city; they are rather conceited, and think themselves better than the rest of the Persians. The king and the royal family, with their Turkish soldiery, are dreaded and hated by them. They look upon the authority of Imam Djuma as superior to that of the king. Fabulous accounts are circulated about the immense wealth of that chief priest, who keeps a thousand *lutis* (strolling players) in his hire. These lutis spread amongst the people wonderful accounts of the chief priest's miraculous power, and it is they who scatter broadcast the vilest slanders concerning the royal family, for the king having power over everybody except the chief priest of Isfahan, the relations between him and Imam Djuma were never of the friendliest kind.

I passed two weeks in Isfahan and had an excellent opportunity to see the noteworthy sights and to observe all the classes of society in the town. We made arrangements with the same leader of the caravan who brought us to this place concerning the continuation of our journey, and almost the entire company met at the appointed time at a caravansary outside the town. We wasted three more days here, and I employed the time in making short excursions in the neighbourhood. Of the remarkable things I saw I will mention only the movable towers of *Munare Djomdjom*. The two towers are on the mosque of the village of *Khaledan*, about an hour's distance from Isfahan. They are about twelve feet high and stand about twenty paces apart. I stepped with my guide on the terrace, and upon his seizing hold of, and shaking with all his might, one of the towers, I became sensible of a motion like that caused by an earthquake not only in the other tower, but in the entire front of the building. This remarkable building, the secret of whose architecture has descended into the grave with its builder, has been considerably damaged by the frequent exhibition of its movableness. The Persians attribute the miracle to the saint reposing beneath it.

We left Isfahan at last, and proceeded on our way in the direction of the mountains lying to the south. Upon reaching an eminence I took another look at the endless mass of houses, gardens and ruins. Our caravan, which consisted of three divisions, two having joined us for our journey to Shiraz, now numbered above 150 animals and about sixty passengers, and even on this much-travelled road we were looked upon as a caravan of considerable size. The combining of the three caravans into one was caused by the fear of certain nomadic Persian tribes who were camped amongst the mountains to the right, and who were in the habit of attacking and plundering smaller caravans either from avarice or as a pastime. Only a few days had passed since a smaller caravan had been roughly treated by them. In the East, however, people are fond of inventing such stories. Many a time one is told, "At this place ten men were killed yesterday," "The day before, at another place, a merchant was set upon and robbed;" but the traveller need not take fright at these accounts, for he may be sure that the events related either happened ten years ago, or did not occur at all. Indeed our party of travellers had no need of the frightful stories with which they had been regaling each other on the eve of their departure to make their courage ooze out, for to a man they were remarkably deficient in that valuable article, the virtue of courage. Since the Persian in general is looked upon in all Asia as a most cowardly creature, who is scared to death by his own shadow, one may easily imagine the state of mind of a caravan consisting chiefly of pilgrims, merchants and mollahs. It was rather amusing to see them keeping close to, and crowding, each other in their fright, although we were only at a distance of two hours from the town. They were conversing in whispers as if a single loudly spoken word might have brought down upon them the most frightful calamities. One man who was conveying wine with which he had loaded four of his mules, was peremptorily made to leave our ranks at the instigation of a devout mollah, lest his sinful merchandise might bring bad luck to the entire company of the truly faithful. It was in vain the poor mule driver whiningly insisted that he had never tasted a drop of wine all his life, and that he was conveying this abhorred beverage to Bombay where the godless Frengis would drink it; in vain he swore by all the saints of the calendar he did not even know if the wine were red or white; he had to leave the caravan and keep a distance of a hundred feet between himself and it.

Next day we arrived at *Kumisheh*, which is near to the dangerous place about which we had heard so many frightful stories. About an hour before our departure my Arab friend, the sacred singer, thought that this was a fitting moment to collect about him the whole company and to chant one of his elegies, in order, as he said, to invoke the prophet's protection on our perilous journey, but in reality that a few coins might wander from the pockets of the deeply affected faithful into his own. The rawzekhan's proposition was immediately acquiesced in. The Persian is prepared at any moment to lament the death of his favourite prophet, particularly of the martyred Hussein; and it does not give him the slightest trouble, though the moment before he may have been in the merriest of moods, to shed copious tears in listening to the singer's elegy. The songster from Bagdad was soon surrounded by the whole company, and he hardly came to the end of the fourth canto of his morning song, when there arose such a wailing and weeping as if the nearest relation of every one of the listeners were lying stark dead before him. The performer usually seizes this moment to rise, tear away his dress from his breast, and to exclaim, clenching his fists: "O ye true believers, behold thus I shall strike my breast with penitence and pity for poor Hussein, yes, for Hussein!" His last words are repeated by all the men of the company; gigantic fists are soon pounding away at stalwart chests, frequently keeping in the pounding such excellent time as to resemble the regular tramp of an approaching troop of horsemen. A pious fellow happened to observe that, with Sunnite perverseness, I did not thump my chest with sufficient violence, and having attentively listened to the sound produced by my fist and not finding it hollow enough, he furiously exclaimed: "Look at this Sunnite dog; he does not consider our Hussein worthy of more powerful strokes on his breast. Just wait; I shall show him how to strike his breast." With this he approached me with his uplifted fist of iron. If he had struck me I should, probably, have had reason to remember it all my life; but thanks to the kind offices of my friends, particularly the Seid, the matter proceeded no further. A friend of mine held his arm back in the nick of time, quieting him by saying: "Let that Sunnite be! though he do not strike his breast in this life, Azrail (the Angel of Death) will beat it all the more for him in the next world."

We safely left the place alleged to be dangerous without having come to harm, and the caravan, now considerably relieved, proceeded on their journey towards *Yezdekhast*. The country around us became more and more flat; the desert, in the centre of which the celebrated city of Yezd is situated, extending to the east. The sun had already risen high when we passed through the arid grass-covered plain, its level stretch being interrupted only here and there by gently undulating ground. I had been informed by my companions that the country abounded in game and especially in gazelles. And, indeed, in looking steadily at a dark dot in the distance, I soon discovered it to be a whole herd of these timid creatures of the desert, who scent the approach of a caravan from afar and fly from them with the swiftness of a bird. I had some difficulty at first in recognizing the gazelles at a distance, the colour of their fur resembling that of the sun-dried grass of the plain; and when my companions called out "The ahuan, the ahuan!" (The gazelles, the gazelles!), I could see nothing, until my eyes became accustomed to distinguish their white hind parts from the dry grass. Just as with us the hare is supposed to be the embodiment of timidity, even so the gazelle is looked upon in the East as the hare's counterpart in this particular. A herd of above a hundred gazelles is seized with a panic at the sudden rising of a bird, or the mere stirring of a leaf. If the hound but approaches the gazelle, it throws itself upon its back with its legs up and looks at one with such a pitiful expression out of its lustrous melancholy eyes, that one cannot help feeling for the poor dumb animal. As my eyes were following the flight of the gazelles, I suddenly caught sight of a mirage rising in the south-east. These deceptive illusions of the air are by no means of infrequent occurrence in the Persian plain. Although they do not equal in grandeur similar atmospheric phenomena in the great desert of Turkestan, yet, even in that fainter form, they never fail to strike the imagination of the traveller. As I was gazing upon the floating forms and buildings, it seemed to me as if they were the same which had delighted my eyes years ago on the great plain of the beautiful Hungarian Alföld (Lowland). Then, too, leaning against the tall pole of a well, I was gazing at the far-stretching plain which, panting and thirsting, was "dreaming of the sea." The mirage recalled my own beautiful country, so far off, and when suddenly a rising cloud of dust concealed the fairy spectacle from my view, it seemed to scatter my day-dreams to the winds.

The province of Fars begins beyond Yezdekhast, and its inhabitants differ from the Persians as much, I should say, as the Neapolitans do from the inhabitants of northern Italy; their complexion is darker, they are more vivacious, their feelings are more excitable, and they are more quickwitted. The greater portion of the inhabitants make a living by the caravans that are passing through their country. *Shulghistan*, our first station in Fars, is noted for the tomb of a saint, supposed to be the son of Imam *Zein ul Abedin*. Of this tomb it is told that, some time ago, it had been attacked by enemies, who were all struck blind upon entering the sanctuary. A blind beggar at the gate of the tomb was shown as one of the sacrilegious band, who desired to end his days repenting. I was sufficiently interested to wish to hear the account from the lips of the blind beggar himself, and questioned him about this occurrence; but he admitted to me that his blindness proceeded from other causes, and that he had never been connected with a band of robbers. Yet he willingly passed himself off for an evil-doer punished by God in order to get his share of the alms distributed by the devout.

In leaving Shulghistan we were joined on our way by a horseman of distinguished appearance, followed by a number of servants, whose place of destination was the same as ours. He seemed to be mustering closely the members of the caravan, as if trying to make up his mind whom he should choose for his associate during the journey. After a while he approached me with the friendliest salutation. I soon found out that he was going to visit the governor of Fars, by orders of the Shah, in order to collect last year's arrears, amounting to 50,000 ducats. The Shah had been repeatedly urging the remittance of the sum, but it was never sent. The Khan was now ordered by the Shah to send the unremitting governor to prison for a few days; and should this punishment fail to produce the desired effect to withdraw for a couple of days his *kallian* (water-pipe) from him. This peculiar method of collecting debts is by no means rare in Persia. The Khan was a person of refinement and culture; he was very tolerant, and to him Sunnite or Shi-ite was the same thing. He saw in me the most travelled and experienced man in the caravan, and had therefore joined me, of which I was all the more glad, as it had procured for me a very agreeable fellow-traveller. When we arrived at our next station, Abade, we took a lodging together, and also took our meals together.

From *Abade* we went towards *Surma*, and we met on our night's march with several smaller caravans, consisting mostly of pilgrims, who were either bound for Kerbela, in the west, or Meshed, in the east. In Persia the number of pilgrims, especially during the seasons of spring and autumn, amounts to hundreds of thousands. The poorest Persian will spend all his savings, nay, even starve, in order to take part in such a pilgrimage. The caravan we met with had come from the neighbourhood of *Bender Bushir*, and was going to Kerbela. The journey there takes sixty days, and the journey back as much again. The lively intercourse on the highways of Persia is chiefly dependent upon these pious travellers. It is no rare thing to see amongst them children ten years of age, and aged women eighty years old. If two such caravans meet on the road, those returning generally tell the pilgrims on their way to the holy places, "Pray for me;" and receive for an answer, "May thy pilgrimage be blessed." Both parties are deeply moved, and generally embrace each other upon these occasions; indeed the most indifferent will feel somewhat affected upon hearing, far off, in the stillness of the night, the *Illahie* (hymns) of the pilgrims. I had heard much to excite my curiosity with regard to our next station. Many notable ruins of ancient times may be seen in *Maderi Suleiman*, and the Persians think that the tomb of King Solomon's mother is amongst them; but I had no difficulty in identifying the village of Maderi Suleiman, lying in the plain of *Passargada*, as the one where the tomb of *Cyrus* is supposed to be. In descending the gentle slope of the low range of mountains and entering the open valley before us, I was delighted to discover on the right of our road several statues gilded by the first rays of the rising sun. The slow pace of the caravan rendered me impatient, and I finally left them, hastening by myself through thin and thick towards the mausoleum, which rose higher and higher as I approached, and when the caravan with their deliberate gait at last reached the station, I was found there seated already on a huge marble step.

XIV.

PERSEPOLIS.

THE first thing that strikes the eyes of the traveller on the flat land of ancient Passargada is that mausoleum, of which Persians say that it contains the remains of King Solomon's mother, but which some antiquarians allege to be the tomb of Cyrus, whilst others, denying this, maintain that it commemorates some unknown hero of antiquity. It is built of huge marble blocks, and stands upon a marble base formed by six marble slabs of enormous thickness placed one upon the other; each slab terrace-like diminishing the higher it is placed, and the whole forming six steps. The structure above it is a room, the floor and ceiling of which consists each of one enormous block of marble. The narrow low entrance is always open. The Mohammedans use the interior of the room for their devotions, and several Korans are always lying about for that purpose. After I had with great difficulty clambered up the huge steps and gained admission to the interior of the mausoleum, I was struck with awe at the sight before me. I gazed for some time with astonishment at the huge blocks, to move which from their places seemed an utter impossibility. The names of numerous celebrated European travellers could be seen carved into the marble steps, whilst the walls were covered with a great many Arabic and Persian inscriptions. I was just engaged in deciphering the latter when a Persian, apparently belonging to the nomadic tribes living in tents in this part of the country, came up to me, evidently in the hope of earning a few pennies by doing a guide's business, and said: "Hadji, there are no such huge blocks to be seen in Bagdad, are there? But come with me, I shall show thee others like them. Come and look at the ruins of ancient Guzi." I immediately followed him to the ruins of the ancient palace, popularly called "Solomon's Throne." At some distance may be seen a large arch of a gate, built of black marble. If a Persian sees a stranger admiring the beauty of these ruins, or astonished at the size of the stones, he invariably volunteers the following remark: "Art thou not aware that Solomon could freely dispose of the *divs* (devils) and all the spirits of the lower regions? It cost him but a nod of his head, and the spirits sailing through the air brought him the largest stones and the most costly objects from India, Tchin-u-Matchin (China) and from Kuhi Kaff.

We continued our journey towards *Sivend*, going for several hours through a mountain gap. We did not visit the village, but went up to an eminence near by, where its inhabitants lived during the summer. We found there about 120 huts standing in a line, close to each other. The whole settlement resembled a bazaar; and as the huts were closed on three sides and always remained wide open on the fourth, the huts and everything in them were open to every one alike, as much as if all the huts had formed but one house. One hundred and twenty families live here together in simple patriarchal fashion; and although there be rich and poor amongst them, a theft rarely occurs. Indeed people said that the population of the whole village were the descendants of one common ancestor, and lived together on terms of the most intimate relationship; and that, even to this day, they were governed by the head of the family, who was both judge and priest to them and lived apart in a white tent.

In leaving this place, on the second of October, we proceeded towards the most interesting part of Persia. The caravan was not far from *Kenare*, in the vicinity of which the celebrated ruins of Persepolis are to be seen. With the prospect of soon seeing these ruins before me, I found the progress of the caravan rather slow, and determined to visit them by myself, after having inquired of some of my companions, who knew the country throughout, the shortest road leading to them. The caravan had left Sivend before midnight, and when we arrived at the promontory where the extensive plain of *Mardesht* begins, I separated from them, and, keeping continually to the left, I followed the mountain track. For some time yet I heard through the calm night the monotonous jingling of the caravan bells. I marched on with watchful eyes, looking out all the time for the much-mentioned ruins, the remarkable architectural monuments of remote antiquity. After lapse of about a quarter of an hour there loomed up in the dubious light of the dawning morning tall forms, looking like so many spectres. The stillness around me seemed awful, and the clatter of my animal's small shoe sounded far away in the unpeopled solitude. I now came to the celebrated steps, so familiar to most people through engravings of them. At sight of them I paused deeply moved, and stood motionless for a few minutes. I dismounted, and, drawing nearer, I went up the steps with feelings of piety and profound veneration, then passed through the gigantic gate to the row of columns. I sat down on a large block and, sunk in deep reverie, gazed upon the columns and the ruins around me; and sitting there for a long time without stirring, it seemed to me as if the spectacle of these ruins of four thousand years ago had turned me, too, into a statue. The sublimity of the ancient monuments of Persepolis cannot fail deeply to affect the traveller from whatever point of view he may have approached them for the first time, even if he has seen them in broad daylight. My feelings then may be easily imagined, who had been longing to see them with feverish impatience, and saw them suddenly burst upon my sight in the spectral twilight of the early dawn. As I sat gazing with wrapt attention at the tall columns, they appeared to me like gigantic forms which had risen from the remote past of forty centuries to tell me, the traveller who had strayed here from the far West, in language mute but eloquent, of the marvels of past ages in the East. I did not awake from my reverie until the sun had risen from behind the mountains and touched with golden tints the heads of the columns, showing their exquisite workmanship. And in a moment, as if a huge curtain had been suddenly drawn aside, a very different spectacle presented itself to my dazzled eyes—Persepolis bathing in a sea of brilliant light. The sombre blocks of marble, the darkling columns and walls all disappeared as if by enchantment, and in their places, glowing in a flood of golden sunshine, beckoned to me on every side exquisitely carved capitals of columns, reliefs of wonderful beauty, all so natural, so fresh as if the last sounds of the chisel had just died away. One sculptured relief shows a solemn procession, in which every man is walking with measured step; on another a troop of prisoners, chained to each other by their necks, are advancing slowly in front of the proud victor; another again represents a gigantic man struggling with a monster. Looking up you see, in several places, a king sitting, with earnest mien, on his throne, before him the sacred fire blazing, and at back of him standing two servants, one holding a long staff, and the other a sun umbrella. The finished accuracy shown in the dresses and the figures is truly admirable; but the wonderful art exhibited in the shaping of the features and in the various expressions of the human countenance is what lends such a peculiar charm to these reliefs, and makes one almost imagine that the cold marble will speak.

I passed three days among these remarkable ruins, which kindle not only the fervid imagination of the young traveller, but rouse the enthusiasm of grave thinkers and antiquarians rich in knowledge and experience. One is at a loss which more to admire, the extraordinary manual skill, or the exquisite taste visible everywhere, in every part of the preserved ruins. Here, as in Egypt, may be seen huge blocks of stone, from forty to fifty feet long, fitted together, in spite of their enormous weight, with such nicety that one can only with great difficulty discover the place where they are joined.

I met in the immediate neighbourhood of Persepolis with nomadic Turks, who were overjoyed at seeing me, a supposed countryman of theirs. The Turkish language is not spoken much in Fars, and these poor people seemed so delighted with the chance of having a talk in their own language, that in the kindness of their hearts they provided me, during my whole stay, with bread and milk, and even took care of my ass. Some of these men advised me strongly not to remain over night at the ruins on account of the innumerable evil spirits that haunted them, and told me that the devs and djins were making an infernal noise. They said that *Thakhti Djemshid* (Djemshid's throne)—the native name for Persepolis—was the work of the fabled king Djemshid.

This king is said to have had a cup, with which he had only to touch his lips, in order to realize all his heart's desires; at the mere touch of the cup, stones would come flying from the east, and artists from the west. The numerous verses and inscriptions on every part of the walls testify to the great respect entertained by the Persians for Persepolis. The legend has it that these buildings stood intact and strong for ever so long a time, and that during that time Persia was happy and flourishing, and no sort of harm or misfortune ever befell her. Later on the Arabs came, and they envied the Shi-ites for these wonderful buildings, and in their envy they mutilated the statues and figures, threw down the columns and left everywhere the traces of their destructive spirit. After them came the Frengis, over Bender Bushir (from India), to gratify their passion for treasures; they ransacked the place and took away with them immense quanties of gold and diamonds. The Frengis carried away besides large blocks of stone for talismans. Since that time adversity and misery had been the lot of Persia; Shiraz was visited by an earthquake, then came the cholera, the famine, and so forth.

This is the account the Persians give of the ruins, but the Turkish Nomads, the remains of the former Seldjuk armies, look at them in a very different light. To them the masterpieces of architecture and sculpture are objects of the utmost indifference, and they will often pull down the proudest and most admirable monument for the sake of obtaining a few ounces of the lead which holds together the several segments or portions of the gigantic columns. The children are delighted to see one of these columns come down by itself; they immediately make a rush at it, and scoop the lead out of the crevices of the stones. Sometimes they manage to obtain, after all this wanton destruction, lead enough for a couple of bullets; but the vandalism of the Turks cares very little about the damage done to works of art.

I felt a special interest in the names of the older and more recent Asiatic travellers, which I found carved in many places about the ruins. I met with even Hebrew inscriptions dating, it is alleged, from the time of the first captivity of the Jews, and written by the unfortunate men then dragged into slavery. Most names were those of renowned English travellers; of German names there were comparatively few, and I grieved at not being able to find a single Hungarian after two days' search. I asked myself if I were the first of my countrymen who had visited this interesting country with its remarkable ruins. Next day, I was delighted to come across the following Hungarian inscription, "Maróthi István, 1839," in a recess of a window, as I was examining the base of an immense structure, built of black marble. I examined my countryman's writing with a childish triumph; and to relieve its loneliness, I added my own name for companionship, writing above the latter, "Eljen a Magyar!" (Hungary for ever!)

A caravan, camping outside the village and consisting mostly of pilgrims returning from Kerbela, was starting a little after midnight. I joined it, and on the following morning I was glad to learn that I had every reason to be satisfied with having done so, for all of the travellers came from *Zerkum*, the place nearest to Shiraz. They had passed the night here, although it is not far from their native place, in order to afford time to their relatives and friends, to whom they had sent information of their approach, to make the necessary preparations for their festive reception. As we drew near the village we were met by crowds of people, who were constantly reinforced by new-comers, and there was no end to shaking of hands, embracing and kissing. Every one of the pilgrims from Kerbela was surrounded by a group of village people, and not only he himself, but his ass, too, were carried home in triumph. As we were marching along the streets of the village, I could not help admiring the patience with which the pilgrims bore the ever increasing felicitations of the villagers. Some of them, especially the stouter ones, were freely perspiring from the many embraces, but they all heroically endured the infliction; nay, they delighted in it, for to have visited Hussein's the beloved martyr's tomb, was tantamount to having been raised above the common herd, and to embrace such a lucky mortal was worth nearly half a pilgrimage to Kerbela.

I left Zerkum in the company of a *tcharvadar* (owner of animals of burden) and his men, and we proceeded together to Shiraz. These people were from Shiraz, and having been absent from their native place for a long time, they were impatient to get there. Every Persian is given to exaggeration in speaking of the sights and wonders of his native city, but these men went beyond anything I had yet experienced in the way of civic glorification, and I could not help looking forward to something extraordinary in Shiraz. The recollection of some verses by Hafiz, full of praises of the shores of *Ruknabad* and the flowery places of *Musalla*, which I had retained in my memory, contributed to raise my expectations to the highest pitch. We had been advancing for about half an hour when the shout of "Ruknabad! Ruknabad!" burst simultaneously from the lips of my companions. I immediately dismounted, thinking we should have to pass over the bridge, crossing the river, and wishing, in doing so, to lead my animal by the bridle; but my pains were all wasted. The Ruknabad river, of which poets deemed it right to sing, had shrunk into an insignificant brook hardly three spans wide, the shallow waters of which gaily leap over its gravel bottom.

I own my expectation about Shiraz received, at this sight, a slight shock, nor were my drooping spirits revived by the appearance of the surrounding country. Cold, bare rocks were staring at me on every side; there was not the slightest trace of vegetation of any kind; yet my companions kept assuring me that we were quite near to Shiraz. We reached at last an opening, called *Tenghi Allah Ekber* (the pass of Allah Ekber) by the Persians. From this place the traveller obtains his first view of the wide-spreading valley below him, in the centre of which rises the city of Shiraz.

XV.

SHIRAZ.

THE sight of Shiraz, standing in the midst of groves of thickly planted cypress trees, is quite a relief for the eye, wearied with the monotonous look-out upon the barren desert and bare rocks. The natives say that looking at the enchanting capital of southern Persia from the spot whence I first saw it, the stranger in his admiration involuntarily bursts out into the customary "Allah Ekber" (God is greatest), and that the place owes its appellation to this exclamation. The eye, wandering over the extensive valley, meets everywhere, as far as it can reach, the exquisite dark green of the cypress. The city is fringed by a garland of cypress gardens, through which a wide brook meanders like a silvery ribbon. Proud edifices rear their heads both inside and outside the walls of the city, the brilliant cupola of the Shah Tchirag mosque looming up most conspicuously. Beyond and opposite to it the far-stretching plain is bordered by a lofty chain of mountains stretching through Kazerun as far as the shores of the Gulf of Persia. Thus the valley is screened by natural walls of rock both to the north and south, and Shiraz stands foremost amongst all the cities of Persia in the matter of climate, fertility and purity of air.

Shiraz owes its fertility especially to its great abundance of water. Its vegetation is so luxuriant that roses and other flowers are blooming throughout the whole year, the plants renewing their sweet-smelling crops every month. The fields are covered with a green sward, and whilst in other parts of Persia the favourite mutton can be got but twice in the year, it can be obtained here throughout all seasons. But what challenges most the admiration of the Western traveller is the exquisitely pure air, the beauty of its blue sky, excelling in these all other parts of Persia, the whole of Asia and I may add every country in the world. The air in Shiraz, in spite of its southern position, is bracing enough, and I do not at all wonder that the people, under the influence of their benign climate, are fond of pleasure, and pass their lives in continual amusements and everlasting merry-making. They have a proverb which says :

> " In Isfahan many scholars and artists may be,
> But dancers, singers and drinkers only in Shiraz you see."

And, indeed, I do not know of a town in Persia, the inhabitants of which are as merry and jovial as those of Shiraz. Centuries have passed by since Hafiz, the glorifier of wine, sung his odes here, but a sojourn of a very few days in the capital of Fars will convince any one that the people of Shiraz have not modified a hair's breadth their views of life since the time of Hafiz. Everybody indulges freely in wine in spite of the rigid inhibition of the Mohammedan law. The poor journeyman, the mechanic, the official, and even the priests, begin their libations as soon as the dusk of evening sets in, and keep up their merry-making until midnight, and even later.

As I had now reached the end of my immediate journey, and intended to make a protracted stay, I took lodgings at the large court of the mosque. I sold my animal, and although the funds I had brought with me were considerably reduced, my future gave me little concern, considering, especially, the abundance and cheapness of food. True to my part of a dervish, I wandered through the streets of the city, on the first day of my arrival, and made the acquaintance of a great many people. Of course, my acquaintances, being zealous Shi-ites, never neglected an opportunity in my presence of cruelly vilifying Omar and his associates; but seeing that I bore their vituperations of my saints very meekly, they were highly pleased with me, and I made so many friends during the first weeks of my stay that they rendered my life very agreeable.

One day, I happened to learn that a European, a native of Sweden, was living in the city and practising as a physician. My love of adventure immediately suggested to me the propriety of paying him a visit; but I determined, as a matter of precaution, to keep up my incognito and to appear before him as a dervish. When I entered his room with the dervish's salutation of "Ya hu! Ya hakk!" the good doctor immediately put his hand in his pocket, in order to get rid of me by a gift of a few coins, the usual way of dismissing a dervish.

"What, dost thou give me money?" I exclaimed. "I come to seek thy confidence, not thy money. I come from a far-off country. I am sent to thee by my chief, to convert thee from the false religion that thou followest and to lead thee to the path of the true faith. I am charged by the Sheikh of Bagdad to make a Mussulman of thee."

The doctor to whom such attempts at proselytizing were by no means new, replied with a suppressed smile :

"This is all very fine, very fine, my dervish, yet it is not usual to try conversion in such a commanding way, but by convincing, affecting and eloquent speech. How canst thou prove to me that thy chief has sent thee to me, and that he can work miracles ?"

"Hast thou any doubts about it ? One syllable from my master is enough to bestow the knowledge of all the sciences and languages of the world. Thou art a Frengi. and speakest probably many tongues. Put me to trial in any language."

The doctor stared at me, and I had some difficulty in maintaining my reserve. Finally he addressed me in Swedish, his native language.

"Swedish," I said, "I know that language as well as thou dost." As a proof I recited to him a few verses from Tegnér's "Frithiofs Saga," which, having been my favourite reading in my youth, came vividly back to my memory. The doctor's surprise knew no bounds. He began to try me in German, and to his astonishment I readily answered him in German, too. He did not fare any better with his attempt to upset me with French and English ; and after having exchanged with him a few words in various languages, I returned to Persian and recited very impressively a verse from the Koran for the good of his soul. The poor man was utterly stupified, but when he began to take to guessing at my real nationality, I abruptly rose and made the following farewell speech : "I will give thee time to reflect until eight o'clock to-morrow morning; either thou wilt turn Mussulman, or thou shalt feel the power of my master."

I returned to my quarters, but I had scarcely got out of bed next morning when I found the good doctor waiting for me. His curiosity did not allow him to wait until I came. I continued the old game with him at first, but finally I dropped the mask, and told him who I was. The delight of the doctor was great, and we embraced as if we had been two brothers. "I immediately thought you were a European," he said, "but your Persian talk made me doubt of it." He inquired about Teheran and his acquaintances there, and insisted, after we had been talking for some time, upon my gathering up my things and following him to his dwelling, in order to remain his guest as long as I desired it. To my Persian friends I pretended that I made my stay with the doctor in order to receive instructions in alchemy from him, a science which he was known to have cultivated before, and, besides, my living with him seemed less strange to them from the fact of Europeans in Shiraz living entirely in Persian fashion. I passed six of the pleasantest weeks at his hospitable house. I chiefly employed my time in studying the customs, manners and modes of life of the interesting inhabitants of Shiraz. The most striking feature about them is their extreme excitability and irritability. Everybody, without exception, carries a two-edged curved poniard in his girdle, and is ready to make use of it on the slightest provocation or difference of opinion. Nor is there another city in Persia where so many lives are taken in such a careless manner. Once I was witnessing a richly dressed Persian walking superciliously along the narrow side walk of the bazaar whilst another Persian came from the opposite direction. The latter, in his hurry, did not know exactly which side to take in order to pass the former, and, as is usually the case on such an occasion, danced before the irate Persian from right to left. The latter, who evidently belonged to the better classes, drew his poniard without another word, and mortally stabbed the innocent man. This happened in broad daylight, in the presence of thousands of people; it may thus be easily imagined what frightful things are occurring in the darkness and seclusion of night. The dreadful cases one daily hears of make one's blood curdle; but the punishment dealt out by the Government is not a whit behind these atrocities in their extreme ferocity. To have the belly split open, the limbs maimed, and to be torn to pieces by horses are, by no means, unusual punishments, and once it happened that the governor caused four culprits to be buried together in a pit and had burning lime poured over them afterwards.

One day, in the company of my kind host, I visited the grave of *Saadi*, the celebrated poet and moralist. It stands in a secluded gorge of the valley, and over it is a very fine building erected by *Kerim Khan* and surrounded by a little garden kept in excellent order. Mounting several steps, we first passed through sundry minor chambers, until we came to a large open hall, in the centre of which rose a marble sarcophagus, bearing masterly inscriptions in Arabic. In the water-basin of the garden there used formerly to be fish, and it is said that the enthusiastic visitors of Saadi's grave would hang golden rings on them, to steal which was looked upon as the greatest sacrilege. There is a small village in the neighbourhood of the grave called *Saadi* in honour of the great poet, and a gate in the city, looking towards the grave, bearing the name of *Dervazi Saadi* (Saadi's gate), as well as a bridge, christened *Pul Saadi;* which are all evidence of the veneration in which he is held to this day. But this great poet and scholar is an object of veneration not only to the people of Persia but to every Mohammedan in the Asiatic world. His *Gulistan* (Grove of Roses, the title of his book) is read with admiration and rapture in the middle of China as well as on the extremest borders of Africa. Wherever schools are attended by Mohammedan youths, there the Gulistan is sure to form the basis of instruction. European scholars have long since appreciated and admired the undying freshness of his style, his brilliant language and his witty and telling similitudes. In one of the chambers of the mausoleum I came across a respectable-looking grey-headed man, whose clean garb and mild aspect formed a strange contrast to the dervish's hat, denoting his calling. With engaging good humour he hastened to address me, and I learned in the course of conversation that he was a native of India, and that, prompted by his veneration for Saadi, he had resigned his rank and given up his wealth at home, in order to pass the remaining days of his life at the tomb of the great man. It is known that Saadi was a dervish himself, but unlike the majority of that tribe who assume the *Khirka* (dervish's garb) in furtherance of their own worldly aims, Saadi went roving about for thirty years meeting with numerous adventures during his wanderings. He was, in turn, a servant, a slave, a lord and celebrated scholar; and he even assumed the religion of the worshippers of Vishnu, in order to extend and increase his knowledge of all things. He despised wealth and the favour of princes, and sought his only happiness in—as the Orientals metaphorically express it—"perforating with the diamond of his soul the precious stones of his experiences, and after gathering them on the string of eloquence, hanging them for a talisman around the neck of posterity." The grave of Hafiz, standing in a larger cemetery, may be seen not far from Saadi's mausoleum. The site of his grave is marked by a monument of white marble erected by Kerim Khan, and the inscription carved upon it is a verse from his own book, the Divan. I frequently visited the grave, and, to my astonishment, found at times a merry carousing company seated about it, drinking their wine; at other times it was surrounded by penitent pilgrims. The former look upon Hafiz as their great master in a life of carelessness and jollity; the latter consider him a saint and come here to beseech him to intercede for them. Some sing his songs while the cheering cup is going the rounds, whilst others deem his book as holy as the Koran itself. When any one wishes to read the fate in store for him, he opens at random either Hafiz or the Koran, reciting the following verses:

Ei Hafizi Shirazi,
Ber men nazr endazi,
Men talibi yek falem,
Tu Kashifi her razi.

(Oh Hafiz, of Shiraz, cast one look upon me; of thee I wish to learn my future fate, for thou art the discoverer of all secrets); and having done his invocation, he studies the page before him, construing its text into a prophecy of good or bad fortune.

I had passed three months in Shiraz, and was so much pleased with the city that I began to turn over in my mind the propriety of spending the winter in the genial climate of Shiraz rather than in Teheran, and going afterwards, when spring came, through Yezd and Tebbes to Khorassan. But the arrival in Shiraz of two European travellers upset all my plans in that direction. One of them was Count Rochechouart, a member of the French Embassy in Teheran, who was travelling with a view to studying the commercial condition of Persia, and the other the Marquis of Doria, a distinguished member of the extraordinary Italian Embassy which came to Persia at the same time that I did, travelling in pursuit of zoological and botanical knowledge. Upon their arrival these distinguished foreigners were received and feasted by the authorities. After the official receptions were over, Dr. Fagergreen, my excellent Swedish friend, invited them to his house, and the table spread before his European guests literally groaned under everything that was good and savoury produced beneath the southern skies of Persia. The doctor's face beamed with inward satisfaction as he rose, glass in hand, to propose a toast in honour of the three nations represented by the guests sitting at his hospitable board. The good man was happiest if he could entertain a European traveller in his house, and overwhelmed him on such occasions with kindness. I had met such a friendly reception and generous treatment at the hands of the kind-hearted doctor, he had proved such an unselfish friend to me, that I became quite attached to him. I therefore received with feelings of keen regret the invitation of Count Rochechouart to accompany him to Teheran, where he was soon going, leaving behind him his Italian fellow-traveller, the Marquis, who intended to prolong his stay in Shiraz in order to enjoy its unrivalled climate. Yet I was bound to accede to the French nobleman's proposal, although it involved an immediate separation from my friend, as I was nearly destitute of everything, and expected to derive some advantages from making the journey back in his company. I had come here in the guise of a begging dervish, and here was a chance to go back as a European traveller, sharing in all the comforts at the disposal of a gentleman travelling in an affair of state and representing His Majesty the Emperor of France. I did not waver long; my mind was soon made up. The Count remained in Shiraz three days longer in order to attend to some matters, and at their expiration we were to return, in forced marches, to Teheran.

On the day of my departure I went to take leave of my generous friend, Dr. Fagergreen. I found him still in his bedroom in the upper story of his house. Our conversation frequently turned upon the probability of our ever meeting again, and whenever I happened to touch upon my Turkestan journey the tears would start to his eyes. I was deeply moved by this heartfelt, genuine sympathy. I had to leave; I embraced him for the last time; I seized his hand to give it a last hearty shake; but at the very moment I received a shock as if the whole house were falling. I glanced at my friend's face—it was as pale as death. "Quick, for the love of God," he cried; "let us call my wife and children, there will be an earthquake. The earthquakes in Shiraz are awful, especially if the shocks begin early in the morning."

We quickly collected his wife and children, and as we came down the narrow staircase into the small yard, we heard an underground noise approaching us with a hollow roar, as if the bowels of the earth were about to open at our feet. The second shock was much more violent than the first had been. The high walls and the surrounding edifices began to totter from side to side with a loud creaking sound, and whilst I was looking up to the sky, the cry of "Yah Allah! Yah Allah!" piercing to the very marrow, was heard from every part of the town. The inhabitants of Shiraz know but too well the frightful consequences of this elemental catastrophe, and the stoutest heart may well quail at the deep roar in the womb of the earth, at the cries of distress above, the very birds fluttering about scared and helpless. For a few moments we stood still, completely paralyzed with fright. My host was the first to regain his composure; he turned to me and said: "We are here in a very narrow place. If this wall happens to come down we shall be all buried beneath it. Take my wife and children to the nearest larger place. I shall remain here, for the mob is apt to take advantage of the general fright to rob and plunder the house." I wished to reply, but the doctor silenced me with a beseeching look, and taking hold of his trembling wife and children, I left without saying another word. We passed through a narrow alley crowded with pale and frightened people. The open space which we reached in a few moments presented a harrowing picture of distress and misery. Women and children were lying on the ground, fainting, screaming and tearing their hair. Others were running to and fro half clad or without any clothing on, as if they had just come out of their baths. A few minutes had sufficed to deprive the whole city of its senses. Amidst all this crying and screaming a couple of mollahs (priests) went about continually repeating that the Frengis sojourning in the city had brought on it this calamity. I began to entertain fears for the safety of my friend, and retraced my steps as fast as I could. As I reached the yard I observed the birds flying about and flapping their wings in a restless and wild manner, which was a sure forerunner of another shock. And indeed very soon we heard the deep roar which usually precedes a violent thunderstorm. The earth shook beneath our feet, and as the shocks came nearer and nearer to the place where we were standing, the shock became so powerful that in spite of all our efforts we lost our equilibrium, and, trying to steady one another, sank together to the ground. I heard a frightful crash, and in another second I had the sensation of water rolling over me, and thought my last moment had come. This was the worst shock; a portion of the wall had given way, and the water which had passed over our bodies came from a neighbouring water-tank. Trembling and frightened, I looked round to see if the building did not threaten to come down on our heads. In this moment of despair the shout of the infuriated mob, "The Frengis are unclean," reached our ears, followed by savage curses, and it seemed as if the mob intended to take the house by storm. "To arms!" cried my friend, but who would have had the courage to enter a house which threatened to come down at any moment? We paused and looked at each other, and then with one accord rushed into the house, returning immediately armed with rifles and pistols. We had now to defend ourselves both against the rage of the elements and the wickedness of man.

These moments will remain for ever engraved in my memory. Suddenly we heard a loud report, and soon after saw dense clouds of dust rising in the air. Fortunately for us a building in the neighbourhood had fallen down and scattered the savage mob. Before long the whole neighbourhood became quiet. We did not feel another shock, but the whole city was wrapped in a dense cloud of dust. The very mountains, lying to the south, had been cleft in twain by these shocks which hurled down their precipitous sides huge blocks of stone and rocks, with a noise like thunder. Seeing that half an hour had passed without a renewal of the shocks, I picked up courage enough to leave the house.

The destruction in the city had been much too cruel for any pen to be able to present a picture of its terrible details. I met Count Rochechouart in the street; with an anxious face he urged our immediate departure. The leave-taking from my friend was short but affectionate. Along the streets the huge cracks and fissures in the walls were yawning at us, as we went on; to the right and to the left—everywhere—nothing but desolation and misery were to be seen, whilst an expression of indescribable discouragement and mute resignation was brooding over the countenances of the people whom we met on our way. Our hearts yearned towards these unfortunates in their present sad plight, but it was, nevertheless, a feeling of relief to find ourselves, after passing through the gates of the city, in the open air again, where our fellow-travellers were awaiting our arrival. Outside there was an immense crowd; those who had run to the open country for safety were watching, with sinking hearts, for those members of their families who had been left behind in the city, and in their unreasoning distress inquired of us, who were perfect strangers to them, if we knew anything about their whereabouts. Words cannot tell with what profound satisfaction I descried at last Tenghi Allah Ekber, the spot from which I had on my arrival admired the romantic situation of Shiraz. Ten years before Shiraz had been visited by an earthquake far more calamitous than the last. There is a legend amongst the people that years and years ago the present site of Shiraz was covered by the waters of a lake, called Deryai Nemek, *i.e.*, the Salt Lake, lying to the east of it, and that the city is doomed to final destruction by this very lake, which will overwhelm it with its tide on the Day of Resurrection. We returned, in forced marches, by the same way on which, three months ago, I had wearily plodded on at the slow pace of caravan travelling. The journey was enlivened by the fascinating conversation of the noble Count and, now and then, by the chase of a herd of gazelles. The Persian horsemen, riding in front, descried them with lynx-eyed quickness, and the fast-running hounds were not long in overtaking them. At times, on our coming to a city, solemn receptions were prepared for us, and, on such occasions, there was no end of complimenting, sweetmeats, and feasting. I came back to Teheran at last, in the middle of January, 1863.

XVI.

PREPARATIONS FOR MY JOURNEY TO CENTRAL ASIA.

I MADE it, of course, my first duty in Teheran to revisit the hospitable circle of my patrons. Here I learned that the war in Herat was at an end, and that, therefore, another obstacle to the carrying out of my programme was cleared away. It has always been customary for the Turkish Embassy to give some assistance to the hadjis (persons who have visited the holy tomb of Mahommed) and to dervishes going every year from Bokhara, Khiva and Khokand, through Persia, to the Turkish Empire. This is a great boon to the poor Sunnite mendicants, who have no chance of ever getting a farthing from the Persian Shi-ites. As a consequence the palace of the Embassy had annually to entertain guests from far-off Turkestan, and upon these occasions I took particular pleasure in having the wild and ragged Tartars come to my room, where I contrived to learn of them a good deal about their country that was interesting. They were quite overwhelmed by my courtesy, and it soon became a familiar saying at the caravansary where these people used to put up, that

Haidar Effendi, the Ambassador of the Sultan, was a man possessing a generous heart, but that Reshid Effendi (your humble servant's assumed name) was something more than that, for he treated the dervishes like brothers, and most likely was, in secret, a dervish himself.

It was nothing to be wondered at, therefore, since I enjoyed such a reputation, that the dervishes should have called first upon me before asking to be admitted to the presence of the Ambassador in chief who frequently would not receive them. Many a time it was through my intercession alone that they were able to obtain assistance in money, or to have some other requests granted. In this way it happened that four hadjis came to see me on the 20th of March, and asked me to introduce them to the Turkish Embassy before whom they desired to lay their complaints against the Persians for levying upon them, on their return from Mecca, the Sunnite tax, the collection of which had been prohibited long ago by the Sultan, a prohibition since ratified by the Shah of Persia. "We do not come to ask money of the Sultan's great ambassador," said they, "we only wish to ensure that henceforth our Sunnite countrymen shall not be compelled to pay a tax on visiting the holy places." These unselfish words from the lips of an Oriental rather puzzled me; I subjected my guests to a closer scrutiny and discovered in them, in spite of the savage expression of their faces, their neglected exterior and the shabbiness of their dress, a certain natural nobility which did not fail to enlist my sympathies. Their spokesman, as a rule, was a hadji from Chinese Tartary, or Eastern Turkestan, as it is actually called; he wore over his tattered garments a new green *djubbe* (an upper garment of cloth) and on

MAKING FRIENDS WITH THE TARTARS.

[Page 138.

his head a white turban of gigantic size. His eyes sparkled with vivacity, and his superiority over the rest of his companions became more and more apparent in the course of the interview. He introduced himself as the Imam (court priest) of the governor of Aksu, one of the provinces of Chinese Tartary, and as a double hadji, having visited twice the holy tomb, and declared that he and his three companions present were the avowed chiefs of a hadji-caravan consisting of twenty-four men. "Our company," he added, "is composed of the young and the old, of the rich and the poor, of the lettered and the unlettered, yet we live in the utmost harmony with each other, for we are all natives of Khokand and Kashgar (the names frequently used to designate the whole of Chinese Tartary), and have no Bokhariotes vipers of humanity amongst us."

The interview had lasted for about an hour, and the frank and open manner of the men deepened the favourable impression they had made upon me at the outset. Although the characteristic features of their race, their careless and shabby attire and the effects of the miseries of a long and fatiguing journey, all combined to give them a wild, almost repulsive appearance; yet throughout the whole interview my mind was busy with the question of the feasibility of undertaking my travels in Central Asia in the company of these very pilgrims. I was thinking that being natives they would be the best guides I could possibly obtain, and it was something to be known to them as Reshid Effendi, and to have been seen by them as such at the Turkish Embassy. I did not hesitate long and told them of my intention to join their caravan. Of course, I was prepared for their putting questions to me about the purposes of my journey, and I was equally clear in my mind that it would be both idle and injurious to tell these men of the scientific researches I had in view. They would have thought it ridiculous for an Effendi, a gentleman, to expose himself to untold dangers for the sake of some ideal object, and indeed might have entertained all sorts of suspicions against me had I told them the truth. I had to resort to a subterfuge which both flattered my guests and advanced my interests. I told them that my soul had been harbouring for a long time the secret but most ardent wish to visit Turkestan (the only country abounding in genuine Islamite virtues) and the saints of Khiva, Samarkand and Bokhara. "This longing desire," I continued, "had brought me from Roum (Turkey), and now after having waited for a year in Persia for a favourable opportunity to gratify it, I had reason to thank God for having sent me, at length, such men as they were, in whose company I could continue my journey and attain the most cherished object of my life."

It was an extraordinary struggle I had to overcome in inventing this pretext, but I sought in vain for another means. My long experience with Orientals of many countries and of various ranks had fully convinced me of the utter uselessness of a straightforward confession of my purposes. I knew that with these simple and ignorant men science and curiosity must be discredited as the chief motors of my errand, and that all my oratorical power would fail to convince them of the possibility that a man living under the patronage of a high official of the Sultan was ready to undergo all the hardships and perils of a distant journey, for the sake of philological inquiries and for ethnographical discoveries. Hard and reluctant as it was, I had to resort to subterfuge, and to assume in their eyes a moral as well as a physical incognito.

The good Tartars looked at me and at each other, in amazement, after I had done speaking. Finally they confessed that they had long ago thought me to be a secret dervish, but that now they were convinced of the truth of their surmises. They declared that they were highly pleased with the distinction I was about to confer upon them by deeming them worthy of my company. Their spokesman Hadji Bilal said: "We are all of us ready to be not only thy friends, but thy servants, but I must call to thy mind that the roads of Turkestan are not so safe as those of Persia and Turkey. Often along our roads we do not see a house for weeks, nor can we get a piece of bread, or even a drop of water. Besides this, we are kept in constant fear of being killed, made prisoners and sold into slavery, or buried by the sands in a hurricane. Therefore ponder this matter well, O Effendi! Thou mightest repent the step later, and we should not like thee to look upon us as the causers of thy misfortune. And, besides, remember that our countrymen are far behind us in matters of experience and knowledge of the world, and with all their hospitality are apt to regard with suspicious eyes every comer from foreign lands. And how wilt thou return, alone, without us?"

The effect of these words upon me may be easily imagined, but my purpose was not to be shaken. I made them easy on the score of their anxiety about me, I told them of the fatigues I had already borne, and my contempt of earthly comforts, particularly of my dislike to the French dress which I was compelled to wear, *ex officio*. I continued that I well knew this world to be nothing but a five days' inn, as our sages say, and that we are moving rapidly from it to give way to others. I laughed to scorn those Mussulmans who instead of caring for the present moment only, turn their thoughts to things which are going to happen years hence. "Oh! take me with you, my friends," I exclaimed; "I must leave this nest of errors, of which I am tired unto loathing."

My request touched them. The chiefs of the dervish-caravan accepted me at once for their fellow-traveller; we embraced and kissed all around, performances by no means pleasant considering the intolerable stench coming from their bodies and clothing. But I scarcely looked at such trifles, the main object of my discourse having been secured. My next step was to hasten to Haidar Effendi, my benefactor, to tell him of my intentions, and to request him to warmly recommend me to the hadjis I was about to introduce to him. He objected at first to the whole plan, and called me mad to wish to go to a country from which none of my predecessors ever returned, and in the society of fellows who were capable of murdering any one for the sake of a few pence. But when my Turkish friends saw that all their arguments were of no avail, they set to work to give me every possible assistance. Haidar Effendi received the hadjis, settled their own matters to their satisfaction, then spoke of me, representing my motives in the way I had put them before the hadjis, commended me to their hospitality and protection, remarking that they, in turn, could count upon his friendly service; "for," he added, "he whom I give in your charge, Reshid Effendi, *is the Sultan's civil officer.*" I was afterwards told that the hadjis, at the audience where I was not present, had solemnly vowed to fulfil their promises. And, indeed, they honourably kept the word they had pledged. When the audience was over the Ambassador asked for a list of the names of the members of the dervish-caravan and distributed about fifteen gold pieces amongst them. This was a munificent gift to people accustomed to live on bread and water and utterly unused to comforts of any kind. The day of our departure was fixed for that day week. Hadji Bilal's visits were very frequent during this time, he bringing with him and introducing to me all his companions, in turn; and I own that their exterior was not apt to inspire confidence. These visits made me suspect that the pious hadji looked on me as a rich prey and was anxious not to lose me. But I conquered my suspicions, and showed the hadji, as a mark of confidence in him, the small sum of money I intended to take with me, requesting him, at the same time, to inform me precisely how I was to dress and what mode of life I should follow in order to be as like to my companions as possible, and not attract any undue attention. He was highly pleased with my request and readily gave me his advice in the matter. In the first place, he said, I was to shave my head and exchange my Turkish costume for that of Bokhara, and in the next place I must leave behind me my bedding, linen and similar articles of luxury. Of course I followed directions, which could be easily complied with, to the smallest point, and was ready to embark in my perilous enterprise three days before the appointed time. I made use of this interval to pay a return visit to the caravansary where my future fellow-travellers were staying. They were living in two small cells, fourteen of them in one, and ten in the other. I never saw in my life so much of raggedness and dirt crowded into such a small space, and the impression this misery then made upon my mind still lives fresh in my memory. Only a few of them were able to perform the journey out of their own means; the rest of them had to resort to begging. When I entered they were busy with a mode of cleansing themselves, the loathsome description of which I will spare my reader, but which, alas! I too had to adopt in course of time.

I was very cordially received by them, and, according to their custom, they immediately prepared some green tea for me, of which it took all my heroism to swallow a Bokhara cup, the green liquid without sugar being the worst thing mortal ever tasted. As a mark of their kind feelings for me they offered me another cup of tea —but I politely declined, my stomach admonishing me that it would refuse to take in any more of the vile stuff. Then there ensued a scene of general embracing; I was looked upon by all of them as their brother, and had this affectionate title bestowed upon me; and, finally, after I had broken bread with every one of them separately, we sat down to settle the definite details of our route. We had two roads to choose from, both equally perilous from the fact of their passing through the desert where the Turkomans are at home. One of the roads by way of Meshed, Merv and Bokhara was less fatiguing, it is true, but it would have taken us through territory inhabited by the Tekke Turkomans, who have the well-deserved reputation of sparing nobody and who would sell the Prophet himself into slavery if he ever fell into their hands. The other road runs through a country inhabited by the Yomut Turkomans, an honest hospitable people; but this road included a desert, where for twenty stations not a drop of drinking water could be obtained. After exchanging our views on the subject we decided in favour of the latter road. "It is better," said the chief of the caravan, "to brave the rudeness of the elements than to expose ourselves to the wickedness of man. God is merciful; we are walking in His ways, and surely He will not desert us." Our decision was now ratified by an oath recited by Hadji Bilal. Whilst he spoke we held up our hands towards Heaven, and when he had finished speaking every one took hold of his beard and said a loud "Amen" to it. Then we rose from our seats, and I was told to join them on the morning of the day after next in order to start on our journey. When I returned to the Embassy a last attempt was made by my friends to turn me from my purpose. They recalled the tragic fate of Conolly, Stoddart, and Moorcroft, and the case of Blocqueville who had fallen into the hands of the Turkomans and was rescued from slavery only by a ransom of ten thousand ducats. But the sad fate of others had no terrors for me and I remained firm in my determination to go.

I took leave of my friends at the Turkish Embassy on the eve of my departure. Only two persons knew of the real destination of my journey; the rest of the European colony thought I was going to Meshed.

XVII.

FROM TEHERAN TO THE LAND OF THE TURKOMANS.

According to appointment, I made my appearance at the caravansary on the 28th day of March, 1863. Those of my friends who could afford to hire a mule or ass to take them to the Persian border were ready, booted and spurred; the poorer, with pilgrim's staffs in their hands, were waiting, too, for the signal of departure. I observed with astonishment that the shabby garments worn by the party in town had been exchanged for other far more ragged ones, hanging down in a thousand tatters and fastened by means of a rope across the back, and learned, to my great surprise, that the miserable dress worn by them in town was their best holiday attire, which was now laid aside in order to save it. But yesterday I fancied myself a beggar in my new costume —to-day I looked fit to be a purple-clad king amidst my companions. Hadji Bilal at last raised his hands for a blessing on our journey, and we had not fairly seized our beards and said our customary Amens, when those of our party who were to walk on foot made a rush towards the gate, in order to get ahead of us who were seated on mules or asses.

The sun had risen to the height of a lance, as the Orientals say, when I turned to give a last farewell look at Teheran, gilded by the early sun, whilst my companions, like pious pilgrims that they were, raised their voices and sang sacred songs. They did not take amiss my not joining them, for they knew that the people of Roum (the inhabitants of European Turkey) were not brought up in such a strict religious way as those of Turkestan, but they hoped that in their society I should soon learn to be more enthusiastic in religious observance.

The caravan numbered twenty-three besides myself; they were all from Khokand and Eastern Turkestan, and mostly natives of Kashgar, Tashkend and Aksu. Their chiefs were Hadji Bilal, of whom I have already spoken, Hadji Sheikh Sultan Mahmud, a fanatic young Tartar, who traced his lineage from a renowned saint, and Hadji Sali Khalifa, who was endeavouring to obtain the rank of an Ishan (the title of Sheikh), and belonged to the half-priestly class. They honoured me with their friendship, and we four were looked upon as the chiefs of the caravan. My name henceforth ceased to be Reshid Effendi and became Hadji Reshid.

We proceeded without any misadventure along the continually rising heights of the mountain chain of Elburz. *Kemerd* was our first station. It offered nothing but a half-ruined hut of mud, in the middle of a desert, its weather-beaten walls threatening to give way at any moment. The rain poured in through the chinks of the roof, and it was difficult to find a handbreadth of dry ground. It was dusk when we arrived, and everybody hurried to get a dry place in the caravansary, myself amongst the pushing crowd. My friend Hadji Bilal set to preparing the *pilar*, and for want of fat, he poured on it grease obtained by melting down some tallow candles. I was of course invited to take my part of this luscious meal, but declined with thanks. Leaving the side of my kind friend, I went amongst the beggars and Persian mule-drivers, and drawing myself up into a corner, I thought, listening to the howling wind and beating rain outdoors in the dark night, of my present miserable condition, compared with that of last night at the palace of the Turkish Embassy, where I was sitting at a sumptuous farewell banquet, given in my honour, the wine glass freely circulating amongst my friends. And now I should have deemed myself happy if I had but room enough to stretch my limbs. To right and left of me fellows, ragged, dirty, ill-smelling and abounding in a variety of little rovers, were affectionately leaning on me; and, to cap the climax of my misery, a Persian mule-driver, afflicted with the gout, sat down near me, now moaning, now screaming with pain, whilst stentorian snoring was going on all around me. My clothes were soaking wet with the rain, and I myself was wet to the skin and shivering as if with a fit of ague. No wonder I could not close my eyes all night, and felt so weak next morning that I could hardly keep my seat decently in the saddle.

We passed the following night much more comfortably in a village called *Ghilar*. We divided into smaller troops, and I joined Hadji Bilal and his intimates. We found quarters in a small room belonging to a peasant, my friend inviting me again to take supper with him. This time I bravely got over my squeamishness; my ravenous appetite made me indulgent towards the nasty smell of the dish and the dirty hands of my companions, who were using them vigorously in helping themselves out of our common plate. The following morning I rose with

A DERVISH FEAST.

[Page 148.

renewed strength, after a refreshing sleep, and began, with less anxiety, to look the future in the face.

I was considerably amused by the remarks made regarding myself, by some Persian villagers, who, with clownish sharp-sightedness, were quick to discover that I was neither a Tartar, nor even an Osmanli, but a Frengi body and soul, availing myself of the society of dervishes in order to visit Central Asia, a land almost inaccessible to Europeans. But of these their surmises they never betrayed a single word to my companions; the Persian Shi-ites' hatred of the Sunnite Central-Asians being such that nothing affords them greater pleasure than to see their mortal enemies imposed upon.

On the fourth day we reached an elevated plateau on which the town of *Firuzkuh* lies at the foot of a mountain topped by a fine ruin. I was charmed by the beauty of both the town and the surrounding country, the houses especially challenging my admiration for the neatness of their architecture. A wide and deep mountain stream winds through the little town in three different directions. Many and large caravans carry from this place oranges, water-melons, sugar-canes, and other products of the Caspian Sea, to Shahrud and Teheran, returning heavily laden with corn, an article of food almost entirely wanting in this mountainous region.

Beyond Firuzkuh our road took us through a most romantic country. The dense forests, spreading endlessly, the far-sounding roar of the huge mountain cataracts, the bottomless abyss yawning between precipitous mountain sides—made me at times almost imagine I saw the most beautiful Alpine scenery of Europe before me. Even my companions, whose sense of appreciation of the beauties of nature was but slightly developed, became quite enthusiastic. We breakfasted near the ruins of *Div-Sefid* (*i.e.*, the white spirit), crowning a rocky peak. One of our Persian fellow-travellers remarked that this rocky habitation in the air was once the favourite resort of the White Giant whom Rustem (the hero of Oriental legends) conquered and drove to the shores of the Caspian Sea; that spirits of the deep then inhabited alone this paradise-like country; and that it was fortunate that there were heroes at that time who could expel these spirits, for surely the modern Persians would be wanting in strength and courage to accomplish the deed.

The Persian travellers who had come with us as far as *Surkh-Abad*, *i.e.*, Red Abode, there took leave of us. The abundant wood and excellent water we found caused immense delight to my Tartars. Whilst at other times six and eight of them would cook by one fire, now each of them kindled a separate fire whereby to prepare his tea. They made use of the very embers, by divesting themselves of their clothes, and two of them holding and drawing tight a piece of clothing at a time over the fire, whilst a third would gently beat it with a small stick. The whole proceeding seemed to me rather mysterious at first, but a peculiar sound, now crackling, now hissing, soon showed that this was a mode of putting to death by fire victims innumerable. The practice, when I first saw it, filled me with disgust; the time arrived, nevertheless, when, for cleanliness' sake, I indulged in it as zealously as any of those present. We were nearly exhausted by our long march on bad roads, and as soon as the dusk of evening approached we were all of us looking for some place to rest in. We should have stopped at many a place in the woods if some Persians had not warned us that the forest was full, particularly at this season, of wild animals who, driven by their predatory instincts, will at night attack strongly built houses, not to speak of human beings camping in the open air. We were especially warned against tigers. In spite of fatigue we were compelled to march on in the woods until late in the night, when we came near several groups of houses, standing apart and called *Heftten*; we settled down near them on the margin of the forest. We decided to keep up a large fire during the whole night, and that each of us should in turn keep watch near the fire. Our nightly fire soon lit up the entire landscape; but the thicket close to us still resounded with the stealthy tread and deep roar of our ferocious enemies. A herd of hungry wild boars were looking out for their prey, and the only way to keep them off was by discharging at intervals our fire-arms at them. The jackals showed most remarkable impudence; they would come quite near us and gambol around us like so many domestic animals, not even minding our sticks. These animals will watch you when you are too absorbed in conversation to keep your eyes on your food or clothing, and catlike pounce upon either, in an unguarded moment, and run away with it. The night passed, however, without any mishap. On the following day I bought for a *penabad* (about two pence and a half) ten large fine and savoury pheasants. My Tartar companions, too, bought a good many, there being a drug of them in the place; owing to their inability to rise in the air in the dense woods, they are killed with sticks by the thousands. For days the excellent roast, furnished by their succulent and finely flavoured flesh, supplied the place of bread, which is very expensive.

We entered *Sari*, which rises in the middle of a marshy country, covered with mud from head to foot, owing to the miserable roads on which we had to pass. The inhabitants, Persian Shi-ites, laughed at our sad appearance, and a troop of urchins pursued us with insults and cries, until we reached the gate of the caravansary. On entering the bazaar, several men, in red-striped costumes and with peculiar head-gears, stood still at our approach, raising their hands and looking at us with great respect. They were Turkomans, residing here, who wished to receive from us, their Sunnite brethren, just come from the Holy Land, a *fatiha** (blessing) while it was still fresh. We had passed scarcely an hour at the caravansary when a number of others made their appearance, bringing with them gifts of food for ourselves and our animals. One of them paid his respects to me, and, following the example of my companions, I gave him a blessing, which he rewarded by a gift of tobacco worth a couple of shillings. I afterwards told Hadji Bilal of it, and he took occasion to remark at this with brightening eyes: "Yes, Effendi, we shall be free before long; we are coming to the land of the Turkomans, our brethren in faith, and as much distinction is awaiting us there as we have to suffer shame, contumely and contempt at the hands of the Persians." I had become such a Sunnite, by this time, that his words caused me real pleasure; forgetting, as all the while I did, the frightful stories I had heard about the savageness and cruelty of the inhabitants of the desert.

We passed two days in Sari. My companions were busy trying to sell their asses, for we were to embark at

* *Fatiha* means the opening chapter of the Koran, and is recited as a blessing.

the next station and wished to avoid the trouble of shipping and taking the animals with us. In Sari we became acquainted with several distinguished members of the Afghan colony, and immediately on our arrival were invited by them to supper. There happened to be other guests, merchants from *Karatape*, whilst we were there, and our Afghan brethren warmly recommended them to the whole caravan. These men served us, with the greatest alacrity, as guides to their native place.

Karatape owes its name to the black hill standing in the centre of the village, one side of it being inhabited by Persians and the other by Afghans. The first thing I did was to climb this hill in order to take a passing glance at the Caspian Sea. From this spot the open sea cannot be seen, it being concealed by a long and narrow strip of land, running far into the sea, and looking, at a distance, like a line wooded with tall trees. All I could descry was the sheet of water between this line and the shore. I then hurried back to our lodgings to see how the preparations for our passage to the Turkoman desert were progressing. After a good deal of inquiry we heard on the following evening that a Turkoman was about to sail directly for Gomushtepe, and was willing, from feelings of kindness, to take all the hadjis with him. He wished us to be ready on the shore early in the morning so as to be able to take advantage of a favourable breeze. Hadji Bilal, Hadji Salih, and myself, the acknowledged triumvirate of the beggar-caravan, immediately went in search of the Turkoman whose name was Yakub. We found him to be a young man still, with an air of boldness about him. He immediately embraced every one of us, and declared himself willing to wait another day in order that we might procure the necessary articles of food. We had here to provide ourselves with flour, rice and other sustenance to last as far as Khiva; the Turkomans themselves coming to this place to make their purchases. Before all, Yakub asked a blessing of Hadji Bilal and Hadji Salih, and as we were turning to leave he called me aside and asked me to remain a few minutes longer. Of course I remained. He confided to me, with some embarrassment, a case of unhappy and unrequited love, of which he was the victim, and that a very clever sorcerer, a Jew who happened to be just then in Karatape, had promised to prepare for him a very powerful *nuskha* (talisman) if he would take to him thirty drops of oil of roses fresh from Mecca, which were absolutely necessary for the writing of the magic formula. "I know," continued Yakub, "that the hadjis bring with them oil of roses and other fragrant articles, and, thou being the youngest of the chiefs of the caravan, I apply to thee and hope thou wilt comply with my request." Our companions had, in truth, brought with them oil of roses, and they at once gave him what he had asked for, to the great delight of the good youth.

Early in the morning of the following day we were all assembled on the shore. We now had each of us, besides our beggars' bags, a sack of flour, and, owing to the shallowness of the shore and the consequent distance of the vessel, which lay about a mile off the land, it took considerable time before we were all of us safely carried by boat to the vessel. The craft was a so-called *keseboy*, carrying a mast and one sail, and engaged in carrying freight; she had brought oil of naptha, pitch and salt from the island of *Tchercken*, and was now sailing back freighted with a small cargo of produce. We had to sit in two rows, close to each other, in order to allow Yakub and his two men space enough easily to move about. Our situation was not of the pleasantest; it was tolerable during the day, but when at night we were oppressed by sleep, we were often compelled to support the burden of a snoring hadji for hours. Two sleepers together would sometimes lean on me, one from the right and another from the left, yet I dared not wake them, for it is considered a great sin to disturb the slumbers of the Faithful.

A favourable westerly wind swelled our sail on the tenth of April, and I enjoyed the sail in the magnificent spring weather as well as I could in my cramped position. A calm set in towards evening; we anchored near the shore, and each of us in turn prepared his tea at the fireplace of the vessel. We arrived on the following day below *Ashurada,* which forms the southernmost point of Russia's possessions in Asia. The place makes a favourable impression upon the traveller coming from Persia. One small and two large Russian men-of-war are permanently in the harbour, for the defence of the Russians in Ashurada and the sailing vessels bound for the place. It happened more than once that, in spite of the strenuous exertions of the military Russian governor, a great number of unfortunate Persians, and not unfrequently Russian sailors, too, were dragged in chains into slavery to Gomushtepe. The Russian vessels are cruising day and night in the Turkoman waters, and every Turkoman vessel, coming from the eastern shore and bound for the shores of southern Persia, must provide itself with a passport, which must be produced in passing Ashurada. At such times the vessel is carefully searched for slaves, arms and other articles forbidden to be carried.

Our Yakub, too, had his papers, which he produced on the evening we arrived at Ashurada, in order that we might go on without further delay. But it being rather late in the evening, the Russian officer put off his visit to the vessels till next morning. We cast anchor not far from the shore. I was uneasy all night at the thought of these Russian officers coming to-morrow to make their visit on board, and possibly being struck by my European features and complexion. I was not afraid of any inhuman treatment, but I feared they might wish me to give up my journey and discover my identity to my companions. The pleasant sound of church bells roused me next morning. My companions told me that this was the Sunday of the infidels and their holiday. One of the men-of-war in our neighbourhood was beflagged all over. I observed, after a while, that a boat, manned by sailors in full uniform, was sent from her to the shore, and returned to the ship immediately with an officer in full uniform. In about ten minutes we were called upon to draw nearer to the Russian vessel, and I perceived that several fair-haired officers were standing near the gangway. The nearer I approached the faster beat my heart, and I tried, as well as I could, to place myself in such a way as not to have to meet their eyes. The day being a holiday the search was made very superficially, their interpreter exchanging a few words with Yakub, whilst the officers were making fun of our party of beggars. I heard one of them say: "Just look, how white this hadji's complexion is," referring in all probability to me whose face was less weatherbeaten and tanned than my companions. Yakub was soon allowed to leave; and, weighing anchor, our vessel, favoured by a fair breeze, bravely ploughed the waters. In a few hours the Turkoman sea-shore, looking like a long, moderately undulating line, rose before our eyes. Yakub and his men took in the sail, the water ceasing to be navigable. We were about a mile and a half from the mouth of the *Gorghen*, along the two shores of which stretches the camp, called Gomushtepe, presenting the appearance of a dense mass of beehives placed close to each other.

XVIII.

GOMUSHTEPE.

WE had to wait out in the sea for a while, until the boats were sent by Yakub to take us to shore. We were conveyed in small detachments to the dry land, Hadji Bilal and myself remaining the last. When we stepped on land we were informed that Yakub had already announced our arrival to Khandjan, the chief of the Gomushtepe, and that the latter was hastening to receive us at once. He was kneeling a few steps from us, engaged in his noon-prayers; and having done, he rose and came towards us with hurried steps. He was a tall, slenderly built, very plainly dressed man, about forty years old, his long beard reaching his breast. He embraced me first, and calling me by my name, cordially bade me welcome. Then came Hadjî Bilal's and Hadji Salih's turn, and our whole caravan being together we all followed him to the tents. The news of our arrival had already spread, and women, children and dogs promiscuously rushed out of the tents to see the pilgrims, who, according to their mollahs (priests), by their mere embrace make the untravelled partakers of divine grace, and sharers, to some extent, in the merit of the pilgrimage. The scene before my eyes was so novel, so surprising, that I did not know which way first to turn my attention; the oddly constructed cloth tents, and the women in their long silk skirts, reaching to their heels, claiming it alike. Besides I had enough to do to satisfy the hundreds of friendly hands extended to me to be shaken. The young and the old, children and women, were striving to get near our persons in order to touch the hadjis, to whose garments the holy dust of Mecca and Medina was still clinging. We arrived in front of the chief Ishan's (priest's) tent quite exhausted by the devout and hospitable reception. We collected in one group waiting for quarters to be assigned to us. The inhabitants who were gathered there almost engaged in a regular scuffle about having us for their guests; every one wished to be the host of one of the poor pilgrims, and much as I had heard of the hospitality of the Nomads, it was all exceeded by what I had now an opportunity of witnessing. The women especially were vociferous in their rivalry, so much so that Khandjan himself was compelled to put an end to their scrambling by making an equitable distribution of the pilgrims. He took me, Hadji Bilal and those belonging to our own set into his own *ova* (tent). In order to reach his tent, which was at the very end of Gomushtepe, we had to pass through the whole camp, extending on both sides of the river Gorghen. This river rises far away in the mountains, abounding in fish to such an extent as to render its waters almost foul at the best of times, and quite undrinkable in summer. Twice I washed in it, and each time my face and hands smelt of fish.

The dusk of evening was approaching when we arrived, tired and exhausted, at Khandjan's tent, hoping to get a little rest. Vain hope! True, there was the tent destined for us, standing near that of Khanjan, on the shore of the Gorghen, but scarcely had we taken possession of it, with the customary ceremony of walking thrice round it and spitting at each of the four corners, than visitors came crowding into the narrow space. They remained till late in the evening asking us thousands of questions which it taxed our whole strength to answer properly. Our host at length took pity on us, and called upon our visitors to leave us to ourselves in order that we might obtain some rest. Supper, consisting of boiled fish and sour milk, was brought us meanwhile by Khandjan's son, a boy twelve years old, called Baba Djan—*i.e.*, literally, the father's soul. The meal was brought into the tent on a large wooden platter by a Persian slave, who dragged a heavy chain after him. He was relieved of the dish by Baba Djan, who placed it before us, and sat down by his father's side, while both looked at us with genuine satisfaction as we fell to with our keen appetites upon the dishes before us. After the meal was over we said our prayers in the customary way. Hadji Bilal raised his hands, every one present following his example, and as he finished by passing his hand over his beard and saying, "Bismillah," Allah Ekber, his action was repeated by everybody. Then Khandjan was congratulated on all sides on account of his guests, and the visitors dispersed.

On the following morning, the 13th of April, as I awoke thoroughly refreshed and invigorated by a night's sound sleep on a tolerably comfortable couch, I found Hadji Bilal standing by my side and was invited by him to take a walk. During the walk he sermonized me a little, telling me that it was time I should doff the rank of Effendi, and become a dervish body and soul. "Thou must have observed," he continued, "that both I and all our companions, without distinction of age, have said our *fatiha* (blessing) on the men. This thou too must now look to. I know that it is not the custom to do so in Roum, but here people will wish it of thee, and they will find it very strange that thou, professing to be a dervish, dost not fulfil the duties of a dervish. Thou knowest the form of blessing; utter it with confidence and a proper expression of devoutness. Thou mayest bestow the *nefes* (holy breath) too, if called to the bed-side of the sick; but ever remember to hold out thy hand, for well do these people know that we dervishes live by our holy trade, and that a present is never amiss with us." He then asked my pardon for having dared to instruct me, but, added, that he meant it for my best. I need not say that I felt much obliged to him for his advice and observations, which were prompted by the genuine interest he took in me.

On this occasion my friend told me also that Khandjan and other Turkomans had been inquiring about me, with a peculiarly mysterious air, and that he succeeded, with great difficulty only, in persuading them that my journey possessed no official character whatever. The Turkomans thought I was going to Khiva and Bokhara on some secret and confidential anti-Russian mission of the Sultan. Hadji Bilal was too sensible to flatly contradict their impressions in the matter, well knowing that they hold the Sultan in high respect, and that I should be benefited by making them think more highly of me.

We returned to our quarters, and found Khandjan with his whole family, his relations and numerous friends, already waiting for us. He brought to us his wife and his aged mother, to obtain for them our blessing. We blessed everybody present, one by one. Khandjan then declared that, guests being according to Turkoman custom the dearest members of the family, we could go about without let or hindrance not only amongst his tribe, the *Kelte*, but also amongst that of Yomut, and that if any of them should so much as dare to touch a hair of our heads, he would know how to obtain satisfaction for such an outrage. "You must remain with us two weeks longer, at least," continued our host, "until some caravan happens to go to Khiva. Take now your rest, visit the other tents; a Turkoman never allows a dervish to leave his tent with an empty hand, and it will do you no harm to fill your bread-sacks well, for it is a long journey from here to Khiva and Bokhara.

We gladly followed his advice. During the first day I went visiting at several of the tents, in the company of Khandjan, or his brother and friends of the family. Later on I went with Hadji Bilal, bestowing blessings, or visiting the sick in company of Hadji Salih, who dabbled considerably in the art of healing. Whilst he gave the medicine, I bestowed the blessing on the patient, and was rewarded for it by the gift of a small piece of cloth, dried fish and other trifles. Whether it was owing to my successful cures or to the curiosity of the people to see the hadji from Roum, I do not know, but certain it is that patients came flocking to me, and I treated them by either bestowing my blessing upon them, or breathing upon them, or writing talismans for them. Here and there sceptical people thought me a political emissary and strongly doubted my dervishship, but I paid very little attention to them.

The number of my acquaintances was daily increasing,

the most prominent people being amongst them. The friendship of Kizil Akhond, whose real name was Mollah Murad, proved to be of particularly great service to to me. The recommendations of this distinguished scholar, who was universally respected, opened the way everywhere. He had in his possession a book which he got, while studying in Bokhara, treating of Mohammedan theology, written in Ottoman-Turkish, which he found some difficulty in understanding; and I had a chance of obliging him by furnishing the proper key to it. He was very much pleased with my conversation, and spoke everywhere in the highest terms of me. especially praising me for my great knowledge of the books of Islam. I managed to secure the kind feelings of Satligh Akhond, another highly respected priest. When I first met him he gave thanks to Providence, in a special prayer, for having permitted him to behold, in my person, a Mussulman from Roum, the true source of the faith; and upon people commenting in his presence on the whiteness of my complexion, he insisted that this was the real *nur-ul-Islam*, the light of Islam shining from my face, and was by the blessing of God the birthright of the Western faithful only. Nor did I fail to cultivate the friendship of Mollah Durdis, who was invested with the rank of a chief judge (Kazi Kelan), for I soon found out that the ulemas were the only class who could exercise any influence over this savage people. As a sort of scholar, I, too, shared in the general esteem, and may cite, in point, the following instance. There were ancient Grecian ruins on the territory of Gomushtepe, probably of a fort built by Alexander the Great, which gave a name to the settlement. These ruins contain the only stone walls to be met with in the whole neighbourhood. It was considered proper,

Gomushtepe being the principal settlement of the Yomuts, to raise there a temple to God, built of stone, particularly as the materials necessary for the same were furnished in abundance at the ruins near by. I was selected by Kizil Akhond, in my capacity of the most learned and experienced dervish, to determine the place and the proper position, in the direction of Mecca (Kibla), of the altar (*mihrab*), a task which I very readily accomplished.

In the company of Kizil Akhond, I made an excursion occupying four days, into the territory of one of the tribes of the Yomuts, living to the east, and the Goklen Turkomans. On returning we were told that Hadji Kari Mesud, one of my companions, living in a tent used as a mosque, had been robbed. The stolen articles were searched for everywhere, but could not be found. Finally the Sheikh or Imam caused it to be publicly announced that he would pronounce a curse against the thief, unless the stolen property were restored to its rightful owner within a given time. The threat had its effect, for scarcely twenty-four hours had passed when the thief made his appearance, penitent and humble, bringing with him not only the stolen property, but some presents of expiation besides. About the same time we received some good news in regard to a caravan which was to go to Khiva. The Khan of Khiva, whom the physicians had ordered to drink buffalo milk for his health, had sent his *kervanbashi* (chief of the caravans) to Astrabad to buy two buffaloes, there being no such animals in his dominions. The kervanbashi had already passed through Gomushtepe, and we were to join his caravan and start at once with him upon his return. A better guide we could not desire, for there was not a man more familiar with the desert than he.

I thought it very strange that many of our party were urging our departure, although these poor people were entertained in the most hospitable manner. "It is impossible for us," they replied to my queries, "to witness any longer the cruelties perpetrated against these poor Persian slaves. It is true they are heretics and that we have to bear much ill-treatment in passing through their country, but what these poor people must suffer exceeds all bounds." The reader may imagine what the fate of these Persian slaves under their Turkoman masters must have been, if even my Tartar companions, who, it is true, know of no slave trade in their own country, had their compassion roused at the spectacle of their sufferings. Usually these poor people are forcibly torn, during the night, from the bosom of their families, and often dragged here covered with wounds. The poor man, once a prisoner, has his clothes taken away and receives instead a few scanty rags barely sufficient to cover his nakedness, and heavy chains are placed upon his limbs, galling his ankles and heels, and causing him cruel pain at every step he takes. In this way he continues for weeks to drag out a miserable existence on coarse food, and to prevent him from running away during the night, an iron collar (*karabogra*) is placed around his neck by which he is chained to a stake, the clanking of his chains betraying his slightest movement. He continues in this sad plight until he is either ransomed by his relations or sent to Khiva or Bokhara to be sold.

There is hardly a Turkoman of the better classes near whose tent the clanking of the chains of a couple of slaves is not heard. Khandjan had also two slaves, youths from eighteen to twenty years old, and my heart ached whenever I saw them dragging their heavy chains after them. I had the additional mortification of being compelled to insult and swear at them in public, as the slightest sympathy shown to them would have roused suspicion in my host, particularly as they addressed me oftener than the others, owing to my knowledge of their language. The younger of our two domestic slaves, a fine youth from Iran, with black curls, begged of me to write his parents a letter, beseeching them, for the love of God, to sell their house and sheep, and ransom him. I did as he requested. Upon one occasion I thought I could pass him, unobserved, a cup of tea, but as he was about to take it from my hands some one entered the tent. I did not, however, lose countenance for one minute; I pretended to have only teased him, and the poor fellow, instead of getting a cup of tea, had to put up with a few gentle blows from me, to keep up my false pretence. Not a night passed during my stay in Gomushtepe without firing being heard from the sea, announcing the arrival of a slaver.

The inhabitants of Gomushtepe were untiring in the arrangement of feasts for devotional purposes, and on such occasions the entire hadji-company had to be present. I once wished to excuse myself, but was ushered out of my tent by a violent poke in the ribs from my would-be host, it being a rule of Turkoman etiquette that "the harder the thrusts, the more cordial the invitation." Upon these festive occasions it is the custom to spread in front of the host's tent a few pieces of cloth, or if the thing is done in great style, carpets, upon which the invited guests seat themselves in groups of six, each group forming a circle. Each of these groups gets a large wooden platter, the contents of which vary in quantity according to the ages and number of the guests, and every one helps himself with his hands, thrusting them into the plate until they reach its bottom. As to the quality of the dishes, the less said about them the better; I will only mention, in parenthesis, that horse's and camel's meat is the order of the day.

Whilst we were the guests of Khandjan he celebrated by a feast the betrothal of his son, a boy of twelve years, with a girl of ten; and, of course, we had to be present at this feast. Originally the betrothal was to have taken place in the following autumn, but he took advantage of our presence to get our blessing for the young couple. A rather remarkable man was the Karaktchi, by whom also an entertainment was arranged in honour of our party. This man, all by himself and being on foot, took three Persians prisoners and drove them a distance of eight miles into slavery. He gave us, as our share, a tenth part of the plunder, being the tithe belonging to the priests and amounting to two krans for each of us; and when we sang, blessing him, the fatiha, the man was beside himself with joy.

After we had passed three weeks in Gomushtepe we began our preparations for the onward journey, Khandjan promising to assist us in every way. We gave up the idea of purchasing camels owing to the expense it involved, and made up our minds to hire, instead, one camel for every two persons, which would carry at the same time the water and the flour of those two. The latter plan, however, would have been attended with considerable difficulty but for the assistance we got from Ilias Beg, who happened to be the very man we wanted for our purposes. This man differed from the others in being less religiously inclined, and being wanting in respect towards our hadjiship, but he observed all the more scrupulously the laws of hospitality. He was a Turkoman from Khiva, and belonged to the tribe of Yomut. Once in every year he used to cross the desert and visit this neighbourhood on business, and whilst on these visits enjoyed during his stay in Gomushtepe the protection of Khandjan, without which he would have been no more safe than any other stranger. He generally came in the autumn and left again in spring with from twenty to thirty camels laden partly with goods of his own, and partly with goods belonging to others. This season he was anxious to take with him a greater number of camels, not caring even if they were without a load, and the conveyance of our party came to him in the nick of time. Khandjan solemnly adjured him to take good care of us. "Thou shalt answer for their safety with thy life, Ilias!" he said, and the latter, fixing his eyes upon the ground, as the Nomads always do when they seem to be in earnest, merely answered: "Thou knowest me." We settled with Ilias to pay him two gold pieces for the hire of every camel we were to use, but that he should convey our water and flour free of charge. The money I had sewn into various parts of my ragged garments, added to what I had received in money for my blessings and cures, would have permitted me to hire a camel by myself, but Hadji Bilal persuaded me not to do so. He represented to me that an appearance of misery, inviting pity, was the best protection against the Nomads, whose predatory instincts are roused at the slightest indication of ease or comfort about a person. He mentioned the names of several of our companions who were well provided with money, but who, for safety's sake, are compelled to be clad in rags and to walk on foot. Yielding to his representations, I, too, hired a camel in common with another man; with this proviso, however, that I should be allowed to make use of a *kedsheve* (two baskets, one hanging on each side of the camel), because of the difficulty I should experience in sitting, with my lame foot cramped up, in the company of another man, for forty long stations. Ilias was not inclined to grant my request, this kedsheve being in the desert an additional burden to the camel, but he finally yielded to the persuasions of Khandjan. It was a source of additional satisfaction to me that I succeeded in securing Hadji Bilal for my neighbour, or rather counterpoise, for he became every day more indispensable to me.

When the bargain was concluded we paid Ilias his hire in advance, according to custom. Hadji Bilal then said a fatiha, and Ilias having smoothed the few thin hairs representing his beard, and answered with an affirmative "Amen," we felt quite easy about the arrangement. We urged him to hasten his departure, but he would make no promises, the time of his starting depending upon that of the kervanbashi of the Khan of Khiva, who was to go in front of the caravan with his buffaloes.

In *Etrek*, a place on the river of the same name and the first station on our road, we were to enjoy the hospitality of *Kulkhan*, the *Karaktchilar piri viz* (graybeard of the robbers), who just then happened to be in Gomushtepe, and to whose special grace we were commended by Khandjan. This old rascal had a morose and repulsive look about him. When he learned that I should be his guest in Etrek he seemed to study my features, and exchanging whispers with Khandjan appeared not to agree with the others. I very soon found out the reason of his distrust. In his youth he had travelled all over Russia, had passed considerable time in Tiflis, and had become tolerably familiar with European life. He told them he had seen men of various nations, the Osmanlis excepted, that the latter, too, are said to be kinsmen of the Turkomans and to resemble them, but that to his surprise there was nothing in my features to indicate the remotest relationship with either. Hadji Bilal remarked to him, in reply, that he was badly informed, as he himself had been living for a long time in Roum, and had never observed the resemblance spoken of by him. Kulkhan was somewhat pacified by this explanation, and, informing us that he would leave for Etrek the day after to-morrow, he told us to hold ourself in readiness for the journey; for, added he, although Etrek was only twelve miles off we could not get there without him, and he was only waiting for the return of his son Kolman from the *alaman* (a predatory venture). He invited us, at the same time, to walk to the lower shore of the Gorghen about noon, when his son would return and gladden us with a rare spectacle. Not having anything to do I was easily persuaded to go and mix with the crowd already assembled there, eagerly waiting for the arrival of their friends. Before long eight Turkoman horsemen were seen advancing in a furious gallop toward the opposite shore, bringing with them about ten spare horses. Eager eyes, full of mute admiration, followed every movement of the young horsemen, who in a second had crossed swimming the Gorghen, reached our shore, dismounted, and were now extending with indescribable gravity their hands to their friends and relations. However much I despised their occupation I could not help feasting my eyes on the manly forms of these young fellows, who in their short riding costumes, their long fair hair falling in curls on their shoulders, and with defiant looks, were the objects of general admiration. At the sight even morose Kulkhan cheered up a little, and after introducing his son, who received Hadji Bilal's blessing, we parted in order to attend to the final preparations for our journey.

XIX.

FROM GOMUSHTEPE TO THE BORDER OF THE DESERT.

WE left Gomushtepe on the following day at noon. We were accompanied by Khandjan and our other friends and acquaintances. They remained with us for an hour, and no matter how often I begged of Khandjan to turn back, I could not induce him to do so. He insisted upon rigorously observing the laws of Turkoman hospitality, lest he might give me cause for complaining of him. It was truly with a heavy heart that I exchanged with him a last farewell embrace, for I had learned to love him as one of the most noble-minded men, who, unselfishly and without the least self-interest, had for a considerable time most hospitably entertained myself and five others. I felt sorry at not being able to make some suitable return for so much kindness, but what I regretted most was my having been compelled to practise deception upon this trustiest of friends by my disguise and compulsory concealments.

We proceeded in a north-eastern direction through an endless plain. Our small caravan, consisting of Ilias's camels and six horses, moved on in close order, we having been informed by Kulkhan that there were such karaktchis in this part of the country who did not acknowledge his authority, and would feel no hesitation at attacking himself, if they thought themselves the stronger party. Ilias gave me as far as Etrek the use of a horse he had got from Kulkhan in order to save me the discomfort of riding on a camel. But whenever we came across a puddle I had to share my saddle with one of our companions, on foot, and he would clutch at my clothes with such violence, that he nearly pulled me from my seat. On one occasion we had to pass through a marsh covered with rushes, which served as a cover for an immense herd of wild hogs or boars. Kulkhan and Ilias had ridden in advance in order to discover some roundabout path, by means of which the caravan might steer clear of these wild animals. As I was cautiously feeling my way with a companion in the saddle, my horse gave a sudden start; and before I well knew what had happened, we were both of us sprawling on the ground. Midst roars of laughter coming from my companions, I heard something like a cross between a squeal and a howl, and turning to discover the place whence these sounds issued, I saw before me two young wild pigs over which I had stumbled. Their mother had frightened my horse, and hearing the squeal of her litter she drew quite near us in a rage, showing her tusks; and she would have made a rush upon us if Shirdjan, the brother of Ilias, had not perceived our perilous position and placed himself with his lance raised high between us and the infuriated animal. The young pigs had, meanwhile, scrambled off, and their mother turned tail and went back to her lair. Kulkhan's son caught the runaway horse and brought it back to me with the remark that I was a lucky man to have escaped being killed by a wild hog, for he who receives his death from such an animal enters the next world in a state of uncleanness, no matter how pious a life he had led, and must suffer the fires of hell for five hundred years before he can be purified again, and even then not completely.

We passed the first night in a group of tents at a cousin's of Kulkhan. They knew already of our coming, and my hungry hadji friends interpreted the smoke rising above the tents, which we saw upon drawing near, as a sign of coming good cheer. The other hadjis and myself were quartered in the narrow tent of Allah Nazr. This aged Turkoman, poor and needy as he was, grew wild with joy at Heaven sending him guests to entertain. A goat was all he possessed, but he killed it to do honour to his guests. The following day he succeeded in getting some bread for us, a thing which had not been in his house for weeks; and upon seeing us surrounding the plate filled with meat and falling to with our tremendous appetites, our host and his aged helpmate, who had seated themselves opposite to us, shed tears of joy, in the literal sense of the word. Allah Nazr would not retain for himself any part of the animal thus offered up to us; its horns and hoofs, which if burnt to powder are used with effect on the galled sores of camels, he gave to Ilias; for me he destined the skin to serve as a vessel for water, having first rubbed it in well with salt, and then carefully dried it in the sun.

Next day we resumed our march. At this station I took for the first time possession of my basket, having sacks of flour placed as a counterpoise in the other basket; for my friend Hadji Bilal wished to deny himself this luxury on that day. We had been going onward for scarcely two hours when we lost sight of green fields and came upon a melancholy soil emitting the pungent smell of salt. We were in the desert. The nearer we approached the mountain ridge called Kara Sengher (black wall) the softer did the soil get under our feet, and it became quite a bog when we came quite near the mountain. The camels, with their legs stretched apart, had every trouble to keep from sliding, and I was threatened every minute with being upset and left on the ground, basket and all. I deemed it wiser to dismount of my own accord, and after a dreadful scramble of one hour and a half succeeded in climbing the Kara Sengher, from whence we shortly afterwards reached Kulkhan's *ova* (tent).

When we arrived there, I was rather startled at being immediately conducted by Kulkhan into his own tent, and being told by him with great emphasis that I should not stir out of it until I was called. A few minutes later I heard him without, scolding his wife and reproaching her with never being able to find the chains when they were needed, and ordering her to find them for him immediately. Upon hearing this I began to suspect that something was wrong. Several times he entered the tent looking about him with gloomy looks, but never addressing a syllable to me. My suspicions increased, and all at once it struck me as strange that Hadji Bilal, who but rarely left me to myself, had not been near me for a considerable time. The most dreadful misgivings overwhelmed me; that fatal clanking of the chains outside the tent still continued. At last I saw that my fears were unfounded, for the chains being forthcoming I found that they were intended for the poor Persian slave who had been dragged with us to this place. Kulkhan afterwards prepared tea, and when we had partaken of it he beckoned to me to follow him to a new tent, adjoining his, especially erected for my use. This was to have been a surprise, and hence came the mysterious manner which had given me such a scare.

I must confess that this was neither the first nor the last time that the grim look and suspicious doings of the Turkomans, who afterwards turned out to be my best friends, filled my mind with all kind of horror. I never felt quite safe as to my future, and the only consolation left to me was my lameness, which made me quite valueless in the eyes of the slave-dealers. Of course, as the time went on, I began to be accustomed to this perpetual anxiety, and in spite of the constant danger in which I found myself, I regained my good humour, and my wit and jokes not only exhilarated my hadji fellows, but even the surliest son of the desert, and the usual remark of the Turkomans was, "That lame hadji of Roum (Turkey) is a jolly fellow; he would make a capital merry-maker."

The inhabitants of Gomushtepe are a civilized community when their mode of life and customs are contrasted with those of the population of Etrek. The cruelties perpetrated by the latter were utterly revolting to the feelings of all of us. We felt therefore sincere satisfaction in learning one evening through a messenger that the kervanbashi would expect us at noon a couple of days later, on the other side of the Etrek (the river of that name), where we were to meet and, joining him, thence proceed on our long march through the desert. Ilias immediately gave orders to get ready, and on the same day we prepared the necessary bread and salted the large pieces of camel's flesh we had received of the Turkomans for our blessings. Who felt happier than I did in stepping on the morning of the following day simultaneously with Hadji Bilal into the kedsheve, and resuming the journey on the back of the camel with its wave-like rocking gait? Kulkhan thought it proper for safety's sake to accompany us during the whole day, for although there were from fifteen to twenty armed men with us, there was reason to fear the attack of a large band of robbers, and the presence of Kulkhan would be of great service, as he was obeyed by the brigands of the entire neighbourhood. In order to avoid the morasses occasioned by the overflowing of the Etrek we had to keep now to the north-west and now to the north-east. At the border of this territory we came across tents, about one hundred and fifty in number, belonging to a Turkoman tribe called *Kan*. Hearing that this was our last station on this side of the great desert, I employed the afternoon, while my companions were sleeping, in letter-writing, intending to send the letters by those who accompanied us and were turning back. Besides the small slips of paper on which I was jotting down my experiences and which I kept concealed among my clothes of Bokhara fashion, I had a Koran with me, which I usually carried in a small bag, and two sheets of white writing paper, upon which I now wrote two letters. One was addressed to Haidar Effendi in Teheran, the other to Khandjan with the request to despatch the letter intended for Haidar Effendi.

On the following morning we reached the banks of the *Etrek*. Its waters were not rapid, but they reached above the haunches of the camels, and the animals in cautiously picking their way fording the stream, caused by their rocking gait our kedsheves to be dipped in the dirty water, now to the right now to the left. We had hardly landed on the opposite side when we were gladdened by the sight of the kervanbashi's long-looked-for caravan, with the three buffaloes at their head, whose safe arrival even the suffering Khan of Khiva could no desire more devoutly than we did. The members of the two caravans very soon fraternized with each other. I appeared to have found little favour with the kervanbashi, but did not discover the cause of his dislike until sometime afterwards. As soon as Amandurdi (the name of our kervanbashi) had assumed the leadership of our caravan, he gave orders that each of us was to provide himself with water, as none would be found on our way for three days. When we had everything in readiness and the camels were laden and harnessed, we and our animals were counted by the kervanbashi, the result being that our caravan was found to consist of eighty camels and forty travellers. Of the latter twenty-six were defenceless hadjis, and the remaining Yomut-Turkomans, one Uzbeg and one Afghan, tolerably well armed. After having mounted our animals we took leave of the men who had escorted us to the border of the desert. The fatiha of leave-taking Hadji Bilal began to sing on the one side, and Khulkan on the other. After the last "Amen," which was followed by the inevitable smoothing of our beards, we parted, and when crossing the Etrek they lost sight of us, they sent after us a parting salute in the shape of loud reports from their firearms. We went due north.

XX.

IN THE DESERT.

THE road we traversed showed no traces of the feet of either man or camels, and taking for our guides the sun during the day, and the polar star during the night, we kept our course straight to the north. The Turkomans call the polar star on account of its immobility Temir Kazik (iron peg). The camels forming a long line and tied together were led by men on foot. In this way we jogged along in the sandy soil without any interruption until late after sunset. The sandy soil gradually ceased and we felt indeed the solid and smooth ground under our feet. The tramp of the camels sounded at a distance, as if they beat time. The day was nearly dawning when we stopped, but we had altogether gone but twenty-four miles; the camels not being allowed to exert themselves in the beginning, and our progress having been delayed, besides, by the slowness of the buffaloes, the most distinguished members of our travelling party, who with their huge bodies were unable to keep pace with the camels. Our rest lasted from dawn till eight o'clock in the morning, and whilst the camels were feeding on thistles and brambles of the desert, we had time to look after our breakfast. We might well call our breakfast an excellent one, for we had a sufficient quanity of water wherewith to wash down our unleavened bread. As we were camping near each other I observed that the kervanbashi, whilst talking with Ilias and the chiefs of the hadji, had been looking at me pointedly several times. I could easily guess the tenor of their conversation, but pretending not to be in the least concerned, I kept on turning the leaves of the Koran with great devotion for a while ; and then, closing the book, I rose and directed my steps towards the little company as if to join them. As I was approaching, both the good Ilias and Hadji Salih hastened to meet me half-way, and calling me aside informed me that the kervanbashi suspected me and was determined not to take me with him to Khiva. He was especially afraid of the wrath of the Khan, for he had brought with him, some years ago, a Frengi envoy to Khiva, who had made an exact drawing of the entire road, not omitting, owing to his infernal skill, a single well or hill. The Khan burning with rage at this, had immediately executed two of the men who had given the traveller information, and spared the life of the kervanbashi only because of some very influential protection the latter had succeeded in enlisting in his favour. "After a good deal of coaxing," my men continued, "we succeeded in prevailing upon him to take thee with him, on condition that thou shalt allow thyself to be searched, in the first place, in order to see if thou dost not carry any drawings or wood pens (lead pencils) with thee such as the Frengis usually have about them, and in the second place, that thou shalt promise not to make any secret memoranda of the roads and mountains ; if thou dost not agree to this he will leave thee behind him in the middle of the desert." I listened to their speech with the utmost patience, but as soon as they were done I assumed the appearance of one angrily excited, and turning to Hadji Salih I said in a voice, loud enough to reach the ears of the kervanbashi: "Hadji, thou sawest me in Teheran and knowest who I am. Tell Amandurdi that it ill becometh an honest man like him to listen to the words of a drunken *binamaz* (a man who does not say his prayers) like this Afghan. It is not permitted to trifle with religion, and if he calls me once more Frengi infidel I shall show him in Khiva what manner of man I am." I spoke the last words in such a loud key as to be heard by every one in the caravan, and my dervish companions became so enraged that, if I had not kept them back, they would have fallen on the spot upon the sottish opium-eating Afghan who had been trying to excite the kervanbashi's suspicions against me. Amandurdi more than any other was startled by this scene, and I heard him replying to every person who came near him to inquire about the occurrence, "God knows!" He was by no means a bad man; on the contrary he was of a kind disposition and very clever; but like all thoroughbred Orientals he was attracted by anything that looked mysterious, and it was this tendency that made him suppose me to be a disguised foreigner, although he never failed to apply to me in questions of religion, having heard in Gomushtepe of my reputation as a scholar. I had succeeded this time in warding off the impending danger, but I felt that the distrust of me was growing apace, and that I should find it exceedingly difficult to make the slightest memoranda even of my travels. I could not even directly inquire after the names of the several stations, and only in a roundabout way, by hook and crook, could I gain some information about one thing or other and set it down afterwards, with great secrecy in my notes. I must recall to the mind of my readers, that the Afghan who set up his mind to cause my ruin, was a runaway from Kandahar at the time when Sir Henry Rawlinson was in command of that place. Mir Mohammed, for this was his name, had an unspeakable hatred against every European, and particularly against the English; and he, supposing me to belong to that nation, was indefatigable in his efforts to penetrate my disguise and to denounce me as a spy, who would speedily be followed by an invading army.

After a short rest we continued our journey, but I observed that after we had been marching for about two hours, the caravan began to slacken pace. A couple of Turkomans had dismounted from their camels and seemed to be carefully investigating right and left the low mounds, a great number of which could be seen everywhere around us. I was informed that Eid Mehemmed, one of our fellow-travellers, was trying to discover the grave of a brother of his, who had fallen hereabouts, last year, in an attack made upon him, after having heroically defended himself. Eid Mehemmed had brought a coffin with him in order to take the remains to Khiva. It might have been two o'clock in the afternoon when the grave was found and the exhumation begun. After the customary prayers and the recital of stray verses from the Koran, ceremonies in which I too had to take part in the most devotional manner, the half-decayed dead body was wrapped in rags and placed in the coffin. When the funeral ceremonies were over Eid Mehemmed baked bread on that place and distributed it among us. We started again, going always north. We had to make up for lost time,

A LIGHT FOR THE COMPASS. *Page* 188.

and the order was given by the kervanbashi to march all night. The weather was fine and, cramped up in my basket, I gazed with intense delight at the starry firmament, the like of which, for transcendental beauty, can be seen nowhere but in the desert. But sleep soon asserted its rights. I had not been asleep an hour when I was roused by several people shouting at me: "Hadji, look at thy *kiblenuma* (compass), we seem to have lost our way." I immediately produced my flint and steel apparatus, and striking sparks with it lit the tinder, by the smouldering fire of which I perceived that we were going east instead of north. The kervanbashi was frightened, thinking we had come near the dangerous marshes, and determined not to move until daybreak. Fortunately we had left the right track only half an hour before when the sky was clouded. In spite of the delay we reached in time the station we were bound for, and turned our tired animals loose to feed upon thistles and similar pasture.

On the 15th of May our road lay through a wild country, intersected, in every direction, by ravines. The poor camels had a great deal to suffer. They are attached to each other in such a manner that one end of the rope is tied to the tail of the camel in front, and the other end is fastened at the nose, through a hole perforated for that purpose, of the camel following it. Now if the poor beast stops from any cause, but for a minute, those before him are tugging away at his nose, in such an unmerciful way, that I have often seen the rope broken. To relieve the poor animals we dismounted several times during our four hours' trudging through the deep sand.

There were three different roads by which the desert might be crossed, but we were as yet kept in ignorance as to which of these the kervanbashi would choose. Owing to the caravan's being liable to be pounced upon by marauders at any minute, it is quite necessary to keep the real route a secret. But at the present stage of our journey it was easy to foretell that we should take the middle road, for our water was giving out; and the tank of water of which we stood in great need lay along that route. This night we were favoured by good fortune on our march, the rope keeping the camels together having broken but twice. When such a thing happens a couple of men are sent after the animals to bring them back, the caravan continuing their march. One of the caravan, however, is selected to keep up a continual conversation with the men sent out, while they are receding, to prevent their missing their way in the dark night. The melancholy sound of this man's voice is their only guide in the pitchlike darkness, and woe to the poor fellows if a contrary wind hinders them from hearing it. On the 16th of May we perceived in a north-eastern direction the mountain-chain of *Korendag* and reached it on the afternoon of the same day. We had been told in Etrek that we might look forward to meeting friendly Yomut-Turkomans at this place, but nevertheless there prevailed a general anxiety on that subject, the fear of the possibility of being attacked by some hostile bands being quite as great as the expectation of meeting the former. We dispatched a brave Turkoman to reconnoitre the neighbourhood. Before long we caught sight of solitary tents, and, our apprehensions being dispelled, we asked ourselves what tribe we were to meet. After all they were Yomuts, and we passed the whole day with them.

I was agreeably surprised to find near the Korendag Mountains some old ruins; the fable attaches to them

THE KARENDAG HILLS. [Page 184.

that they are the ruins of Kaaba, God having from His special love for the Turkomans placed the Kaaba here first, but that Goklen, a lame blue devil, pulled it down, whereupon God carried the Kaaba to Mecca. And this was the reason why the Turkomans lived in constant enmity with and war against the Goklens, who have descended from Goklen.

The Nomads sojourning in the environs came flocking to see the caravan and to engage in trade with some of its members. In the evening, we being ready to start, one of the buffalo cows presented the caravan with a healthy calf to the kervanbashi's intense satisfaction. On the road it occurred to him that the calf was too feeble to follow us on foot, and that he must find a place for it on the back of one of the camels. Myself and Hadji Bilal being the only ones occupying a kedsheve he naturally thought of us, and asked that one of us should give up our place to the newborn animal. Hadji Bilal resigned his basket with the utmost readiness, alleging that he did so out of kind feelings for me, who could not with my lame foot find accommodation everywhere. But no sooner did my counterpoise occupy the hadji's place than I discovered the real cause of his great complaisance—the calf was exhaling a pestiferous smell. It was passable at nights, interfering but occasionally with my slumbers, but during the day, when the sun shone out hot, I could hardly bear my sweet-smelling neighbour. Fortunately for me this agony did not last long, the calf departing this life three days afterwards.

From the spot where we started on the 18th of May, it was calculated that the Great Balkan was distant two days' march and Khiva a march of twelve days. Our guides hoped we should find rain water on the flat lands. We had last filled our canteens from the miry water of the two miserable water-tanks of Korendag, and such as it was, it had become, through being shaken up on the camels' backs, a liquid mass of mud, loathsome both to the smell and taste. We had, nevertheless, to be very economical in the use of it, for there was no prospect of obtaining any water before passing the Great Balkan. Our marching from this time onwards became more regular. We usually made three stoppages daily, of one hour and a half, and two hours' duration. The first was before daybreak, when we would bake one day's ration of bread, the second at noon, to afford some rest to both animals and men, and the third before sunset, in order to eat our modest supper, consisting of a little bread and of a few drops of water carefully doled out. The soil of the country through which we passed was a hard-baked clay producing scantily and at intervals a few blades of sickly grass. The blazing sun marked the whole surface with a thousand burning cracks. It is frightfully wearisome for the traveller to see before him everlastingly the boundless plain from which every vestige of life is banished, so much so that even the reaching of a new station is quite a relief, as it affords some rest from the rocking motion of the camel.

On the following day, about noon, the Little Balkan Mountains loomed up before us in the hazy distance. The Turkomans spoke to me in the most laudatory strain of the extent and size of this mountain chain as well as of its beauty and wealth in minerals. The kervanbashi, otherwise always wakeful, feeling oppressed by sleep as the evening set in, left the caravan under the care of the leader of the camels, who led us into such danger that we were all near losing our lives. There are at the foot of the Balkan many salt marshes, covered with a thick white surface, formed by deposits of salt, which it is difficult to distinguish from the solid ground. Into one of these the substitute of the kervanbashi had taken us, and we had already advanced so far that the animals, owing to the shakiness of the ground under their feet, refused to go on in spite of all urging. We quickly jumped off our animals, and my fright may be imagined when upon touching ground I had a rocking sensation as if seated on a swing, the ground apparently giving way under my feet. The panic became general. Finally the kervanbashi called out that every one should remain where he was until sunrise, when we should be able to extricate ourselves from our perilous position. For three mortal hours we dared not stir and had to remain motionless in our places, having besides to suffer from the pungent soda smell, making our heads dizzy. At length the gray streak in the east assumed the rosy tints of dawn for which our hearts had been longing. With considerable trouble and exertion the caravan succeeded in getting out of this miry pitfall and in retracing their steps to the solid track. Had we advanced but a little farther into the salt marshes, part of the caravan, if not the whole, would have been doomed to certain destruction.

On the 20th of May we reached the *Little Balkan*, which stretches from the south-east to the north-west We marched on along its foot on that day and the whole day following. The kervanbashi declared that we had but just now reached the veritable desert. We soon came to the ancient bed of the Oxus, and crossing it we entered on the opposite side a high plateau. By and by the Balkan mountain chain vanished in the blue distance, and the desert in all its awful grandeur spread before us. Man is overwhelmed here by the idea of the infinite. The impression produced by the absence of all sounds, by the very change in the colour and appearance of the sun, is indescribable. Up to this time I always thought that the charm of the desert existed chiefly in the heated imagination of enthusiastic travellers, but I lived to be undeceived in this my supposition.

We camped near *Yeti Siri* on the 22nd of May. This place owes its name to seven wells which stood there in ancient times, and most of which are now dry. In one or two of them some little water may be found even now, but it is undrinkable owing to its salty taste and nasty smell. The kervanbashi comforted us with the hope of finding rain-water towards evening, but at this moment I was not disposed to exchange the remaining little water (abundantly mixed as it was with mud) which was left in my canteen for the ill-smelling contents of the wells. The animals were watered, and several of the men eagerly competed with them in drinking from this water. After resting a little we resumed our march and, on our way, happened to observe, on a sand mound, raised above the smaller heaps of sand, two empty kedsheves. In the opinion of my fellow-travellers these wooden baskets had belonged to some persons who died on this spot; and the Turkomans hold in veneration every object once possessed by man. Strange anomaly! to look upon selling men into slavery and carrying desolation into a country as commendable acts, and to couple with such views a tender feeling of piety for a wooden basket—because, forsooth, a man had once sat in it.

We went towards evening with the kervanbashi and a couple of Turkomans, on foot, to look for the hoped-for rain-water. We were all well armed, and went in search of water in different directions. I followed the kervanbashi—with whom I had been on the best terms since the last collision with him. Suddenly he caught sight of footprints in the sand and, lighting our tinder, we followed them up by its feeble light, to the mouth of a cavern. We entered after a slight hesitation, and beheld there, to our utmost horror, a man in perfectly savage condition, with long, unkempt hair and beard, and enormous finger nails, wrapped in chamois skins. At our sight he, too, started, and seizing his lance made a rush at us. I retreated as quickly as I could, but my companion remained perfectly calm, and dropping the arm he had raised, and saying in a low voice, "Aman bol!" (Peace be with thee!), he left the dreadful place. Not daring to ask too many questions, I learned from the kervanbashi, on returning, that the man we saw was "Kanli dir" (a man stained with blood). I was afterwards told that this unhappy being had fled from righteous revenge for bloodshed, and had been wandering for years, summer and winter, in the wilderness.

Our companions, like ourselves, returned with empty hands from their search for water, of which not the slightest indication could be found. It was an appalling thought that the few drops of muddy dregs I still possessed would be used up to-day. That evening I ate a few pieces of bread soaked in boiling water, for I had heard that the water lost its bitter taste by boiling. I determined patiently to bear everything, for in comparison to many of my companions I had every reason to be satisfied with my condition, inasmuch as I was in good health and they were suffering a great deal from the consequences of their having drunk from the brackish water. Some of the Turkomans were suspected of having secreted a quantity of drinkable water. But to rely upon being supplied, in the desert, with water belonging to another person, would be the height of madness; and indeed any one wishing to borrow or to beg water in the desert is looked upon as demented. I had lost my appetite and could not swallow even a few bits of bread. I dropped on the ground, exhausted and weak, and pitied my hard fate, when all at once I saw every one rising and flocking around the kervanbashi, and some persons beckoning to me to join them with my canteen. The word "water" was enough to infuse new life into me; I jumped up from the ground I had been lying on, and on reaching the crowd I saw the kervanbashi dealing out about two glasses of clear sweet water to every member of the caravan. This brave Turkoman afterwards told us that for years he had been in the habit of storing away in secret places large quantities of water, to distribute it in times of great need, when every one is benefited by it. This is a great *sevab* (pious act), for a Turkoman proverb says: "One drop of water given to the thirsting in the desert will wash away the sins of a hundred years."

It is just as hard to determine the greatness of such a good action as it is to describe the enjoyment afforded by one swallow of sweet water. My craving for food was gone, I did not feel any more hunger, and thought I could bear being without water for three days. As far as drinking was concerned I was all right again, but it had gone all wrong with my bread. From want of appetite and in a fit of indolence I thought that instead of using wood for fuel, which it took some time to get as it was at some distance, I would use camel's dung—the regular fuel of the desert—but of this too I had gathered rather less than was needed. I placed the dough into the hot ashes, but there was not heat enough to bake it into bread, even if it had been left there for a week.

I quickly ran off to gather some wood, but it was quite dark when I returned. I immediately set to kindling a little fire, but no sooner was it perceived by the kervan-bashi, than he called out to ask "If I wished to betray by the smoke our caravans to the enemy?" I had to put out the fire at once, and take with me the unleavened bread half done.

On the 23rd of May the rays of the sun beat down upon our heads with a scorching heat. The sand to the depth of a foot became so hot, that even the most hardened Asiatic who had never worn either shoe or boot on his feet, was compelled to fasten around them a piece of leather, sandal fashion. It was only ten years later, when a Russian army led by Colonel Markusoff had crossed this part of the desert, that I learnt that the heat in the month of May reached the height of fifty-four degrees Réaumur (about 152 degrees Fahrenheit) in the sun! No wonder that the effect of the refreshing beverage of yesterday was soon gone, and that I began to be tantalized anew by thirst. At noon we were informed by the kervanbashi that we were not far from Kahriman Ata, a place of resort for pilgrimages. In duty bound we had to dismount and walk for a quarter of an hour until we reached the saint's grave, where we performed our devotions. My distress may be easily imagined at being compelled, worn out with the heat and half dead with thirst, to join the band of pilgrims. The tombs rose on an eminence; they crowded around it and yelled out, with dry throats, *telkins* and citations from the Koran. Oh cruel saint, I thought within myself, couldst thou not have managed to get thyself buried in some other place, in order to save me the tortures of this pilgrimage! Choking and out of breath I sank down on the grave, which was about thirty feet long, and covered with rams' horns, the ram's horn being looked upon in Central Asia as a symbol of supremacy. The kervanbashi told us that the saint resting in his grave had been a giant, as tall as the grave was long, and that ever so long ago he had defended the wells hereabouts against evil spirits who had threatened to block them up with stones. The innumerable smaller mounds, surrounding the saint's grave, marked the places where poor travellers, who had lost their lives in different places of the desert either by the hands of robbers or by elemental visitations, were sleeping their eternal sleep. Hearing of the wells placed under the patronage of the saint, my heart was gladdened with a new hope, for I thought we should find drinkable water in the neighbourhood. I hastened to be amongst the first to arrive at the designated spot. I caught sight of a brownish puddle-like spring, and helped myself to its water by taking some into the hollow of my hand. It was as cold as ice, but when I brought it near my lips I had to leave it untasted, it was so brackish, bitter, and ill-smelling. My depression became extreme; for the first time I began to be seriously alarmed about my future.

Luckily for us a heavy rain storm came up during the night, the rain descending in large drops, and towards morning we came to the extremest edge of the sand. It took us three days to pass through it. We were sure of finding on to-day's road in the loamy ground an abundance of rain water. The kervanbashi, judging by the numerous footprints of gazells and wild asses, anticipated with certainty the accomplishment of our hope, but, volunteering no opinion of his own, only pressed forward, and very soon discovered with his lynx eyes, at a great distance, a pool of rain-

A WELL IN THE DESERT.

[Page 192.

water. Su! Su! (water! water!) was on everybody's lips when the kervanbashi had communicated his discovery. We arrived there towards noon, and met on our way, besides the large pool we had seen at a distance, numerous pits filled with the sweetest rain-water. I was the first to run up to them, not to drink, but to fill my goatskin and other vessels with the precious fluid before it became muddy and murky with being stirred up. A quarter of an hour later everybody sat at his breakfast with a feeling of infinite delight.

From this station to Khiva we could without interruption fill our skins with sweet water, and our further progress became, comparatively speaking, contrasted with our former experiences, a pleasure trip. In the evening we reached a place where everything pointed to the mastery of a genuine spring, and camped amidst small lakes set in frames of verdant meadows. My thoughts involuntarily reverted to my sorrowful plight of yesterday, and it was with some difficulty I could persuade myself that the landscape before me was not an idle dream. To add to our satisfaction, the kervanbashi announced to the caravan that the danger from attacks was over, and that we should be permitted to build fires after to-night. Our Turkoman fellow-travellers attributed the abundance of water to the fact that we, the hadjis, had been with them. We refilled our canteens and gaily proceeded on our journey.

XXI.

IN KHIVA.

TOWARDS evening we arrived at the ravine beyond which spread the so-called plain of *Kaflankir* (Tigerland). The ascent to this table-land, which is about three hundred feet high, was excessively fatiguing to men and animals alike. The Turkomans allege that Kaflankir had been anciently an island formed by two arms of the Oxus, which were flowing all around it. It is undeniable that this tract of land differs greatly from the surrounding wilderness in its structure, the luxuriance of its vegetation and the great number of animals it harbours. We had met, it is true, thus far with solitary gazelles and wild asses on our march, but here we saw them browsing in flocks by hundreds. On one occasion we saw an immense cloud of dust approaching from the north, coming nearer and nearer. The kervanbashi and the Turkomans immediately seized their arms, and their impatience increased the nearer the cloud drew. We finally succeeded in discovering that it was caused, apparently, by a troop of horsemen advancing in full gallop, in a regular line. The Turkomans dropped their arms.

AN ASININE ARMY.

[*Page* 195.

Fifty paces from us we perceived a herd of animals wildly running and almost concealed by the dust; and one minute later we heard a sound reminding one of the sudden halt of a troop of a thousand horsemen in line. We saw before us innumerable wild asses, stopping suddenly in serried ranks. These strong and lively animals stood staring at us for a second, and then started away like the whirlwind in a western direction.

On the 28th of May we came to *Shor Gol* (salt lake) in the plateau of Kaflankir. We took a rest of six hours in order to go through the ablutions commanded by Islam, which for some time we had been compelled to neglect. On this occasion my fellow-travellers opened their bundles, and every one of them found a spare shirt in it; I was the only one who had none. Hadji Bilal offered me the loan of one, but I declined it with thanks, well knowing that in my apparent poverty lay my greatest security. My face was covered by a layer of dust an inch thick. I had numerous occasions, in the desert, to wash it off, but I preferred keeping it on as a protection against the heat of the sun. Truth to tell, not only myself, but all the others were dreadfully disfigured by the *teyemmun*, or washing with the sand, the substitute for the ablutions with water, ordered by the Prophet to travellers in the desert. After my friends had been washing and dressing, I saw only what great lords they looked like in comparison to me. Several of them offered to lend me parts of their wardrobe, but I thanked them cordially, and in refusing their kind offers, I announced to them that I should wait until the Khan of Khiva supplied me with a garment.

We had been toiling on for four days in the high plateau of Kaflandir, when one morning my eyes were gladdened by the sight of numerous tents on our right and left. The occupants of these tents came flocking out to meet us, receiving us with the friendly greeting of "Aman gheldinghiz!" (Happily come!) Ilias having many friends amongst the people who were encamped here, he proceeded at once to procure from them hot bread and other Kurban (they were just then celebrating this, one of the most important holidays of Islam) gifts. He came back very soon from his errand, loaded down with meat, bread, and *kimiss* (a sharp and acid beverage brewed of mare's milk), all of which he distributed amongst us. Before long nomads living at a greater distance were arriving to shake hands with us, and thus perform an act pleasing to God. For our share in this pious act we were remembered by gifts of great quantities of camel's, horse's and sheep's flesh.

As we were preparing our tea on the evening of the 30th of May, we were startled by the wild scampering of the camels which we had turned loose. Before we had time to investigate the cause of their fright, five horsemen appeared all of a sudden keeping straight towards us at the top of their horses' speed. We, too, immediately ran to our arms, and in a second we stood prepared to meet them. But the horsemen slackened their pace and the Turkomans soon discovered that they had been mistaken in supposing them to be hostile, for they only wanted to go with us as members of our caravan.

On the following morning we came to an Uzbeg village belonging to *Akyap* (the white canal). At this place we had left entirely behind us the wilderness lying between Gomushtepe and Khiva. Here I saw Uzbegs for the first time, and I found them very kind and friendly people. As usual we made, with our visits, the round of all the houses, and earned with our fatihas a plentiful harvest. We might still have reached Ilias's dwelling-place on the same day, but he had his dose of vanity and did not wish us to arrive there unexpectedly. We therefore passed the night, within two hours' march of his home, at the house of a rich uncle of his, who entertained us most sumptuously. In the interval he sent word of our arrival to his wife, and next morning, on the 1st of June, we entered the village of Akyap. The numerous kinsmen and friends of Ilias came out to meet us, receiving us most cordially. To me he offered a handsome tent, for my quarters, but I preferred his garden, for my soul had long been yearning for the shade of trees. After a brief rest we resumed our march towards the capital, which we reached in safety on the following day. The capital, seen at a distance, surrounded by gardens and surmounted by its many towers and cupolas, makes a pleasing impression upon the traveller. In entering through the main gate of the city I could not shake off a certain fear of being found out or suspected by the Khan of Khiva, whose cruelty was condemned by the Tartars themselves, and at whose hands I had reason to expect a much sterner treatment than even from the Turkomans. I had heard that the Khan makes a slave of every stranger suspected by him, and that only recently this had been the sad fate of a Hindoo, alleged to be of princely origin. But by this time I was accustomed to brave almost any danger without losing my presence of mind. I therefore kept perfectly cool, and only busied myself devising schemes by means of which I might outwit the superstitious tyrant. I had collected, on the way, reliable and full information about every prominent man in Khiva who had visited Constantinople. The name of a certain Shukrullah Bey, who had there passed ten years in the capacity of an ambassador to the Sublime Porte, was most frequently mentioned, in this connection. I had a sort of hazy recollection of having met this man at the house of the Turkish Secretary of State. This Shukrullah Bey, I reflected, knows Stambul well; he must be familiar with the language and manners current with its better classes. Now I should pretend to a former acquaintanceship with him, and force it upon him whether he wants it or no; and as I thought myself fully capable of acting the character of a man from Stambul to such a perfection as to impose upon a native of that place, I felt sure that I should not be suspected by the late ambassador of the Khan of Khiva, who would be thus obliged in a manner to countenance me.

Many people were already waiting for us at the gate, offering us bread and dried fruit. For years there had not arrived such a numerous party of hadjis; and people came crowding around, and gaping at us from every street in the city. We were greeted on all sides by the words, "Aman essen gheldinghiz!" (Happily arrived!) "Ha shahbazim! Ha arslanim!" (My falcon! My lion!) As soon as we arrived at the bazaar, Hadji Bilal began with a *telkin* (a hymn). My voice being the loudest of all, I could not help being moved upon people kissing my hands, feet, and even the loosely hanging rags of my garment, as if I had been some first-class saint or had just descended from heaven. We put up, according to the custom of the country, at the caravansary, used at the same time for a Custom House, and I set out, before long, in search of Shukrullah Bey. I had been told that he was now without any employment or office, and was living in a cell at the Medresse of Mehemmed Emin, the finest building in Khiva. I introduced myself to him through one of his attendants as an Effendi come from Stambul, adding that I had known him there and wished to pay him my respects in passing through Khiva. The old gentleman was quite astonished at so strange an occurrence and came out himself to receive me, but was quite startled upon seeing before him a tattered beggar in rags. He nevertheless took me into his room, and no sooner had I pronounced a few words with the genuine Stambul accent, than he began to inquire, with increasing interest, after his friends at the Turkish capital, the political configurations, the new Sultan, and so forth. When, in the course of conversation, we became better acquainted, Shukrullah Bey thus apostrophized me: "For the love of God, what has induced thee, Effendi, to came from Stambul, that earthly paradise, to these fearful countries?" I then told him that I belonged to an order of dervishes, that my *pir* (spiritual chief) had sent me on this journey, and that a *murid* (a novice) is bound to obey the commands of the *pir*, even at the risk of his life. My new acquaintance was highly pleased with my explanations, and only wished to know the name of the dervish order to which I belonged, and when I told him that of the *Nakishbend*, he became aware that Bokhara was the object of my pilgrimage. He was desirous of immediately arranging quarters at the Medresse for me, but I declined, excusing myself by mentioning my fellow-travellers whom I had left behind, and went away promising to renew my visit very soon.

An officer from the Court came to me on the following day, bringing with him presents, destined for me, from the Khan, and orders from the latter to make my appearance at the *ark* (palace) that very evening, in order to bestow on him, the Khan, my fatiha, it being the Hazret's (his majesty's) most cherished wish to receive the blessing of a dervish coming from the Holy Land. I told him I should obey. I called upon Shukrullah Bey in the afternoon, as he wished to be present at the audience, and was conducted by him to the palace of the Khan. On our way there he gave me directions how to comport myself, and described to me the ceremonial I was to observe on being presented to the Khan. He informed me, at the same time, that not being on good terms with the *mehter* (minister), who looked on him as his rival, his, Shukrullah Bey's, recommendation might perhaps injure me rather than be of benefit to me. But following the prevailing custom, I nevertheless had myself first introduced to the mehter. His ante-chamber, it being audience day, was cramful of people who, on our entrance, respectfully made way for us, standing aside. Some women present were pointing at me, saying: "This is the dervish from Constantinople, who will bestow benediction on our Khan. May the Lord hearken to his words!"

I found the mehter in a porch, surrounded by his men, who smiled at every word uttered by him. His dark complexion and long beard reaching to his chest showed him to be a Persian. When he saw me approaching him he said something to his attendants. I marched up boldly to him, saluted him with becoming gravity, and immediately sat down in the principal place belonging by rights to a dervish. After saying the customary prayer, followed by every one's stroking his beard, and responding with a loud "Amen," I exchanged the usual formal courtesies with the mehter. Then he told me that the Hazret—at which word everybody rose from his seat—wished to see me, but that he would be very glad if I could produce a couple of

AUDIENCE WITH THE KHAN OF KHIVA.

[Page 201

lines from the Embassy at Teheran or the Sultan. I replied that my journey had no worldly aims, that I required nothing of anybody, but that for the safety of my person I had brought with me a firman provided with the *tugra* (the Sultan's seal). In saying this I handed the mehter my passport, which he kissed with great reverence, rubbing the seal against his forehead: then he rose and said he would give the document to the Khan. Shortly afterwards he returned, announcing to me that the Khan was ready to receive me. Shukrullah Bey entered first, and I had to wait until the necessary preparations were made. Although I was introduced as a dervish, the Khan had been informed by Shukrullah Bey that I knew every distinguished pasha in Constantinople. After a while I was taken by the arm by two officers, the curtain was drawn aside, and I saw before me *Seid Mehemmed Khan Padishahi Kharezm*, the Khan of Khiva, seated on a terrace-like platform, a round velvet cushion supporting one arm, and holding a short gold sceptre in his other hand. Strictly adhering to the ceremonial prescribed for me, I lifted my hand, all present and the Khan himself following my example, recited a brief *sura*, a short passage from the Koran, two *alahumu sellahs* (God be praised) and a short prayer. As the Khan was taking hold of his beard in order to respond with "Amen" at the termination of the prayer every one called out, "Kabul bolgai!" (May thy prayer be heard!) Thereupon I drew near the prince, who held out his hand, and after having gone through the *mussafeha* (the salutation prescribed by the Koran—the two persons in giving a greeting extend an outstretched hand to each other), I retreated a few steps, and there was an end to the ceremony. The Khan now commenced to make inquiries about the object of my journey, and the impression the Turkomans, the great desert, and Khiva had made upon me. I replied that I had undergone a great many trials and sufferings, but that the sight of the *Hazret's djemal mubarek* (his Majesty's blessed beauty) compensated me abundantly for all my sufferings. "I thank Allah," I continued, "for allowing me to have this extraordinary good fortune, and I believe that I must look upon this signal favour of *Kismet* (fate) as a good omen for the safe progress of my journey." I was asked by the Khan if I intended to remain a long time in Khiva, and whether I was provided with the necessary wherewithal for my journey. I answered to him that before continuing my journey I intended visiting the graves of all the saints reposing in the blessed soil of the Khanate, and that as to being provided with the needful travelling expenses, we dervishes did not trouble ourselves about such worldly trifles; the *nefes* (holy spirit) which was given to me by my *pir* (chief of the dervish order) on my journey would sustain life in me for four or five days without taking any food. Therefore I had no other wish but that God might prolong his Majesty's life to one hundred and twenty years.

My words seemed to have pleased his Royal Majesty, for he ordered that I should be given twenty gold pieces and a strong ass. I did not accept the money, under the pretext that it was a sin for a dervish to be possessed of money, but accepted the animal, adding, however, the request to select, if possible, a white one, for it was one of that colour which the sacred law prescribed for pilgrimages. I was about to withdraw, when I was asked by the Khan to be at least his guest during the short time I intended to pass at the capital, and to accept during this time from his treasury, daily, two *tenghes* (a sixpence) for my board. This offer, too, was declined with thanks, and I retired after having given my final benediction. Upon returning, I was greeted most respectfully with *selam aleikums* (Peace be unto you!) by the people who were thronging the court-yard of the palace and the bazaar. I did not breathe freely until I found myself in safety within the four walls of my cell.

Every feature in the Khan's face betrayed the debauched, worn-out, dull-minded, inhuman tyrant; his eyes were deeply sunken, his lips of a pallid white, and his voice was shaky. I was profoundly thankful for his exceptional kindness to me, and was pleased to think that I now could employ the time I had in wandering through the Khanate to my heart's content without any interference.

There was not much to be seen at the capital itself, and what little there was worthy of note might have been easily looked at in a couple of days. But my time was entirely taken up by invitations from the Khan, the government officials and prominent merchants. Since it had become generally known that I was in the good graces of the king, everybody wished me and my dervish companions to be his guests. It was a real torture for me to have to accept six and even eight invitations a day. I recall with a shudder, to this day, the number of times I had to sit down, early in the morning, between three and four o'clock, to a plate of rice swimming in a gravy of mutton fat. The *Toshebaz* (the name of the cloister where I was quartered) comprised a mosque and a large water-tank, and was therefore looked upon as a public building, and continually swarming with visitors. This offered me a very good opportunity observing the dress, the mode of life and all the doings of the Uzbegs, and to become personally acquainted with several of them. The men wear tall pyramid-shaped fur caps on their head, and enormously large boots of Russian leather of shapeless bulk on their feet, besides which their costume consists in summer of only a long shirt. The women wear turbans of immense size, consisting of from fifteen to twenty Russian pocket handkerchiefs rolled one into the other, and are compelled, poor creatures, to drag jars of water during the greatest heat, having on their feet tremendously large boots, and muffled up in their manifold dresses. Often women were stopping at my door asking for a little *khakishifa* (health-powder) which the pilgrims bring with them from *Medina*, from the house of the Prophet, and which is used as a medicine against all sorts of ailings; or they would beg for a *nefes* (holy breath) and give a detailed account of their bodily sufferings. I had, of course, to comply with all requests, and touching the sore place I blew or breathed on it three times. Thereupon the patient heaved a deep sigh, and many of them insisted that they immediately felt relieved from pain. Both I and my hadji friends had reason to be gratified with the brilliant success of our dealing in the holy breath, for I myself earned fifteen gold pieces for the heavenly article.

I soon had occasion to become convinced that the mehter, the Khan's minister, was trying to injure me for no other reason except that he hated Shukrullah Bey, who patronized me. He could not very well doubt my being a Turk, but he endeavoured to make the Khan believe that I had put on the dervishship as a mask merely for some secret mission from the Sultan on which I was now going to Bokhara. Information of his per-

A ROAD IN CENTRAL ASIA. [*Page* 205.

fidiousness had already reached me, and I was not at all surprised at being again invited to the Khan's court, a few days only after my first audience. A large company was present, and he received me immediately with the question, if it was true that I was versed in worldly knowledge too, and that I could write in a flowery style. He wished me to write something for him in the fashion of Stambul, which he was very desirous to see. I very well knew that the request was made in consequence of the mehter's machinations against me, who enjoyed the reputation of being clever in fine and flowery writing and had made inquiries respecting me of my hadji-companions. I produced my writing materials and wrote as follows: "High, mighty and terrible king and lord! I, thy poorest humblest servant, immersed in thy royal graces, keeping before my eyes the proverb that every fine writer is a fool, have hitherto occupied myself but little with studies of fine writing. On the other hand I recalled that other saying, that every fault becomes a virtue as soon as it pleases the king, and found courage to write down these lines."

These high-sounding titles pleased the Khan very much, but the mehter was too stupid to perceive the drift of my allusions. I was told to sit down and, having been treated with bread and tea, called upon by the Khan to come and talk with him. Politics were, this time, the exclusive topic of our conversation, but I, remaining faithful to the character of a dervish, showed but little interest in the matter, and every word had to be forced out of me. All this while the mehter was attentively listening and keenly scanning the expression of my countenance in the hope of my saying something to justify his suspicions, but it was all to no purpose. The Khan sent me away again with the repeated assurance of his good graces, and told me to draw upon his treasurer for my daily stipend. He ordered a *yasaul* (a court officer) to take me to the treasurer. I found the treasurer, who paid me at once the sum as directed, singularly employed. He was arranging the *khilat* (robe of honour), that is, those garments which were destined to be sent to the camp in order to invest with them the heroes, in reward of their bravery. There were four different sorts of silk suits of clothing, all of them the most glaring colours, richly embroidered with flowers in gold; and dividing them into four groups, he called them suits of four heads, suits of twelve heads, suits of twenty and of forty heads. This nomenclature struck me as very odd, all the more so as there was not the slightest trace of a head to be seen on those garments. Instead of answering my question the treasurer told me to meet him in the large public square on the following morning. I was there at the appointed time. I found about a hundred horsemen, who had just arrived from the camp, covered with dust, each of them leading a couple of prisoners, amongst them women and children, who were tied either to the horses tails or the saddle bows, each horseman bringing with him, besides, a sack which was thrown across the saddle. As soon as they arrived each of them handed over the prisoners, he had brought with him, as a present to the Khan, or some other grandee of the land; then they removed the sacks from the saddles and taking hold of the two sides of the one end they spilled their contents on the ground as one does with potatoes. But these were human heads, the heads of slaughtered enemies, which were rolling at the feet of the official who wrote down their number. He first carefully counted the number of heads brought by each horseman and then gave a receipt for the same, the servant kicking them meanwhile into a heap. The horsemen galloped away with their receipts, which were drafts upon the treasurer for their respective rewards, in the shape of robes of honour of four, twenty or forty heads.

The Yasaul who was to take me to the treasurer had, before doing so, another order to attend to; I was therefore obliged to go with him. There were three hundred Tchaudor (a Turkoman tribe) prisoners of war in the third courtyard, and it was in reference to these that the Yasaul had received the Khan's orders. These unfortunate people were all covered with rags, and looked, owing to their fear of death and the starving they had to undergo for days past, like dead men risen from their graves. They were already divided into two groups, those under forty years of age who were fit to be sold as slaves or to be made a present of, and those who owing to their position or advanced age are looked upon as *aksakals* (graybeards or chieftains), and were subject to the punishments meted out by the Khan. Those of the first class were led away by their escorts, in bands of fifteen tied to each other by iron collars. The second group were anticipating with patient resignation, like sheep taken to the slaughter-house, the horrible fate in store for them. Part of them were sent to the block or to the gallows; eight of them, of an advanced age, lay down on their backs at a hint from the executioner. In this situation their hands and feet were tied, and he, kneeling on their chests, and stabbing with a sharp knife the eyes of each of them, in turn, deprived them of their eyesight. After he had accomplished his cruel task he wiped his bloody knife on the gray beard of one of his victims. It was a dreadful sight to see these miserable people, after the fetters had been removed from their hands and feet, in their groping attempts to rise from the ground. Some knocked their heads against one another, others sank to the ground again from sheer exhaustion, moaning and beating the ground with their feet in their agony. I shall think with horror of this scene as long as I live.

I made an excursion of two weeks' duration, in the society of my friend Shukrullah, into the interior as far as Kungrat. On my return I found my companions impatient at their prolonged stay; they were urging our departure on the following day, the ever-increasing heat filling them with anxiety with reference to our journey to Bokhara. I immediately called upon Shukrullah, who had shown me so much kindness during my stay in Khiva, in order to take leave of him. I was deeply affected when this noble old man begged of me to abandon my scheme of going to Bokhara, drawing a most frightful picture of *Bokharai Sherif*, (Bokhara the noble). He told me of the suspicious disposition of the *Emir* (ruling prince), who treated every stranger as an enemy. He confided to me as a great secret, that an Osmanli, who had been sent there as a teacher by the soldiers of Reshid Pasha, and wished to return two years later to Stambul, had been assassinated by the Emir's orders. His well-meant advice had, of course, no effect upon me, and tears were glistening in the eyes of the old man when we exchanged the farewell kiss.

I bestowed upon the Khan, too, my blessing, upon taking leave. He asked me to come back by the way of Khiva as he wished to send with me an ambassador to Constantinople, whose mission it would be to obtain from the new Sultan the customary confirmation for himself. I replied that it was sinful to think of the future, but we should see by and by what *Kismet* (fate) ordains. I then took leave of every one whose acquaintance I had made, or whose friendship I had gained, during my stay of one month in Khiva.

XXII.

FROM KHIVA TO BOKHARA.

WE met for our departure in the cool and shady yard of the Toshebaz. The charity and liberality of the inhabitants of Khiva was manifestly traceable in the altered appearance of the mendicant caravan. The moth-eaten fur caps which we had adopted amongst the Turkomans had given way to turbans of spotless white. The conglomeration of tatters, dignified by the name of apparel, was gone, and the very travelling outfit was far superior to our former holiday apparel. Our bags were filled to bursting, and we experienced great satisfaction in observing that even the poorest of us was provided with an ass, however diminutive. The time for carrying black flour with me was now over; its place was supplied by white cakes, and my store contained such luxuries as rice, butter and sugar. The only article I would not change was my dress. I had been presented with a shirt, it is true, but I did not put it on, thinking that such superfluities, for which the time had not come yet, might have an effeminate effect upon me. It was rather late in the afternoon of the 2nd of June when, having happily got over the never-ending benedictions and farewell embraces, our party left Khiva. The over-zealous ran after us for half an hour, shedding copious tears and saying to us in taking leave: "Who knows when Khiva will be again so fortunate as to have so many pious men for guests within her walls!" *Godshe* was the name of the small town where we passed the first night. Here we put up for the first time at a *kalenterkhane,* that is, an inn for the separate and special accommodation of dervishes which it is customary for every larger community to provide. From here to *Khanka* we uninterruptedly passed through cultivated land. In the kalenterkhane at Khanka I found two half-naked dervishes, who were just in the act of abandoning themselves to the indulgence of opium-eating when I entered. They at once asked me to join them, offering me a goodly dose thereof, and were quite astonished to hear me refuse their kind proffer. They were not to be easily baffled in their friendly attentions, and treated me to tea instead. While I drank my tea they swallowed their poppy-seed poison. In half an hour's time the drug had taken effect; they were both in the realms of the happy; but while the face of the one sleeper wore an expression of joy and delight, the agonies of terrible fear were depicted in the countenance of the other.

Towards evening on the day of our departure from Khanka we came to the Oxus. The spring rains must have considerably swelled the volume of its waters, forcing them beyond their ordinary bed; for I found the river much more considerable than I imagined it to be. The yellow water of the Oxus is not so good in its bed as it is in the canals issuing from it, or in its side-branches where the water, flowing more slowly, is apt to cool off sooner. Where the sand is settling in the Oxus, there the water for sweetness and purity has no rival in the world. Toll must be paid for crossing the Oxus, but the payment of it will in itself not pass a person; one must also be provided with a *petek* (a license to cross). The hadjis had one passport, in common; I had myself been given a separate one which ran thus: "Be it known to the guards on the frontier and the collectors of customs and tolls that Hadji Mollah Abdur-Reshid Effendi was granted a license. Let nobody molest or interfere with him."

Our transportation across the river commenced at ten o'clock in the forenoon; and it was sundown when we reached the opposite shore. We might have crossed the mighty river itself in half an hour's time, but on its smaller side-branches we ran aground; the sandbanks, every ten minutes, forcing the passengers and animals to disembark in order that the ferry-boat might be pushed off into deeper water, and more time being lost getting on board again. The shipping and the unloading of the asses, particularly the stubborn ones, gave no end of troublesome and hard work; the passengers being compelled, for the most part, to carry the animals bodily from and into the boat. There is one laughable scene before my eyes at this very moment; how tall, rawboned Hadji Yakub packed his little ass on his back, gathering up in his fists the struggling legs of the frightened animal, which meekly leant its head on the neck of the hadji. Our caravan could proceed but very slowly. When we were near *Akkamish* (white reed), the kervanbashi, two others, and myself, trusting to the speed of our animals, took advantage of the tardy progress of the caravan, and turned aside to visit *Shurakhan*, where the weekly fair was being held, in order to replenish our provisions.

Shurakhan consists chiefly of those three hundred shops which are open two days a week, and where the permanent inhabitants of the neighbouring country and the nomads happening to camp there, can obtain the necessaries of life. I entrusted my companions with the making of the needful purchases, and sauntered away to the kalenterkhane, outside the place. Here I met again with several dervishes whose frames, reduced to mere skeletons, plainly showed their indulgence in *bang* (opium prepared from hemp). Bang is most universally used for intoxicating purposes in Khiva, and the sinful indulgence in it by many arises from the fact that the Koran forbidding the use of wine and other spirituous liquors, the transgression of that commandment is punished with death by the government. I returned to the fair to join my friends, but it was with great difficulty that I succeeded in pushing my way through the swarming multitude. Everybody was on horseback, buyers as well as sellers. Kirghiz women on horseback were vending *kimiss* (a sourish beverage prepared from mare's milk) in large skin jugs, and it was amusing to see with what dexterity they put the mouth of the jug to the lips of their customer, who was on horseback too, without ever spilling a single drop. At the caravan they had been looking out for us with the greatest impatience, and we resumed our march at sunset, for henceforth we were to travel at night only. As we marched on by the light of the moon, the spectacle was indeed entrancing—the moving caravan and its fantastic shadows, upon which the pale moon shed its mysterious silvery light, flanked on the right by the Oxus rolling its darkling waters with a hoarse murmur, on the left the awful desert of Tartary stretching its endless vista. We met with some Kirghiz Nomads on the following day, and I seized the opportunity of addressing a few words to a Kirghiz woman, asking her if she did not weary of this roving gipsy life of hers. "We cannot be so indolent," she answered, "as you mollahs are, and spend the entire day in one place. Man must move about, the sun, the moon, the stars, the water, animals, birds, fish, all are moving; only the dead and the earth lie motionless."

As we were continuing our march along the willow-covered shores of the Oxus, we were met by five merchants from Khiva, on horseback, who had made their way from Bokhara to this point in four days, and who, moreover, brought us the cheering news that the roads were perfectly safe and that most likely we should on the following day meet with the caravan they had left.

It was at the break of day on the fourth of July when we suddenly stumbled upon two men, in an entirely nude state, who in a pitiful voice could only repeat, "A piece of bread! a piece of bread!" and then fainted away. They were at once given some bread, water and mutton fat, and recovering themselves they told us that they were sailors from Hevaves, had been attacke by a band of Tekke-Turkoman robbers, numbering about one hundred and fifty, and had been robbed by them of their boat, their clothing, their bread and everything else they had. "For the love of God," they said, "run or hide, for you are sure to come across them in a couple of hours, and although you are pious pilgrims, they will strip you of everything and leave you naked in the wilderness, for the Kafir (infidel) Tekke is capable of everything."

No sooner did the kervanbashi hear the name of Tekke mentioned than he gave instant orders to retrace our steps. We were to retreat as fast as was compatible with the pace of the poor, heavily laden camels. Of course it was well-nigh an impossibility to get away with camels from Turkoman horses, but we counted that it would take until morning for one hundred and fifty horsemen to cross the river, and whilst they were cautiously reconnoitring we might safely reach Tunuklu. There we intended to fill our canteens with water and then to turn into the desert of *Khalata*, where we hoped to escape from the pursuit of the Tekkes. After tremendous exertions we arrived with our animals quite exhausted in Tunuklu. Here we had to remain until our animals were rested and fed, for in their present condition they could not have reached the first station in the desert. We passed three mortal hours in unquestionable anxiety, making our preparations for the awful journey, and the sun had not set when our caravan was wending its way, from the ruins of Tunuklu, along the road leading to Khalata.

Knowing the terrors of the desert as we did, one may easily imagine with what feelings myself and my fellow-travellers commenced this new journey through the desert. We had travelled from Gomushtepe to Khiva in the month of May, and now we were in July; then we found some rain-water, now we should not find even salt-water. With what longing did we look at the Oxus, on whose bosom the setting sun was casting a halo of light, as it receded, to the right, from our sight. The very animals, dumb as they were, kept their eyes continuously in that direction. The sky was covered already with stars when we reached the sandy desert. We proceeded as noiselessly as possible for fear of attracting the attention of the Turkomans whom we thought not to be far off. They could not possibly see us in the darkness of the night, and the moon would rise late. The soft ground prevented the noise of the tramp of the animals being heard, and the only thing we apprehended was that one of our animals might take it into its head to give us a specimen of its charming voice. Fortunately the spirit of singing did not descend on any of them. About midnight we reached a place where all of us had to dismount, as the animals were wading knee deep in the fine sand.

Our station on the morning of the 5th of July was called *Adamkirilgan*, that is, man destroyer, and one glance taken at the surrounding objects was sufficient to prove the propriety of this appellation. As far as the eye could reach, nothing but sand, sand, now like the stormy sea lashing itself into tremendous waves, now again presenting the spectacle of the rippling caused by gentle breezes on the bosom of a calm lake. No bird can be seen in the air, nor insect on the earth; all the eye can discover here and there are the sad signs of decay, the skeletons of lost men and animals, which are placed in a heap by the travellers in order to serve them as a guide. Here, of course, we were safe from the Turkomans, for there is no horse in the world capable of walking the distance of one station through this sand. According to our kervanbashi's statement the journey from Tunuklu to Bokhara, generally took six days, three through the sand and three on solid ground, covered here and there with grass. We had to fear then, altogether, one day's or one and a half day's want of water. But I observed on the very first day that the water of the Oxus we had with us upset all our calculations, as it diminished with frightful rapidity in spite of our utmost economy, a phenomenon which I attributed to evaporation. Everybody of course guards his skin most carefully, and jealously hugs it close to his bosom when asleep. We marched six hours every day in spite of the dreadful heat, wishing to get out of the sandy desert as soon as possible; for if we happened to be caught dozing in the sand for only a few seconds by the murderous *tebbad* wind, the lives of the whole caravan would be in danger, whilst on the solid ground of the desert beyond, such a tebbad visitation involved only an attack of high fever. The forced march had worn out our camels to such an extent that two of them died on the 6th of July.

Our toilsome march had now lasted three days; the scorching heat enervated us all and reduced our strength. Two of our poorer companions, who had been compelled, owing to the inferiority of their animals, to trudge by their side on foot, had consumed all the water they had, and became, for want of it, so sick that they had to be tied to the backs of the camels, being unable both to walk and to sit upright. They were covered up besides. As long as their voices did not desert them, they were constantly begging for water. It is the pitiful truth, alas! that their best friends denied them the boon of a few drops of the life-giving elixir, and it was reserved for grim death to be more generous and relieve one of them from the pangs of thirst on reaching Medemin Bulag, at which place he expired. I was near the unhappy man when he had breathed his last. His tongue had turned quite black, his throat was of a grayish white, but his features were not overmuch discomposed, except his mouth, which was gaping, owing to the shrunken state of his lips. I am not sure if the bathing of water would have been of any benefit to the poor fellow, but the thought that nobody attempted to save the dying man by offering him one swallow of water did not cease to haunt me for many a day to come. The father hides his liquid store from his son, the brother from his brother, for every drop of it not only represents life but relief from the dreadful torture of thirst, the fear of the latter banishing that self-sacrifice and generous-mindedness which we often have an opportunity to witness on other occasions of danger and peril.

The Khalata mountains which signalize the beginning of the hard-soiled desert, were not yet within sight. Our camels were unable to proceed, their weakness and fatigue necessitating a further stay of one day, the fourth day, amid the burning sand of the desert. My store of water was reduced to about six glasses of water, which I kept in my leather flask; of this I durst not drink more than a drop at a time, the consequence being that I was constantly suffering from thirst. To my horror I discovered a black spot in the middle part of my tongue, and this was sufficient to make me at once swallow one half of my store. I thought I was saved, but on the following morning a burning sensation accompanied by a violent headache made itself felt, more and more, and by the time the Khalata mountains loomed up in the distant horizon like towering blue clouds, my strength gradually failed me. The nearer we drew to the mountains the scarcer the sand became, and every eye was eagerly looking out for some herd or shepherd's hut. All of a sudden some one called the kervanbashi's attention to an approaching cloud of dust, who seeing it became deadly pale with fright, and exclaimed: "This is the tebbad." Every one dismounted at once from the camels. The animals were quicker to feel the approach of the stifling wind and had knelt down, roaring loud, on the ground, laying down their long necks flat before them, and trying to hide their heads in the sand. We used the animals as a bulwark against the coming storm, crouching down near them, and hardly had we time to do so when the wind swept over our heads with a deep roar, covering us with a layer of sand of the thickness of half an inch, its first grains burning as like drops of fiery rain. Had we been attacked by the tebbad five miles more inland, we should have been all irretrievably destroyed. I did not observe the symptoms of fever attended with vomiting which are said to be the effects of this wind, but the atmosphere became sensibly heavier and more oppressive.

We scrambled up when it was over, and found to our intense satisfaction after a short while that the sand was gone. From three roads which led from the edge of the sandy desert to Bokhara we chose the shortest one, and resuming our march we came, towards evening, across several wells that had not been visited, even by herdsmen, this year. The water we found in them was unfit for man, but the animals drank their fill from it. We were all of us in the last stages of exhaustion, and nothing but hope kept up the spark of life within our enfeebled frames. Coming to the next station I was not able to get off my animal without assistance, and was taken down and laid on the ground. I felt a dreadful internal fire and my head stupified by the violence of the headache. My pen has no power to describe the tortures of thirst unallayed which I underwent at that moment, nor do I think there is any more painful mode of death, for I had hitherto bravely faced all kind of dangers, keeping up my manhood—but now I was completely broken down; I felt my power of resistance had deserted me and had no hopes of ever surviving the night. Towards noon we took up our march again; I fell asleep, and on awaking on the 10th of July I found myself lying on the ground in a mud hut, surrounded by men with long beards whom I at once recognized as natives of Iran. They first administered to me tepid milk, then I had to take some sour milk mixed with salt and water, called *ayran* by them, and very soon recovered my strength from the combined effect of both these beverages. I now learned that, together with my companions, we were the guests of a couple of Persian slaves camping here, in the desert, at a distance of forty miles from Bokhara, they having charge of flocks of sheep, but being very sparingly provided with bread and water, so as to prevent them from making an attempt to escape. Yet these Persians, poor slaves as they were, had the broad charitableness which gives water to their ancient and inveterate foes, the Sunnite mollahs. They became particularly kind to me when they heard me addressing them in their native language, the Persian. The sight of a child-boy only five years old, who was also a slave, inspired me with feelings of profoundest pity. He had been taken prisoner two years ago, together with his father; and being asked the particulars of his life he answered: "My father has bought (ransomed) himself; nor am I to remain a slave above two years, for my father will earn the necessary money to set me free by that time." The poor child had hardly a rag to cover his nakedness, and his skin was as dark and hard as tanned leather.

After a little while we journeyed on again, not without being presented at our departure with some water by the unfortunate Persians. At daybreak on the 11th day of July we came to the borders of a lake of sweet water. At last there was an end to death from want of water, and to all fear of winds, robbers and other perils. At this point we entered Bokhara proper, and upon arriving after a march of two hours at *Khakemir* (the land of the Emir), the dwelling-place of the kervanbashi, we found the surrounding country in a fair state of cultivation. Here we had to pass the night whilst, according to the laws of the country, information was sent to the officer of customs and to the official reporter, in order that they might come and search and examine us before we were allowed to enter the city of Bokhara. A special messenger was dispatched by us for that purpose, and early in the morning of the following day three officers of the Emir made their appearance to collect the customs and, more particularly, to gather information about ourselves and neighbouring countries. After we had finished our business with them we set off at once, and having walked amidst gardens and cultivated lands for about half an hour, we caught sight of Bokharai Sherif (noble Bokhara, as it is called by Central-Asians) with its rude towers, on the top of which storks were building their nests.

XXIII.

IN BOKHARA.

WE marched into Bokhara on the 12th of July, and betook ourselves straight to the spacious *tekkie* (convent), shaded by trees, which, forming a regular square, is provided with forty-eight cells on the ground floor. The chief of this building was the descendant of some saint, the court-priest of the Emir, and a man enjoying universal respect. Hadji Salih, my intimate friend and companion, had been at one time a pupil of this holy man, our present host, and, in that capacity, he took upon himself at once to introduce me and the more prominent members of our party to him. The recommendation and introduction coming from such a source, we were received in the most friendly manner by the chief of the tekkie; and having indulged in half an hour's conversation with me, his satisfaction seemed to know no bounds, and he loudly expressed his regret at the Badevlet's (his Majesty the Emir's) absence from Bokhara, which prevented him from taking me to the Emir at once. He immediately ordered a separate cell, in the most acceptable location near the mosque, to be assigned to me, one of my neighbours being a learned mollah, and the other Hadji Salih. The tekkie was full of celebrities, and I had happened to light on the principal nest of religious fanaticism in Bokhara. The official reporter had given information of my arrival as an event of great importance, and Rahmet-Bi, the first officer of the Emir and commander-in-chief in Bokhara during the Emir's absence on his campaigns in Kokhand, was making inquiries of the hadjis about me, on the first day of my stay. But as the Emir's power does not extend to the tekkie, the inquisitiveness of his first officer was made so little account of, that nobody had thought it worth while to inform me of the same. In speaking of me my friends said: "Hadji Reshid is not only a good Mussulman, but a learned mollah besides; and he who entertains a suspicion against him commits a most grievous sin."

On the following day I went out with Hadji Salih and four others of our party, to take a look at the city and its bazaar. Although the squalid and rickety buildings and the streets covered with sand, one foot thick, did not tend to place "noble Bokhara" in the most favourable or imposing light, yet upon entering the bazaar and beholding the thronging multitude animating it, I could not refrain from being intensely interested at the novel sight. The beauty and wealth of the bazaar were not the things that surprised me, so much as the immense and multifarious variety in races, dress and manners which struck the eye everywhere. The type of Iran was visible in the faces of a great portion of the people; but the Tartar features, which could be seen in all their shades, from the Uzbeg to the wild Kirghiz, claimed my particular attention owing to their prominence. The last, and generally the Turanian race, may be distinguished from the people of Iran by their heavy and awkward gait. Jews and Hindoos could be seen in great numbers, too. I cast, now and then, a stealthy glance at the contents of the shops, finding in them but few goods of the manufacture of Western Europe, but Russian manufactures were all the more extensively represented in them. Home-made articles have a separate place assigned to them in the bazaar, and it is to this place that the Kirghizes, the Kiptchaks, the Kalmuks and the inhabitants of Chinese Tartary resort to make their purchases of clothing.

After loitering about and observing for nearly three hours I became so exhausted with fatigue that I had to request my guide, Hadji Salih, to allow me to take some rest. He led me, through the tea bazaar, to a place called the "Divanbeg's Reservoir." It was a tolerably regular square, in the centre of which a lake, flagged with stones and shaded by magnificent elm trees, was visible. The place is encircled by tea-shops, in which gigantic *samovars* (teapots), manufactured in Russia especially for Bokhara, are standing. In numerous shops are sold candies, sweetmeats, bread and fruit, around which thousands of gourmands and hungry people swarm. A mosque stands on one side of the palace, in front of which dervishes and *meddahs* (story-tellers) recount the heroic deeds of renowned prophets and warriors, distorting their features in every possible way as they do so, to a large and curious audience. As we were entering the square we saw a procession of fifteen dervishes from the cloister of Nakishbend pass before our eyes. It was a sight not to be easily forgotten—the mad jumping about of these dervishes, in their wild fanaticism, with tall caps on their heads and their long flowing hair, waving their sticks, and bellowing forth in chorus a hymn, the several strophes of which were first sung to them by their gray-headed chief.

Although I had put on a costume, such as they wore in Bokhara, and the sun had disfigured my face to such an extent that my own good mother would not have recognized me, I was followed, nevertheless, by a crowd of curious people, whose embraces and hand-shaking became very annoying to me. Judging by my gigantic turban and the large Koran suspended from my neck, they evidently took me to be some ishan or Sheikh, and there was no way to escape the unpleasantness. While in Bokhara, its people never, during the whole time of my stay there, suspected me, although they are rather cunning and distrustful. They would come to me for benedictions, listen to my recitals in public places, but never a farthing did I get from them.

The authorities did not trust me as implicitly as the people did. Rahmet-Bi, the Emir's chief officer whom I have mentioned before, could not assail me publicly, but he pestered me with spies whose business it was to engage me in conversation, dragging into it all the time the Frengistan name, in the hope of seeing me betray myself before them, through some inadvertent remark. Failing in this method they thought to frighten me by stray remarks, such as that the Frengis covet the possession of Bokhara, and that several of their spies and emissaries had already met with condign punishment. Or they would talk of some Frengis (unfortunate Italians) who had come to Bokhara a couple of days ago, and were arrested owing to their alleged importation of several boxes of tea, sprinkled with diamond dust, for the purpose of poisoning the entire population of the sacred city. These spies were for the most part hadjis who had been living for years in Constantinople, and were now trying to test my knowledge of the language and the circumstances of that place. To get rid of their obtrusions I pretended to a feeling of indignation and impatience at their everlasting discussion of the Frengi. "Why," said I to them, "I have left Constantinople for this very reason, to get rid of the sight of these Frengis who have robbed the devil of his reason. I am now, thank God, in noble Bokhara, and have no wish to waste here my time on speaking about them."

At one time again one of the servants of Rahmet-Bi brought to me, by orders of his master, a thin little man, requesting me to examine the individual, and then tell if he were an Arab from Damaskus, as he claimed to be. Immediately on his entering I was struck by his features, and set him down at once for a European. I was strengthened in this opinion after having talked with him a while, for I found his pronunciation not to be the true Arabic at all. He told me he was going to China to visit the grave there of some saint. He was visibly embarrassed in the course of our conversation. I rather regret not having met him afterwards, for I strongly suspect he was acting the same part I was.

The commander-in-chief, finding himself foiled in his attempts to draw me out by spies, invited me to a *pilar* (a dish of rice and meat) at his house, where a brilliant galaxy of the representatives of the ulema world of Bokhara were awaiting my appearance. As soon as I entered and looked about me I saw at once that the whole company were assembled to sit in judgment upon my case; that a hard task awaited me, and that my powers of dissimulation would have to pass through a fiery ordeal. I thought best to anticipate their design, and instead of giving them time to address questions to me,

I boldly plunged into a discussion of some religious dogmas and requested their opinions concerning them. My zeal met with applause at the hands of the pious assemblage, and a very heated dispute arising soon after, in which I was careful not to take any part, concerning some mooted points in the sacred book, I took occasion to loudly declare the mental superiority of the mollahs of Bokhara over the ulemas of Constantinople. At length, my trial ended with my triumph; the learned mollahs gave Rahmet-Bi to understand by nods and winks and words, that his official reporter had been outrageously mistaken, and that there could not be the slightest doubt about my identity.

During my whole stay in Bokhara the heat was intolerable, and I had to undergo besides the additional infliction of drinking warm water as a preventative against getting the *rishte*, viz., the filaria medinensis, with which every tenth person here is afflicted. People in Bokhara think as little of feeling in summer an itching sensation in their feet or any part of their bodies, as Europeans do of a cold. The itching is followed after a while by a red spot, from the centre of which a worm of the thickness of a thread issues to the length at times, of several yards, and it must be carefully unwound in the course of a couple of days. This is the regular course of the disease, which is otherwise unaccompanied by any pain. But if the worm happens to break whilst being unwound, inflammation sets in, and six to ten appear where there had been one before, compelling the patient to keep his bed midst great sufferings for a week. The more courageous gets the rishte at once removed from his body, by having it cut out. The barbers in Bokhara perform the operation with considerable skill; the spot where the itching is felt is cut open in an instant, the worm removed, and the wound heals in a very short time.

Bokhara is supplied with water from the Zerefshan (gold-scattering) river by means of open aqueducts. The canal is sunk to a sufficient depth, but not kept clean. As it frequently happens to run dry, the water coming in again is received by the populace with shouts and screams of delight. First of all the people, young and old, dive into the basin and take a regular bath; then comes the turn of the horses, cows, and asses, followed by the dogs. When this general bathing of man and beast is over any further going into it is forbidden; the water settles somewhat and becomes clear again, but it remains, nevertheless, tainted with dirt and messes of all kinds.

There is something of the metropolitan character, withal, about Bokhara, at least it was so to a man like myself who had been wandering for a considerable time through the deserts of Central Asia. I had good hot bread, I could get tea, fruit and cooked eatables; I even went to the length of having two shirts made for myself, and indeed got to like the comforts of civilized life to such an extent that it was with a pang of regret that I listened to my companions talking of the preparations I should make for our departure, as they wished to reach their distant Eastern homes before the setting in of winter. I intended, at all events, to accompany them as far as Samarkand, where I might easily happen to meet the Emir, in which case my fellow-hadjis would be of great service to me. There, in Samarkand, I should then have to choose either to continue the journey to Kokhand and Kashgar, in their company, or to return by myself to Teheran by way of Herat. I was warmly urged by Hadji Bilal and Hadji Salih to remain with them, but in order to afford me every facility, in case I would not be persuaded by them and insisted upon leaving them at Samarkand, they made me acquainted with a kervanbashi from Herat, who was staying in Bokhara with one hundred and fifty camels, and was going to leave for his home, Herat, in three weeks. *Molla Zeman* was the name of the kervanbashi; he had known my friends for a long time, and they recommended me to him in such cordial terms as if I had been their brother. It was consequently arranged between me and Molla Zeman, that in case I made up my mind to return from Samarkand I should meet him in three weeks at Kerki, on the other side of the Oxus.

Before saying good-bye to Bokhara I shall make some mention of the place where I first met him. It was one of those caravansaries where the unfortunate slaves are put up for sale. The Turkoman karaktchi, who hunts the Persians, cannot afford to wait a long time for his money, he therefore usually sells his human booty to some wealthier Turkoman, who makes a business of buying a good many of them, and then takes a large troop of slaves to Bokhara to be sold there. He then sells as many as he can during the first days after his arrival, the rest which he is not able to dispose of he hands over to the dellal to be sold for him; the latter is the person who does the real wholesale business in slaves. Slaves of from three to sixty years of age, unless from some cause or other they have become crippled, are constantly for sale in the marts of Bokhara and Khiva. The tenets of their religion, it is true, forbid them to sell into slavery any but unbelievers, but hypocritical Bokhara knows how to elude the law. Besides the Shi-ite Persians, who are declared to be unbelievers by the Sunnite law, any number of Sunnite true believers are sold into slavery, conscience being salved by the simple process of compelling them before their sale and by the most cruel tortures to confess to being Shi-ites.

The male slave who is exposed for sale is publicly examined, and the seller is bound to guarantee that the article sold by him is without a flaw. The hour in which a slave gets out of the clutches of the slave-dealer is his happiest, for it is impossible that such ill-treatment could await him, even at the hand of the worst master, as he endures whilst in the warehouses of the dealer in human flesh. The prices paid for the slaves vary according to the political situation, being favourable or unfavourable, as the Turkomans send their *alamans* (robber-bands) into the neighbouring countries. At the time of my visit the price paid for an able-bodied strong man was from forty to fifty tillas (from £2 10s. to £3 10s.); but at the time when the Persians were defeated near Merv, and 10,000 prisoners were taken, a man could be bought at the low price of from three to four tillas. This abominable traffic, I am happy to remark, has since the time of my sojourn in Bokhara, if not entirely ceased, yet certainly greatly abated; and it is very probable that ere long slaves will not be exposed for sale at all in Central Asia. For the cessation of this horrible practice we are indebted to Russia, who has forbidden the slave trade in her own Asiatic possessions, as well as in the countries under her protection. Nor can the Turkomans, the chief men-stealers, continue as before their inroads into Persia to carry away men and cattle.

We had already passed eighteen days in Bokhara, and my friends being unwilling to remain any longer, we had to proceed on our journey to Samarkand. Our purses, too, were at a rather low ebb, for in Bokhara we got nothing beyond hand-shaking. All that we had saved up in Khiva was spent by us in Bokhara. I had to sell even my animal; and many of my companions sharing my fate, we were compelled to hire a waggon in order to continue our journey. Some of our fellow-hadjis said good-bye to us here, and many and affectionate were the leave-takings and embraces.

Before leaving I paid a farewell visit to Rahmet-Bi, who was kind enough to furnish me with a letter of recommendation for Samarkand, and made me promise that I would get myself introduced to the Emir.

Our first station was the village of Bahaeddin, the burial-place of the celebrated saint, Baha-ed-din Nakishbend, who, after Mohammed, is esteemed most highly in Turkestan. It is the firm belief of a native of Bokhara, that the mere exclamation of his "Oh! Bahaeddin, dispeller of danger," is sufficient to protect him against every peril. Crowds are constantly flocking from the city to visit the grave of this holy man, three hundred asses being steadily engaged in the conveying of these pious pilgrims. These asses are celebrated for their peculiarity of going almost at a racing pace to Bahaeddin, whilst on their return trip to Bokhara their sluggish pace cannot be accelerated even by administering blows to them. The people of Bokhara ascribe this curious humour of the sagacious animal to the attachment which their patron saint is apt to beget even in the bosoms of dumb animals.

The road to Samarkand leads for the most part through well-cultivated fields, populous and nicely built villages. We halted at five stations on this road. Now that I was drawing near Samarkand all my curiosity and interest revived to see this Mecca of my longings of old.

Mount Tchobanata, at the foot of which the city spreads, was already visible, and climbing up an eminence we saw Samarkand, the city of Timur, before us in all its pomp and splendour, shining out, with fairy-like enchantment, with its many coloured cupolas and towers, illumined by the rosy hue of the rising sun.

SAMARKAND

[Page 284.

XXIV.

IN SAMARKAND.

THE Tadjiks maintain to this day that *Samarkand*, this ancient city of Central Asia, is the centre of the world. And it does, in truth, excel all the other cities of Central Asia, in its ancient monuments as well as in the splendour of its mosques, its grand tombs and new structures. We put up at a large caravansary where hadjis are provided with free quarters, but having been invited on the day of our arrival to establish my quarters as a guest in a private house near the tomb of Timur, I readily accepted the invitation and left the caravansary. I was agreeably surprised to find in my host an officer of the Emir who was charged with the superintendence of the Emir's palace at Samarkand. The return of the Emir, who was about to terminate a successful campaign at Kokhand, having been announced to take place in a few days, my fellow-travellers determined to oblige me by putting off their departure from Samarkand until I had an opportunity to see the Emir and find suitable companions for my return journey. I employed my time, in the meanwhile, in looking at the remarkable sights in the city, of which a greater variety is offered here than in any city in Central Asia. Being a hadji I had, of course, to begin with the saints. There are here about a hundred holy places to be visited, and the pilgrims do their visiting by a certain established rote, according to the superior claims of persons and places to sanctity. I would not deviate from the observance of this routine, and looked at everything, in its proper turn, down to the smallest object, with the zeal and devotion becoming the character I was acting. Amongst the many, I will mention in passing only the mosque of Timur; that castle in one of the halls of which the celebrated *Kök-Tach* (*i.e.*, green stone) is still to be seen upon which the great Emir had his throne erected, when its hall was crowded with vassals who hied from all the quarters of the world to do him homage; at that time when three messengers on horseback were always standing ready in the precincts of the amphitheatrically constructed hall to blazon forth the edicts of the conqueror of the world to the remotest corner of it. The tomb of Timur and its many brilliant medresses are worth mentioning, too. Only a portion of the latter are used as dwelling-places, and many of them are threatened with decay. The medresse of Hanim, once so grand, is in ruins now, and in vain did I search within mouldering walls for even a trace of the renowned Armenian and Greek library which Timur is alleged to have brought to Samarkand to form one of the ornaments of his capital.

Whilst I was in Samarkand crowds were always thronging in the bazaars as well as in the public places and streets, to which the soldiers returning from the war contributed, to a great extent. The number of its regular population hardly exceeds fifteen to twenty thousand inhabitants, two-thirds of whom are Uzbegs, and one-third Tadjiks. The Emir, whose seat of government is properly speaking in Bokhara, used to spend two or three months during the summer in Samarkand, owing to its more elevated position and more genial climate.

I had now passed eight days in Samarkand, and I finally came to the conclusion to return to the West by way of Herat, taking the route I have mentioned before. Hadji Bilal still insisted on taking me with him to Aksu, promising to send me safely to Mecca by way of Yarkend, Thibet and Cashmere, or, if favoured by luck, to Peking by way of Komul. But Hadji Salih was opposed to the plan, laying stress on the great distance and the scantiness of my means. "As far as Aksu, and even Komul," he said, "thou wouldst experience no difficulty, for Mussulmans and brothers are living along the road, and they would have regard for you as a dervish from Roum; but beyond thou wilt meet unbelievers only, who, it is true, will not hurt thee, but will not give you anything either. Therefore be advised, and return to Teheran by way of Herat, with the men we have selected for your travelling companions.

There was a struggle going on within me for a while. To have travelled by land to Peking, through the ancient fastnesses of the Tartars, Khirgizes, Mongols, and Chinese, where even Marco Polo would not have dared to place his feet—would have been indeed a feat without a parallel! The voice of moderation prevailed with me after all. I reflected that it would be a pity to risk losing the fruits of the experiences hitherto gathered, however trifling they might be, by embarking in an enterprise of great uncertainty and undoubted danger. And putting off was not giving up; I was only thirty-one years old, and what I could not well do to-day I might accomplish at some future day. I made up my mind to return.

My preparations for the journey had advanced considerably when the Emir made his triumphal entry into Samarkand. Its taking place had been announced for some days past, and a great multitude had collected on the *righistan* (principal public place), to witness the show, but I cannot say that any special pomp was displayed in the pageant. The procession was headed by two hundred sherbazes, wearing over the uncouth Bokhara costume some sort of overall of skin, to which piece of additional dress they were indebted for their being called regular troops. They were followed by horsemen with banners and kettledrums, and behind these, at some distance, came Emir Mozaffar ed-din, surrounded by his higher officers and chief men. The Emir was forty-two years old, of middle size, rather stout, but very pleasant in appearance, with fine black eyes and a thin beard. After the Emir came Kiptchaks—rude, martial warriors with features nearly Mongolian, armed with bows and arrows and shields.

The Emir caused a feast to be arranged for the people on the day of his arrival, several gigantic cauldrons being erected, on that occasion, on the righistan, in which the princely pilar was being cooked. Into each of these cauldrons was thrown a sack of rice, three sheep chopped up, a large pan of mutton fat, enough to make five pounds of tallow candles, and a small sack of carrots. Then ensued a scene of eating and drinking beggaring all description.

An *arz*, that is a day for public audiences, was proclaimed for the following day. I took advantage of this occasion to present myself in the company of my friends to the Emir. As we were entering the interior of the city, we were startled to find ourselves stopped by a Mehrem, who gave us to understand that his Badevlet (majesty) wished to see me alone, without my companions. My friends were this time of my opinion, that this message boded ill to me. But what was to be done but to follow the Mehrem to the palace. After being made to wait for about an hour I was conducted into a room where I found the Emir reclining on a mattress of red cloth, amidst books and papers lying about. I recited a short Sura, accompanying it with the usual prayer for the welfare of the governing prince, and after saying amen, to which the Emir responded, I sat down in close vicinity to him without having first received his invitation to do so. The Emir was struck by my bold behaviour, which was in fact in perfect keeping with the character of a dervish. He fixed his eyes severely on mine as if wishing to embarrass me, and said :

"Hadji ! I hear thou hast come from Roum to visit the graves of Baha-ed-din and the other holy men of Turkestan ?"

"Yes, takhsir (sir) ! and, besides, to be edified by thy blessed beauty."

"Strange ; and hast thou no other object in coming here from such distant lands ?"

"No, takhsir ! It has ever been the warmest wish of my heart to visit noble Bokhara and enchanting Samarkand, upon whose sacred ground, as is justly observed by Sheikh Djelal, men should walk with their heads rather than their feet. Besides, this is my only vocation, and I having been roaming now through the world for many a day as a *djihangheste*" (a wanderer through the world).

"How is this, a djihangheste with thy lame foot? This is very strange indeed."

"Let me be thy victim, takhsir ! (This phrase answers our "I beg your pardon, sir.") Thy glorious ancestor Timur—may he rest in peace—was afflicted in the same way, and yet he became a *djihanghir*" (a conqueror of the world).

Having bantered me in this preliminary conversation, the Emir inquired what sort of impression Bokhara and Samarkand had made upon me. My answers, which I took occasion to interlard with copious citations of Persian poetry, seemed to make a favourable impression upon the Emir, who was a mollah himself and spoke Arabic pretty well; but I was not altogether sure yet of my success with him. After the audience had lasted for a quarter of an hour he summoned a servant, and telling him something in a cautious undertone he bade me follow the servant.

I quickly rose from my sitting posture and followed as I had been bid. The servant led me through a number of yards and halls, whilst my mind was at the time cruelly agitated by fears and misgivings as to my fate; my perplexed imagination conjuring up pictures of horror and seeing myself already travelling on the road to the rack and that dreadful death which was ever present to my mind. My guide showed me, after a good deal of wandering about, into a dark room, conveying to me by a sign that I should expect him here. I stood still, in what state of mind any one can guess. I counted the moments with feverish excitement—when the door opened again. A few seconds yet of suspense and the servant approached at last, and by the light of the opening door I saw him holding in his hand, instead of the frightful instruments of the executioner, a parcel carefully folded up. In it I found a highly ornamental suit of clothing, and an amount of money destined for my onward journey, sent to me as a present by the Emir.

As soon as I obtained possession of the parcel I hastened away to my companions, wild with joy at my escape. They were quite as glad of my success as I myself had been. I subsequently learned that Rahmet-Bi had sent the Emir an equivocating report about me, in consequence of which I was received with diffidence at first by the Emir, but succeeded in dissipating his mistrust, thanks to the glibness of my tongue.

My fellow-hadjis now advised me to leave Samarkand at once, and not even to sojourn at *Karshi*, but to cross over as quickly as possible to the other side of the Oxus, and await there in the midst of the hospitable *Ersari-Turkomans* the arrival of the caravan bound for Herat. I took their advice. The hour of parting was at hand. I feel my pen is too feeble to give an adequate picture of the parting scene. For six months we had been sharing in all the dangers connected with travelling in the desert; we had in common defied robbers, borne the raging elements, and braved hunger and thirst. No wonder then that the barriers of position, age and nationality were all broken down, and that we had come to look on ourselves as one family. It may be easily imagined with what heavy hearts we looked forward to the sad moment when we should have to separate. There is hardly anything more painful to the heart of a true man than to see those ties severed which common hardships, the exchange of mutual acts of friendship and devotion, have firmly knit together. And mine, especially, I own it, nearly broke at the thought of the double-dealing I had to practise upon these friends of mine—the best I had in the world, who had preserved my life—even in these last moments leaving them in the dark as to my identity. But those who know the fanaticism of the Moslems, and the danger I should have exposed myself to by divulging the truth even at the moment of farewell, will surely find no fault with my reserve.

After recommending me most warmly to a couple of pilgrims with whom I was to go to Mecca, in terms such as one uses in committing to the charge of another that which is dearest, a brother or a son, they remained with me until I had passed through the gates of the city, outside of which my new fellow-travellers were already waiting for me with their hired waggons. The sun was setting when, tearing myself away from the last embrace, I stepped into the vehicle. We were all crying like very children. My friends remained standing and looking after me for a long while, holding up their hands towards heaven and beseeching the blessing of Allah on my head. Often and often I turned back to get a last look at my faithful friends, but they soon disappeared from view, and I saw nothing but the cupolas of Samarkand bathed in the pale light of the rising moon.

XXV.

FROM SAMARKAND TO HERAT.

I DID not remain long with my new fellow-travellers from the Khanate of Kokhand. But I attached myself all the more closely to a young mollah from Kungrat by the name of Ishak, who wished to go with me to Mecca. He was a kind-hearted youth, as poor as myself, and looking upon me as his master, he was always ready to serve and oblige me.

The road from Samarkand follows the direction of the road to Bokhara up to the hill whence we saw the city for the first time. The next day found us already in the desert. In truth, however, compared to the other deserts through which I had passed, it might have been more fitly denominated an extensive grassy plain or a prairie. One meets here everywhere with herdsmen, owing to the numerous wells around which nomadic Uzbegs have their tents erected. The wells are for the most part very deep, and near them are tanks forming reservoirs for water, of stone or wood, at which the cattle are watered. To avoid the fatiguing labour of drawing water from the wells with buckets which are exceedingly small, the herdsmen attach the rope of the bucket to the saddle of a mule, passing it over a pulley, making thus the mule perform the work of drawing water. Quite a picturesque scene is presented by such a well, the flocks of sheep wandering or resting near it with their serious shepherds, and I was forcibly reminded by it of similar sights in the Lowlands of Hungary. On the second day after our departure we met a caravan coming from Karshi, near one of the wells. One of this caravan, a young woman who had been sold by her husband to an old Tadjik, and had discovered the infamous transaction after she reached the desert, was tearing her hair, bitterly wailing and crying, and upon catching sight of me she frantically rushed up to where I stood and exclaimed: "My hadji, thou hast read books: where is it written that a Mussulman may sell his wife, the mother of his children?" In vain I told the Tadjik that to do so was to commit a grievous sin, he only composedly smiled; the judge at Karshi apparently not having shared my views, the buyer felt quite sure as to the validity of the bargain.

We proceeded but slowly owing to the excessive heat, and it took two days and three nights to reach *Karshi.* Nakhsheb was the ancient name of Karshi, and as a city it ranks second in the Khanate of Bokhara in extent and commercial importance. I went in search of an Uzbeg by the name of Ishan Hassan, to whom my friends had given me a letter of introduction. I found him and was very cordially received by him. He advised me to buy an ass, cattle being very cheap in Karshi, and to purchase with my remaining money knives, needles, thread, glass beads, Bokhara-made pocket-handkerchiefs, and particularly carnelians brought here from India, and to trade with these articles amongst the nomadic people we should meet along our road. All the hadjis do the same thing. In exchange for a needle or a couple of glass beads you get bread and melons enough to last a whole day. I saw that the good man was right, and went on the very same day with the Kungrat mollah to make the intended purchases. One half of my khurdjin was full of my manuscripts, mostly of literary and historical contents, which I bought in the bazaar of Bokhara; the other half was used by me as a storehouse for my wares, and thus I became at once an antiquarian, a dealer in fashionable articles, a hadji and a mollah, deriving an additional source of income from the sale of benedictions, nefesses, amulets, and similar wonderful articles.

After a stay of three days I left, in company of the mollah Ishak and two other hadjis, for Kerki, about fifty-six miles distant from Karshi. After three days' travelling we reached the Oxus in the morning, at a place where there was a small fort on our side of the shore, and on the opposite side on a steep height the frontier fort surrounded by the small town of *Kerki*. The Oxus flowing between the two forts is here nearly twice the width of the Danube near Budapest, but owing to its rapid current, which drove us considerably out of our course, it took us fully three hours to cross over. The boatmen were very clever, and would not accept anything of us for ferrying us over. But scarcely had we placed our feet on the shore when the *deryabeghi* (the river officer) of the governor of Kerki stopped us, accusing us of being runaway slaves intending to return to Persia, and compelling us to follow him immediately with all our luggage and things to the castle of the governor. My surprise and terror may be easily imagined. Three of my companions whose speech and features at once betrayed their origin were allowed to go free before long. I did not fare quite so well; things would not pass off so smoothly with me, they making all kinds of objections; but finally I flew into a rage, and exchanging the Turco-Tartar dialect I had been using for that of Constantinople, I emphatically insisted either upon having my passport shown to the Bi (governor) at once, or upon being taken into his presence.

At the noise I made the *toptchubashi* (an officer of artillery), who was of Persian origin, said something in a whisper to the deryabeghi. Then he took me aside, and telling me that he had gone several times to Stambul, from Tebriz, his native city, he knew very well persons belonging to Roum, and I might be perfectly quiet, as no harm would befall me.

Every stranger must submit to this searching investigation; for as slaves who had become free and were returning home had to pay a tax of two gold pieces at the border, there were many of them who resorted to all kinds of subterfuges and disguises to steal unrecognized over the frontiers. The servant who had taken my passport to the governor soon returned, not only bringing back with him my papers, but a present of five tenghis which the governor had sent me.

I was very sorry to learn that Mollah Zeman, the chief of the caravan going from Bokhara to Herat, was not expected to make his appearance before the lapse of eight or ten days. I consequently left in company of Mollah Ishak to go amongst the Ersari-Turkomans living in the neighbourhood. Here I entered once the house of Khalfa Niyaz, an ishan who had inherited sanctity, science, and authority from his father. He had a cloister of his own, and had obtained a special license from Mecca to recite sacred poems. In reading, he always had a cup filled with water placed by his side, and would spit into the water whenever he had finished reading a poem. The saliva thus permeated by the sanctity of the words he would then sell as a miraculous panacea to the highest bidder.

As we had an abundance of leisure, my faithful mollah and I, we visited the Lebab-Turkomans, (viz., Turkomans on the bank). We were given quarters in the yard of an abandoned mosque. In the evening hours the Turkomans would bring with them one of their poetical tales, or a poem out of their collections of songs, and I was in the habit of reading it out aloud to them. It was delightful to have them sitting around me in the stilly night within view of the Oxus rolling onward, they listening to me with rapt attention while I read about the brave feats of one of their heroes.

One evening the reading had lasted as late as midnight. I was quite fagged out, and, forgetting to heed the advice I had been frequently given not to lie down near a building in ruins, I stretched my weary limbs close to a wall and very soon fell asleep. I might have slept for an hour when I was suddenly roused by a painful sensation. I jumped up screaming; I thought a hundred poisoned needles had run into my leg. The spot from which the pain proceeded was a small point near the big toe of my right foot. My cries roused an old Turkoman, lying nearest to me, who, without asking any questions, immediately broke out in the following comforting apostrophe: "Unhappy hadji! thou wast bitten by a scorpion, and that at the unlucky season of the *saratan* (canicular or dog days). God have mercy on thee!" Saying these words he seized my foot, and tightly swathing my foot so as almost to sever it from the heel, he immediately applied his mouth to the wounded spot, and began to suck at it with such a violence that I felt it passing through my whole body.

Another soon took his place, and re-swathing my foot twice they left me to my fate, with the sorry comfort that it would be decided before next morning's prayers whether it would please Allah to free me from my pain or from the vanities of this world. Although I was quite stupified with being thrown about, and the burning and stinging pain which kept on increasing in intensity, my memory still reverted in a dull, mechanical way to a recollection of the fact that the scorpions of Belkh were known in ancient times for their venomous nature. My distress was rendered more intolerable by my fears, and that I had given up every hope during the many hours of suffering was proved by the circumstance that, totally unmindful of my incognito, I had broken out into such moans and plaintive exclamations as seemed to be quite outlandish to the Tartars, who, as I subsequently learned, were in the habit of bursting out into shouts of joy on an occasion of this kind. In a few seconds the pain had darted from the tips of my toes to the top of my head, rushing up and down like a stream of fire, but being confined nevertheless to my right side only. The tortures I was suffering beggar all description, and losing all further interest in life I dashed my head against the ground reckless of all consequences, and seeking relief in death. This action of suicidal violence was speedily remarked by the others, and they, taking no heed of my remonstrance, tied me securely to a tree. Thus I continued to be in a prostrate, half-fainting condition for several hours, staring fixedly at the starry vault above me, whilst the cold sweat of agony was gathering in heavy drops on my forehead. The Pleiades were slowly moving towards the west, the beloved West, which I despaired of ever seeing again. Being perfectly conscious I looked forward to the hour of prayer with its sounds of devotion, or rather to the dawn of day. Meanwhile gentle sleep stole over me, sealing my burning eyelids, but I was soon roused from my beneficent slumbers by the monotonous: "La Illah, il Allah!"

When I awoke and began to arrange my ideas I thought I felt a slight cessation of the pain. The burning and stinging sensation grew less and less violent, and about the time that the sun had risen to the height of a lance, I could attempt to stand on my foot, although very feebly and clumsily yet. My companions assured me that the morning prayer had the effect of exorcising the devil which had crept into my body by means of the bite of the scorpion. Of course I dared not suggest any doubts as to this pious version of my cure, but was too well pleased under any circumstances to have got over this dreadful night, the horrors of which will be ever present in my memory.

After having waited for many weary days for the arrival of the caravan from Herat we were at length informed that the looked-for event was near at hand. I immediately hastened to Kerki, in the hope of starting at once. But my hopes in this direction were doomed to disappointment. There were about forty freed slaves from Persia and Herat in the caravan of Mollah Zeman, who were now on their way home under his dearly-paid protection. In journeying alone these poor freedmen run the risk of being pounced upon and sold into slavery again. These former slaves returning home must pay toll here, and this gave occasion to a great deal of noisy demonstration, the kervanbashi having stated the number of slaves at a lower figure than was warranted by the actual facts, whilst the officer of customs claimed toll for others not slaves, setting down every person who was not known to him to be free as a slave, and demanding toll for him. And as neither of them would yield, but stood up in defence of their respective allegations, the hubbub and anger seemed to be in a fair way of never subsiding. It took the entire day to examine the goods, the men, the camels, and the asses. We left at last, not, however, without the escort of the officer of the customs, who kept a vigilant eye upon the caravan lest some straggling travellers might join it at some by-path. He did not leave us until we had crossed the frontiers of Bokhara, and had proceeded on our journey through the desert.

At the first station I gathered that there were a great number of people, besides myself, in the caravan who were longing to set their eyes on the southernmost border of Central Asia. The freedmen appeared to seek our company by preference, that is, the company of the hadjis, and by their joining us I had occasion to hear of truly affecting instances of the misery of some. Near me was sitting a grayheaded old man who had just ransomed his son, aged thirty, in Bokhara, and was taking him back to the arms of a young wife and infants. He had to purchase his son's freedom by sacrificing all he had, the ransom amounting to fifty gold pieces. "I shall rather bear poverty," he said, "than see my son in chains." His home was in Khaf, in Eastern Persia. Not far from me there was lying a muscular man, whose hair had turned gray with mental agony. A few years ago the Turkomans had carried away into slavery his wife, his sister, and six children. For a whole year he had wearily to drag his steps through Khiva and Bokhara before he could find a trace of them. When he had succeeded in tracking them a heavy blow was in store for him. His wife and the two smallest of the children as well as his sister had perished from the hardships of slavery, and of the four remaining children he could purchase the freedom of only the two younger ones; the two elder ones, girls, who had blossomed into beautiful lasses, being rated too high and above the amount of ransom he could afford to pay. There was a group of an aged woman and a young man that attracted our attention. They were mother and son, he a young man from Herat, and she fifty years old. He had purchased the liberty of his mother. Two years before, as she was travelling in the company of her husband and eldest son, they were attacked and made prisoners. Her husband and son were massacred before her eyes, and she was sold into slavery at Bokhara for twenty gold pieces. When her younger son found her and offered to ransom her, they doubled the amount as soon as they recognized him as a son, rapaciously speculating in his filial affection. Let me mention the case of another unfortunate man who had been sold into slavery about eight years previously, and was ransomed after about six years of slavery by his father. On their way home, when but a few hours' march from their native town, both father and son were fallen upon by Turkomans, who immediately carried them to Bokhara to be sold. Now they had both regained their freedom and were returning home.

We were following a southern course, through an interminable level plain destitute of vegetation with the exception of a species of thistle, growing sparsely, which furnishes a sweet morsel for the camel. It is rather wonderful how these animals will pull off with their tongues and swallow a plant the mere touch of which is apt to wound the most callous hand.

On the following morning we reached the ruins of the

town of *Andkhuy.* The caravan and all its members were camping at the lower end of what had been formerly the town, none of the travellers daring to stray away owing to the known predatory dispositions of the inhabitants. The camels of Andkhuy are in greater demand than any other in Turkestan, especially the breed known as Ner, distinguished for the abundance and length of hair on their necks and breasts, their slender build and extraordinary strength. Andkhuy has about two thousand houses, which form the town proper, and about three thousand tents scattered about in the immediate neighbourhood, the edge of the desert and its oases. We were very near becoming engaged in a regular customs war here. In the absence of the Khan, his Vizier wanted to become rich all of a sudden at the expense of the travellers, claiming from them preposterously large tolls, and our kervanbashi was already at loggerheads with him, owing to the extortion attempted by him. From high words it soon came to blows, and, the inhabitants siding with the caravan, both sides were seriously arming and preparing themselves for the worst. Fortunately for the belligerents, the Khan, who was a kind and good-natured man, just then happened to return from a campaign, and by lowering the exaggerated demands of the Vizier he immediately restored order, and matters were amicably arranged. He warned us, as we left, to be on our guard against the Turkomans who, taking advantage of political imbroglios, were infesting the roads. We felt, however, but slight apprehension on that score, the number of our caravan having doubled at Andkhuy, by fresh accessions of travellers.

Our nearest larger station after Andkhuy was *Maimene.* Our caravan camped here outside the town, whilst I myself put up at the *tekkie* (convent) of a certain Ishan Eyub, to whom I had been given a letter of introduction by Hadji Salih. The following day I set up my shop at the corner of a street. My stock of wares, however, was quite reduced owing to the fact that I had not replenished it since the first purchases I had made. One of my companions came up to me and said in a tone of warning and compassion: "Hadji Reshid, half of thy knives, needles, and glass beads, thou hast already eaten up, the other half, together with thy ear, will follow in a short time; what will then become of thee?" The man was perfectly right, but what was I to do? My future caused me many an anxious thought, the Persian border being far away, with winter approaching. I comforted myself very soon, however, with the remembrance of my former experiences amongst the Uzbegs, whom I knew never to allow a hadji or a beggar to leave their door empty-handed. I was sure of bread and fruit, and, now and then, even of a gift of some piece of clothing; and with these I hoped to be able to get on in my journey.

No difficulties about the tolls retained us at Maimene, but the kervanbashi and more prominent merchants of our caravan put off their departure on account of their own private affairs. They wished to attend two or three horse fairs at least, the prices of these animals being very low here. The horses are brought to the fair by the Uzbegs and Turkomans of the environs, and are carried from here to Herat, Kandahar, Kabul, and often to India. Horses which I saw sold in Persia for thirty to forty gold pieces apiece, could be bought here at one hundred to one hundred and sixty tenghis (a tenghi being about ninepence).

Our road now lay continuously through mountainous

regions. Upon reaching the border of Maimene, we were confronted again by a Yuzbashi, performing the office of frontier's guard, who levied upon us an additional toll under the title of whip money, this being the third toll we had to pay within the Khanate of Maimene. A merchant from Herat to whom I complained about this extortion, observed to me: "Thank God we are called upon to pay toll only. In former days travelling in these parts was most dangerous, for the Khan himself was plundering the caravans."

A troop of *Djemshidis* who were sent by the Khan from *Bala Murgab*, for our protection against predatory tribes through whose territories we were to pass, joined us at the frontier, forming our escort. I was informed that our caravan had not been exposed to such imminent danger as awaited them here during the whole journey from Bokhara. We kept our eyes open, carefully glancing to the right and left, and cautiously surveying every little hill we passed. Thus we journeyed on in the greatest suspense, but it was in all probability owing to the size of the caravan and its watchfulness that we escaped being attacked. On the following day we came to a mountain pass, leading to the river Murgab. This road is at places so very steep and so very narrow that a laden camel can pass with great difficulty only. On awaking next morning, I found myself in a valley encircled by high mountains, presenting a most charming picture, with the Murgab winding through with its clear green waters. It took us half an hour to find a convenient place for fording the river. The horses were sent in first, then followed the camels, and after these came the asses. It is a well-known fact that asses fear more the water and mire than fire or death. I therefore deemed it advisable first to place the bag in which I had my papers on the back of a camel, and then, seating myself in the empty saddle on my ass, to urge it on in its passage through the water. At the very first steps the animal took on the gravel-covered bottom of the rapid stream, I had a presentiment of some coming evil. I was eager to dismount, but it was too late, my quadruped had already stumbled and fallen, but starting up at the bursts of laughter from the shore he quickly recovered his equipoise, and rushed back to the dry land. The involuntary bath was especially disagreeable, because I had no change of clothes, and was therefore compelled to cover myself up with carpets and sacks whilst my apparel was getting dry.

At *Murgab*, as everywhere else, the first and only difficulty we encountered was in the matter of the imposts levied upon us. During the whole journey people were constantly repeating that in Afghanistan, which begins on the left shore of the Murgab river, they imposed no tolls on the freed slaves, at least. But this was a mistake. The Khan of the Djemshidis bargained in person with our kervanbashi as to the fees to be paid on the goods, animals, and slaves, and he exacted a larger amount than had been asked by any one else. Even the hadjis were made to pay nearly two shillings each for every ass. The enormous imposts laid on the poor travelling public of Central Asia render commercial intercourse nearly impossible, and the rich treasures growing wild in those regions go, in consequence of these outrageous tolls, to waste and ruin. We lost four days at *Bala Murgab*. It takes four days to go to Herat from Bala Murgab on horseback, and as much again with camels, the road passing through a hilly region; but these calculations offered no standard for the time it would take our caravan to get there, as our camels were very heavily laden. Crossing over the lofty *Telkhghuzar* mountain, we reached before long a place called Kale No, and here again the monotony of our journey was varied by a slight difficulty about toll matters. The road from here to Herat continued through lofty mountains. On the snow-covered peak of Mount *Serabend* our teeth were nearly chattering with the intense cold, although we continuously kept up large fires. On the third day the road went down hill, and we safely dropped into the valley again; reaching, after a day's march, Kerrukh, one of the border villages of Herat.

At the time the caravan left Herat for Bokhara it was spring, and Herat was then besieged by the Afghans under Dost Mohammed. Six months had passed since the news of the capture of the city; its pillage and destruction had reached us long ago, and the intense longing of those of our caravan who were from Herat to see again their families, friends, and houses may therefore be easily imagined. We were, nevertheless, made to wait a whole day until the officer of the Customs, who had come already upon us in the morning, had, in the overbearing and supercilious manner peculiar to the Afghans, finished making up, with a great deal of ado, an extensive list of every traveller, animal, and each piece of goods we had with us. I had imagined Afghanistan to be a country with somewhat of a regular administration; nay, I had fondly hoped that my sufferings would terminate here, and that I might dispense henceforth with the assumption of the character of a dervish. Alas! I was sadly mistaken. Nowhere had we been treated in such a brutal manner as we were treated here by the Afghan Customs collectors. We had to pay duty on the very clothes we wore, with the exception of the shirt. On my ass I had to pay a duty of six krans, and he who was not able to pay had simply all his things confiscated.

Towards evening, when the plundering was over, the governor of Kerrukh, who has the rank of a major, made his appearance in order that he might examine us. At me he took a good long look, evidently being struck by my foreign features, and immediately summoned the kervanbashi to make some whispered inquiries about me. He then called me to come near him, made me sit down, and treated me with marked politeness. Whilst talking with me he studiously turned the conversation on Bokhara, smiling always in a mysterious way as he did so. But I remained faithful to the part I had assumed. On taking leave he wanted to shake hands with me in the English fashion, but I anticipated the motion of his hand by raising mine as if in the act of bestowing a *fatiha* upon him, whereupon he left me with a laugh. We were finally allowed to leave Kerrukh, and entered Herat on the following morning after a toilsome journey of six weeks.

XXVI.

IN HERAT AND BEYOND IT.

THE large, flourishing valley, intersected by canals, in the centre of which the city of Herat is situated, is called *Djolghei-Herat* (the Plain of Herat). I saw with surprise how rapidly the wounds inflicted by war had healed. But two months ago savage Afghan hordes had been camping in the neighbourhood, trampling down and laying waste everything, and behold! to-day the fields and vineyards are boasting of their intensest verdure, and the meadows are covered with a luxuriant sward dotted all over with field-flowers, making them look like embroidered work.

We entered by the gate of *Dervaze-Irak* (viz., the Gate of Irak). The gate itself and the houses surrounding it were one mass of ruins. Not far from the gate, in the interior of the city, was a lofty fortification, which, owing to its phenomena, was more particularly exposed to the hostile missiles, and now there was nothing left of it but a heap of stones. The wooden framework from door and window was gone, it having been used up as fuel, of which there was great scarcity in the city during the siege. In the deserted openings of the houses were seen naked Afghans and Hindoos squatting, worthy keepers of a city in ruins. At every step I advanced the desolation became more appalling; entire quarters of the town were empty and deserted. The bazaar alone, or rather that part of it covered with the cupola, which has withstood many a siege, presented an interesting picture of life characteristic of the confluence of Persia, India, and Central Asia at this place. It was a wonderful sight to see the astonishing variety of types, complexions, and costumes amongst Afghans, Hindoos, Turkomans, Persians, and Jews. The Afghan, whose national costume consists of a shirt, drawers, and a dirty blanket, assumes sometimes the English red coat, but on his head he wears the never-failing picturesque Hindoo-Afghan turban. The more civilized affect in part the Persian dress. Arms are the universal fashion; private citizens as well as soldiers seldom come to the bazaar without sword and shield, and persons wishing to look distinguished carry with them a whole arsenal. The Afghan is both in appearance and demeanour the rudest and most savage, every one passing him with a great show of humility, but never did people hate a conqueror more intensely than those of Herat the Afghan. The surging, variegated crowd before me was pleasant to look at. There were moments when, seeing Afghan soldiers in English uniforms and with shakos on their heads, I thought that after all I was now in a country where I had nothing to fear from Islamite fanaticism, and that I might drop the mask which had become intolerable to me. But only for a moment, for upon reflection I could not help remembering that I was in the East, where appearances are most deceptive.

As I mentioned before, my purse was quite empty,

and as soon as I arrived in Herat I was compelled to sell my ass. The poor beast had grown quite thin with the fatigues of the journey, and all I could get for him did not amount to more than twenty-six krans, of which sum I had to spend immediately five krans for duty, and in discharge of various small debts I had contracted. My situation was anything but a pleasant one. In the matter of bread I could still manage somehow; but the nights being very cold, I had to suffer intensely, in spite of the hardness of my body, in being compelled to sleep, thinly clad, on the bare ground in roofless ruins, with nothing to cover myself up with. The only thought that infused a more hopeful spirit in me was the reflection that Persia was but at a distance of ten days' march from Herat. But to get there was a task of enormous difficulty. By myself I could not possibly go, and the caravan intending to go to Meshed was but just forming, waiting for an accession to its numbers and a more auspicious time for starting, as the Tekke Turkomans not only infested the roads at that time, but had boldly advanced as far as the gates of the city, kidnapping people and pillaging villages and caravans. My companions, too, who had come with me from Samarkand and Kerki, had all dispersed; and no one but Mollah Ishak, my honest companion from Kungrat, remained with me. He would go begging for food and fuel during the day and prepare the supper in the evening; and then it was only with the greatest difficulty that I could persuade the good fellow to share the modest meal with me out of the same plate. This Mollah Ishak acted in fact a most interesting part in my adventures, and he is at this present moment a Hungarian citizen and an *employé* at the library of the Hungarian Academy of Sciences.

I tried everything in my power to procure myself the necessary travelling expenses. I waited upon the reigning prince, Serdar Mehemmed Yakub Khan, a youth sixteen years old, and the son of the then king of Afghanistan. The king had entrusted this youth with the government of the conquered province, he having had to hasten to Kabul where his own brothers were plotting to deprive him of his throne. The young prince was residing in a palace very much battered by the siege. He was dressed in a uniform with a high-standing collar, and would sit, most of the time, in an arm-chair at the window; and when wearied with the great number of petitioners which it was his official duty to receive, he would order military drills and manœuvres to be executed on the place below his window and inspect them from there.

As I was stepping into the courtyard of the palace in the company of Mollah Ishak, the military drill was just at its height. Near the door of the reception hall a crowd of servants, military men and petitioners were lounging. Thanks to my huge turban and pilgrim-like appearance every one made way for me, and I could reach the hall without interference from anybody. When I stepped into the hall I found the prince seated as usual in his arm-chair, with the Vizier on his right side, whilst ranged along the wall were standing other officers, mollahs, and people from Herat. In front of the prince were the keeper of the seal and four or five servants. As became my position as a dervish I entered with the customary salutation, and exciting no sort of comment by it, I went up straight to the prince, seating myself between him and the Vizier, after having pushed aside the latter, a stout Afghan, to make room for me. There was a general laugh at this intermezzo, but I kept my countenance and immediately raised my hand to recite the customary prayer. The prince looked at me fixedly during the prayer. I observed an expression of surprise and hesitation stealing over his face, and after I had said "Amen," and the whole company smoothing their beards responded to it, he jumped up from his chair, and pointing at me with his finger, he exclaimed, laughing and yet half astonished, "I swear by God, thou art an Englishman!"

A loud burst of laughter followed the original remark of the young prince, but he, in no wise disconcerted, approached, stood up in front of me, and then clapping his hands like a child who had guessed right at something he added, "Let me be thy victim! confess thou art an Ingiliz in disguise." But I now pretended to act as if the joke had been carried too far for my forbearance, and said: "*Sahib mekum* (stop this); dost thou know the proverb—'he who even in fun takes a true believer to be an unbeliever, becomes one himself?' Give me rather something for my *fatiha* that I may continue my journey." My grave looks and the citation made by me somewhat perplexed the young prince, and sitting down again, half ashamed of himself, he excused himself by saying that he had never seen a dervish from Bokhara with such features. I answered him that I was not from Bokhara but from Constantinople; and having shown him as a proof my passport and spoken to him about his cousin Djelaleddin Khan, who had visited Mecca and Constantinople in 1860 and met with a most distinguished reception on the part of the Sultan, he seemed to be perfectly satisfied. My passport passed from hand to hand, everybody approved of its contents, and the prince giving me a couple of krans called upon me to visit him again whilst I remained in Herat, an invitation of which I did not fail to avail myself.*

Time dragged on heavily while I was waiting for a caravan at Herat, and I grew very impatient at the delay. There was a sad and depressing air about the city, terror of the savage conqueror could be read in every face, and the recent siege and devastation continued to form the ever-recurring topics of conversation. At length, on the 10th of November, 1863, I left this entrance-gate to Central Asia, joining a larger caravan going to Meshed, with which I was to accomplish the remaining portion of my journey. The caravan consisted of two thousand persons, half of whom were Hezares from Kabul who, for the most part poor and miserable, were proceeding with their kith and kin on a pilgrimage to the shrines of Shi-ite saints. The caravan forming thus a large body of men, its members were subdivided again into smaller bands. I was assigned to a troop of Afghans from Kandahar, who were dealing in furs and indigo, and were conveying these articles of merchandise to Persia.

Our road took us through several smaller places. Near the village of *Shebesh* begins a large forest, spreading on the banks of the Heri, which serves as a hiding-place for the lurking Turkomans. *Kuhsun* was the last place in

* It may interest my readers to know that it was the same prince who afterwards succeeded his father Shir Ali Khan upon the throne of Kabul. In spite of having proved himself at the beginning of his career to be a valiant soldier, he nevertheless turned afterwards a cowardly man in the hands of his fanatic subjects by participating in the murder of Sir Louis Cavagnari and the rest of the English officers who took part in the British Mission to Kabul. In spite of his undoubted crime, the English Government did not put him to death—which he fully deserved—but interned him in India, where he is now living on a generous pension with his family. The miserable wretch is always boasting, as I am told, of having been the only Asiatic who penetrated my incognito.

the territory of Herat; and here we were again delayed for two days in order to settle for the last duty levied upon us by Afghan rapacity. On the following day we observed, from the tower of the caravansary, an immense cloud of dust rolling on towards the village. The shout of "Turkomans! Turkomans!" was heard on all sides. The terror shown at the caravansary and in the village beggars all description. When the cloud of dust came near enough to allow us to see by whom it was raised, we discovered to our relief a herd of wild asses, who, after coming quite near the village, turned round and fled towards the desert. From Kuhsun to the Persian frontier extends the region, owning no master, which is overrun by the alamans (bands of robbers), despatched there by the tribes of the Tekkès, Salors, and Sariks, who push their raids as far south as Khaf and even Bihrdjan. These bands, numbering about a hundred horsemen, attack the villages, capture the inhabitants and drive away the flocks.

Although our caravan was so very large, it was nevertheless thought prudent to reinforce our great numbers by an escort composed of every man in Kuhsun able to carry arms. I thought that I had emptied the cup of bitter sufferings to the very dregs during my wandering through Central Asia, but it was reserved for the journey from Herat to Meshed to convince me that there may be miseries greater still than those I had already endured. To this day I ask myself with astonishment how my body, used to European life, could brave all these hardships. I was utterly destitute of money, of everything, and to satisfy my daily wants I was thrown upon the charity of the Afghans and Tadjiks, from whom I begged right and left and got what I could. The Tadjiks were poor pilgrims, themselves but scantily supplied with the bare necessaries of life. And as to the Afghans, their known avarice and meanness of character might give me a dispensation from telling how hard it was to excite their pity. I fared best when we happened to pitch our tents near some inhabited village. In such a case my Tartar and I divided the village between us; I would go in one direction and beg for wood and fuel, whilst he would go in another begging for bread and flour, and on meeting again we would exchange parts.

The inhabitants of this region, though very poor themselves, did not turn a deaf ear to our appeals for charity. With food we were tolerably supplied, poor and mean as it was in quality; but what caused us the most terrible suffering was the bitter cold prevailing towards autumn in this part of the world. Such was the effect of the cold cutting blasts coming from the north-eastern plains that the intense cold would pierce through the thickest cloak in which a person might wrap himself; and the animals themselves came very near being benumbed by it. All the way from Shebesh until we were two stations from Meshed, I had to pass the night in the open air, lying on the hard frozen ground, in the ragged dervish dress which I had on me, and which served the purposes of both pillow and coverlet. Many a time I would not dare to close my eyes for fear of freezing to death. I besought the hard-hearted Afghans to let me have one of their spare horse blankets; with chattering teeth and in a most piteous voice I vainly appealed for hours together to the cruel barbarians bundled up in their warm fur skin cloaks. They only jeered at me, saying, "Dance, hadji, and thou wilt get warm." The high plateaus of Eastern Persia will for ever rank in my memory with the sand of the deserts of Central Asia.

Near Kafir-Kale we met with a caravan coming from

Meshed. From a member of this caravan I learned that Colonel Dolmage, an English officer in the Persian service, an old acquaintance of mine, was still residing in Meshed, a piece of news which was very welcome to me. Ferimon was the first village inhabited by Persians, and a warm stable made me forget the sufferings of many a day past. At length, on the twelfth day after our departure from Herat, the gilded cupolas of Imam Riza loomed up before our eyes. We had reached the city of Meshed, for the sight of which I had been longing; and my heart bounded with joy as I first caught sight of it.

Besides, in approaching Meshed, there were other motives—motives of humanity—at play, which quickened my pulse and made my heart beat with something of the regained dignity of a man who escapes from moral slavery. In Meshed I was at length to be restored to myself; I was to fling off, to some extent, the artful disguises with which, in fear of life, limb and liberty, I had had to surround myself, to discard the shameful rags which lowered me in my own estimation, to put an end to the pitiful anxieties to which I had been continually exposed, and last not least to exchange a life of hardship, discomforts and privations for one of comparative ease and comfort. Nor did I entertain the usual fears, which haunted me elsewhere, as to the reception I might meet at the hands of the authorities; the governor of the province was an enlightened prince, an uncle of the king of Persia, and under his auspices the government was conducted, in appearance at least, more in accordance with European ideas. To all these cheering reflections was added the hope of meeting and embracing again, after all these weary wanderings, an old friend of mine—perhaps the solitary European who had pitched his tent so far east and was now living in Meshed.

Under all these combined impressions the very cupola, under which the mortal remains of Imam Riza repose, blazing with its resplendent light far into the outlying country, seemed to me a beacon which was to guide me to a harbour of safety. I even caught the enthusiasm of the thousands of people who were flocking to the tomb of the saint, and could almost imagine myself one of the pilgrims who hail with emotions of unutterable thankfulness and pious joy the sight of the holy place, after having wearily wandered over the immense distances from their several homes, India, Turkestan or Afghanistan.

Here as elsewhere, near holy places, the pious Shi-ites, on coming within sight of it, are prompted, by their feelings of devotion and gratitude at having been permitted to behold the glories of the city of Meshed, to offer up some tangible tokens of their sentiments by heaping up stones, adorning trees and bushes with rags representing all the colours of the rainbow, and the singing of sacred songs and the chanting of hymns.

It may not be uninteresting to know who this Imam Riza is, the renown of whose sanctity has made such a lasting and deep impression upon the minds of a large portion of the Eastern world. Of the twelve Imams he is the eighth. He was a contemporary of the Caliph Maamun, a son of the famous Harun el Rashid. This Caliph's envy and jealousy of Imam Riza was roused by the general esteem in which he was held, and the unbounded devotion which was shown to him by the sect of Shi-ites, then already very numerous, but not daring yet to enter publicly into the area of religious sectarianism. He was banished by the Caliph to Tus, a town in the vicinity of the present site of Meshed. The banishment had not the desired effect; in his abode of humiliation he became again the object of general veneration, so the Caliph had poison administered to him in a cup of wine, thus ridding himself of a dangerous and hated rival. The memory of his name did not die with him; from a beloved leader of a sect he rose to be a martyred saint, and the very name of Meshed is synonymous with a place of martyrdom. His death in exile seems to have especially commended him to the imagination of the travelling public as their patron saint; and he was honoured, in this, his quality, with the title of Sultan al Gureba (Prince of Strangers). Nor is it difficult to appreciate the enthusiasm of the travellers in approaching the holy city. Apart from their pious feelings for their safe arrival here, it means their having securely steered their way through all the dangers of the long road, not the least of which is the possible capture by Turkomans.

XXVII.

IN MESHED.

NATURE seemed to have put on her holiday garb as we were approaching the city. The weather was splendid; it was one of those fine autumnal mornings which are so common in the Eastern part of Persia. The road leading to the city passes through a bare almost level tract, its monotony being relieved only here and there by a few hills. The contrast which the city presented to the unromantic aspect of the environs was all the more striking. With its bright and flashing cupolas, and surrounded by gardens, it lay there like a rich and glittering gem embedded in a rare setting of leafy verdure. My gaze was fixed upon the buildings that seemed to detach themselves as we approached from the confused mass presented at a distance. For the time being I was utterly lost in thought, careless of the movements of the caravan, and even my looking at the city was more in a dreamy vacant way than for the purpose of gratifying my curiosity. The traveller had for once merged in the human being; casting aside all interest in historical reminiscences, not even caring to recall the names of the great saints whose splendid tombs formed the attraction of the place, I fairly rioted in the consciousness of being able now to turn my back upon the black and ugly experiences of the past, and looked forward to the attractive vista of a bright future.

I was roused from these pleasant reveries by our entrance through the Dervaze Herat (Herat Gate). We passed along the wide and long street of Pajin Khiaban (Lower Alley), and proceeded towards the Sahni Sherif (the Holy Vestibule). A very pleasing sight is offered by the broad canal, winding through the city, its banks studded with trees which spread a pleasant shade; indeed this is a feature rendering Meshed one of the most attractive cities in Iran. The concourse of people, representing all the nations of Asia who are adherents of the Shi-ite faith, gives a most striking character to the streets, which are pulsating with stirring life. Every variety of costume prevalent in Persia and the whole of Eastern Asia meet the eye wherever you look. It does not take long to realize the fact that Meshed is one of the strongholds of Shi-itism. The proud Sunnites, the Turkoman and Uzbeg, walk about with an humble and apologetic air as if to beg pardon of those whom he oppressed in his own home; whilst the men of Bokhara, Hezare, India and Herat are treading proudly and lightly on a ground which seems to inspire them with a consciousness of their superiority—their forms erect, their carriage haughty and independent and their looks scornful and defiant. The Sunnite is by no means, however, exposed to any danger of retaliation on the part of those whose compatriots have often been the victims of his ferocity. In Iran he is safe, but he cannot shake off a guilty sense of the merited retribution his cruelty amply deserves, and the impress of this unpleasant consciousness betrays itself in his movements and demeanour.

Especially during the bright days of autumn the streets are crowded with a dense mass of humanity, rolling in an endless stream along the thoroughfares, and in vain does the eye attempt to find a resting-place amid the varied confusion of the spectacle, nor is it possible in the throng of conflicting sights to treasure up some distinct recollection which might shape itself into a reminiscence at some future day. The neighbourhood of the magnificent building of the Imam for several hundred paces forms the centre of most bewildering sights and sounds. Standing beside their booths or stands, or in front of their shops, on both sides of the street, on the banks of the canal, and moving through the streets, are to be seen and heard a multitude of men, active, scrambling, energetic, carrying their wares on their heads, shoulders, or in their hands, pushing through the crowd, offering them vociferously for sale, and producing a strange din and noise whilst they recommend them to buyers with their sing-song cries. It seems utterly impossible to elbow your way through this compact mass of humanity, and yet there is a sort of order in this wild confusion, for an actual block but seldom occurs. Trying to disentangle from this surging crowd the elements that compose it, you will see that it is made up of foot passengers, men on horseback, laden camels, strings of mules, fastened to each other lengthwise, loaded with bales of merchandize, or bearing travelling-baskets, out of which pretty, half-veiled ladies peep coquettishly at you, all of them passing to and fro, going or coming through the gates of the city. The great business of pilgrimage is being meanwhile briskly carried on, the stereotyped watchwords are passed around; the departing pilgrim being invariably saluted with a "*Ziareti Khabul*" (May thy pilgrimage be accepted), and the new arrival with an "*Iltimasi dua*" (Pray for me). The mendicant class, the parasites on the holy tree of pilgrimage, ply their business with remarkable success, keeping the even tenor of their own way, and never allowing themselves to be disconcerted or abashed by the chaos reigning around them or any rebuffs of which they may be the recipients. The new-comers are their victims; on these they fasten, and he must be very clever who can get away unscathed from them. The Seids (descendants of the prophet), these princes of Eastern beggardom, are conspicuous alike for their huge green turbans and their untiring importunity; with their keen eagle's eyes they descry and pounce at once upon the stranger, offering their services as the fittest guides to the holy places. So the chorus of singing, yelling and shouting goes on swelling until it grows to be a mighty deafening roar, and the movement in the streets seems to be getting every moment more and more complicated and chaotic. Nor is the scene always free from violence, for you see the excitable mule-driver from Shiraz forcing his way with curses through the crowd, hitting wildly about him, those nearest him scampering away yelling and screaming. Yet this scene of confusion is only an apparent one, especially to the unfamiliar eye of the European, who cannot separate order from quiet, for an attempt to push your way through the throng is attended with no evil consequences or harm; every one is sure to reach safely the place he is bound for. This bustling life, however, was quite agreeable to me after the experience of the dull and stolid constraint so characteristic of the cities of Turkestan which I had lately seen.

I now wished to meet as soon as possible my English

friend, Colonel Dolmage, of whom I spoke before. First of all I entered a caravansary in order to wash myself, and to put in some kind of decent order my tattered toilet. This done, the next thing was to find the house where my friend lived. It is always a ticklish thing to go about in Meshed inquiring after the whereabouts of a Frengi, but it becomes immeasurably so in the case of a person like me—who bore about him the unmistakable garb, gait and mien of a hadji—undertaking to do it. By dint of perseverance and much ingenious cross-questioning I stood at last in front of his house. Almost overcome with emotion I knocked at the door. I heard footsteps approaching, and a moment later a servant opened the door. The portal was as quickly re-shut in my face, for the servant just deigning to glance at me, overwhelmed me with a volley of oaths, and slammed the door. My emotion disappeared in the twinkling of an eye, and angry and impatient at this unexpected rebuff, I vigorously set to rapping at the door again. The servant reappeared, and this time I gave him no opportunity for parley or remark, but went past him into the court without vouchsafing a solitary word of explanation to him. The man was quite dumbfounded with what seemed to him my impertinence, but recovering himself soon, he asked me roughly what I, a hadji, wanted with his master, who, as I knew, was an unbeliever. I very emphatically told him that this did not concern him, but that he should without delay advise his master that a stranger from Bokhara wished to see him.

Whilst the servant was gone, I leisurely found my way into a room, on entering which I was struck with the sight of the furniture, which vividly recalled European comfort and civilization. The furniture was quite plain, merely a table and chairs, but to my unaccustomed eye they looked like an epitome of all the things towards which my orphaned heart was warming. Yes, these lifeless, homely objects of daily use seemed sanctified to me, and I stood gazing at them as if they were things of life. A newspaper on the table, the *Levant Herald*, caught my eyes next, and to seize it and devour its contents was the work of a moment. How many things had happened since I had a newspaper in my hands! Every item of news, the humblest and that of the highest political importance, possessed an equally intense interest for me, and immersed in the perusal of its columns I even forgot Colonel Dolmage, who had softly entered and was now standing before me. Dressed in a European uniform, a fine specimen of British manhood, he looked at me silently, searchingly, but I vainly watched for a look of recognition. Thus standing face to face for a few moments, the situation became almost painful. To be sure the ravages which hunger, thirst, cold, anxiety, and the thousand trials of the journey had made in my appearance, sadly altered my looks, and no wonder the young colonel failed to recall in the ragged hadji before him his former acquaintance. I broke in upon the silence by exclaiming in English, "What, Colonel, do you not recognize me?" The familiar voice dispelled like a charm his uncertainty as to who I was, and in an instant we were locked in a close embrace. He now remembered everything, knew even something by hearsay of the perilous journey I had ventured upon, and, seeing the pitiful condition I was in, tears of manly compassion rose to the young officer's eyes.

Distinctions of class, profession, or nationality, entering so largely into European life, separating man from man, lose their hold upon Europeans meeting in the distant East. The great West, seen at that distance, becomes their common country; they are drawn together by the bond of common views, feelings and modes of thought which obliterate the artificial lines of nationality—nay, they feel for, and treat each other as only blood relations and brothers would in Europe. Colonel Dolmage's conduct towards me illustrated this in a conspicuous manner. His very first question, accompanied by a look of almost tender sympathy, "For God's sake, what have you been doing? what has happened to you?" made me feel like a long-lost brother who had found his way home again. I saw the terrible alterations and the sad havoc which hardships had made in my appearance reflected in his questions and accompanying looks. He was a most sympathizing listener to the story of my late experiences, and it was rather late in the evening when I rose to leave him.

Colonel Dolmage proved my staunch friend during the four weeks I stayed in Meshed, and although I dare say I occasioned him no little trouble, I found him unflagging in his zeal for my welfare. Not only did his kind offices largely contribute to making my stay in Meshed an exceedingly pleasant one, but to his generosity and active friendship I was chiefly indebted for the means which enabled me to proceed on my journey with renewed vigour and a cheerful mind. And no matter what unpleasantnesses the interest he bore me drew upon him, his invariable good humour and friendly conduct to me remained unaltered.

Upon my arrival in Meshed, after having visited Colonel Dolmage, I felt, above all, the necessity of recuperating somewhat before turning my attention to the remarkable sights of the city. The first few days, therefore, I entirely devoted to rest, a species of *dolce far niente* which did infinite good to both body and mind, invigorating the one and brightening the other. After my few days' rest I returned with redoubled interest to the main duty of a traveller, to see, observe, inquire, and remember. Nor is there any other city in Eastern Persia abounding in such a variety of curiosities as may be seen here. Indeed I was sorely puzzled which way first to turn my attention. Rich in monuments appealing alike to the student of history, the curious in holy things, and the literary man—it is hard to know where to begin.

Probably led by the dervish instinct, developed in me by months of devout pilgrimage, I found myself entering the Sahni Sherif, looking about me with unfeigned admiration. The quick eyes of several loitering Seids did not fail to discover the stranger and the Sunnite pilgrim in me; and I was soon surrounded by them, each anxious to acquaint me with the notable features and wonders of the holy tomb. That the sanctuary at which Conolly, Fraser, Burnes, Chanikoff, nay, the official Eastwick himself, endeavoured from a safe distance to steal a hasty glance, was thrown open to me, and I was almost forced to enter it by the hungry descendants of the prophet, involuntarily recurred to my mind as I declined the services proffered by them. For, truth to tell, the months of compulsory pilgrimage I had gone through had strangely palled my appetite for holy sights appertaining to Islamism, and I felt relieved when I was left to myself to continue my observations. My attention was next engaged by the monument lying to the left of the Sahn, and the splendid mosque of Gowher Shah. The former of these two buildings surpasses in magnificence and richness the most renowned tombs to which the Mohammedan world perform their devout pilgrimages, not even excepting those of Medina, Nedjef, Kerbela and Kum. It is inlaid with gold inside and outside. Much of its former glory is gone, and many of its richest ornaments have been carried away at different periods of time by Uzbegs, Afghans and others. Since the monument was first erected it has been several times plundered. Meshed suffered most at the hands of Abdul Mumin, Khan of Bokhara, in 1587, when entering it at the head of the Uzbegs the city was sacked and its inhabitants carried into slavery. It was laid waste again by the Afghans, and at different times civil wars spread desolation within its very walls. The golden ball on the top of the dome of the tomb, weighing four hundred pounds, is said to have been removed by the impious hands of the sons of Nadir, and several jewels of great price passed, in later times, into the unhallowed possession of the rebel leader Salar. But in spite of the ruthless conduct of foreign enemies and the violence of intestine war, the tomb still harbours an immense amount of treasure. The walls of the monument are fairly resplendent with jewels and trinkets of the rarest kinds offered up to their favourite saint by the devout Shi-ites. The eye is dazzled by the splendour of the pious gifts, consisting of precious ornaments of every imaginable shape, a headgear shaped like a plumed crest (*djikka*) of diamonds, a shield and sabre studded with rubies and emeralds, massive candelabra of great weight, costly bracelets, and necklaces of incalculable value.

The sight without and the sights within court a like amount of admiration, and the balance is constantly preponderating, now in one now in the other direction. Without the cupola and the towers with their rich incrustations of gold, within the massive fretted work and grating of silver, the artistically stained windows, the construction of the done denoting a fine perception of refinement and elegance in form, and rich Oriental carpet stuffs with diamonds and precious stones woven into them, continually challenged and divided my wondering interest. This cold and glittering accumulation of wealth was not wanting in the touch of humanity which warmed it into a scene of life and bustle. The groups within were not mere sight-seers, come to gratify their curiosity. They were pious visitors at a holy shrine, with silent devotion stamped upon their features, denoting ecstasy, enthusiasm, deep contrition, humble self-abasement, and every shade of religious joy and sadness, which none so well as the faces of Islamite devotees know how to express or simulate; whilst to their lips rose muttered prayers, interrupted by guttural yells, their chests were heaving with wild sobs. Those who did not know their prayers by heart, or could not read from the tablets inscribed with them, which were suspended from the grating, had them repeated by the leader of the group they belonged to. All seem anxious to propitiate the divinity by acts and prayers of praise or humiliation in order to secure a place in the dwellings of the blessed and happy. One all-absorbing feeling seems to inspire at such a moment men of all races and classes alike, whether they be lords, merchants, or servants—the cautious dwellers in Central Asia, the shrewd men from Isfahan and Shiraz, the guileless Turks, or the ferocious Bakhtiaris and Kurds. None are too high or too low for the performance of acts of pious tenderness; the sons of Khans, the Mirzas and the poor peasants mingle freely together; and it is a touching and sublime spectacle, indeed, to see these sons of Asia, both rude and refined, pressing forward to kiss, with unfeigned humility, the silver trellis, the padlock hanging from the door of the grating and the hallowed ground itself. Mingling with this pious crowd, pushing their way to the groups and bystanders, directly soliciting alms, or offering their services as guides, exhorting, praying, explaining, felicitating; in one word, doing all they can to excite the charity of the spectators and to obtain some gift, are the Seids and priests. Upon them the sublimity of the spectacle is lost; their souls are dead to every other influence except that of insatiable greed. The pilgrim leaves the shrine with awe-struck backward step, and on leaving it and standing outside the gate in the open air, his heart swells with a holy triumph; his soul is washed clean from the stain of his former sins, and he may plod on now in blissful security for the remainder of his mundane existence. Nor is this all. Like the pilgrim to Mecca, whose visit to this holy place earns him the coveted title of hadji, he may henceforth assume the equally honoured surname of Meshedi, and prefix it to his name, with the privilege of having it engraved on his signet, and on his tombstone when he is gathered to his forefathers.

Of the mosque of Gowher Shah, which I visited next, the Persians say with great justice, that whilst the monument of Imam Riza is more gorgeous, the mosque far surpasses it architecturally. The mosque is situated in the same court, opposite to the monument. The *kashi* work (glazed tiles) enters largely into the structure inside and outside, and there is an artistic beauty about it which more than compensates for the comparative absence of richer materials such as gold and silver. The lofty portal is admirable, both for the elegance of its design, and the rich colouring it derives from the many-hued and brilliant kashi work, especially when lit up by the rays of the sun. The gate is of the same style as those I saw in Herat and Samarkand; it is certain that they all date from the reign of Shahrukh Mirza, nor is it unlikely that they were the work of the same architect. The Medrese Khanum in Samarkand, and the Musalla in Herat may be more magnificent and luxurious, but in point of artistic beauty they did not surpass the one at Meshed, and, indeed, I am tempted to award the latter the palm of superior beauty.

Shaping my course after that of the numerous pilgrims and beggars, who all went in the same direction on leaving this splendid building, I went to the refectory of Imam Riza, or as the natives call it, *Ashbaz Khanei Hazret* (the kitchen of his highness). The Hazret, so his holiness is entitled, *par excellence*, enjoys the reputation of being immensely rich. He is very hospitable, and every new-comer has the choice of becoming his guest; but this hospitality is limited in point of time to seven days only. The wealthier pilgrims rarely take advantage of this liberal arrangement, but the poorer classes eagerly avail themselves of the privilege of boarding and lodging at his Highness's expense. The convenience of the guest is cared for on a very large scale, and the vast machinery of baths and caravansaries, boarding-houses and soap-boiling houses, of which his Highness is the owner, is put in motion in order to satisfy the various wants of the strangers flocking to the Hazret. I could not resist the temptation of adding one more experience to those for which I was indebted to my Oriental disguise. Indeed, hunger did not attract me, for the table of Colonel Dolmage was supplied with everything I could desire. I went to the place where the hungry were fed, my Bokhariot dress being a safe passport to the delights of an Asiatic meal. I squatted down, unheeded in the midst of the crowd of hungry Shi-ite and Sunnite pilgrims. Very soon large dishes of smoking rice were brought in by a troop of servants. Rancid fat and damaged rice, of the kind of which I had already collected reminiscences enough to last me for a lifetime, made up the delicious dish, which gave me but a mean opinion of the boasted riches of his Highness. I pretended to be as eager about fishing out my share of it as any other, splashing about with my fist in the plate, but thought it best to save my appetite for a more favourable occasion, and felt no little relieved when the dishes were removed.

The avarice and greediness, so characteristic of the Persians, induce me to believe that their admiration for Imam Riza is owing, not so much to the renown of his sanctity and the inviolable right of asylum belonging to him, as to the vast and fabulous wealth of which he is supposed to be the owner. They are extremely jealous of the visits of unprivileged persons to the holy places; Hindoos, Jews and Armenians not being allowed to approach within sight of them, for their very glances at a distance of five hundred paces are supposed to profane and desecrate them.

An accident led me to discover the precarious condition in which the Jews were living in Meshed. I met one day in the streets of Meshed a former fellow-traveller of mine, on my journey from Bokhara. As he was about to pass on without heeding me, I called out after him, knowing him to be a Jew, "Yehudi, Yehudi." He hurriedly came up to me and said confidentially in a low voice: "For God's sake, Hadji, do not call me a Jew here. Beyond these walls I belong to my nation, but here I must play the Moslem." It was the old story over again of persecution fanned by bigotry and fanaticism, and taken advantage of by murderers and robbers.

The cause of their present distress and their fear of being recognized as Jews dates from an occurrence which had happened several years ago in Meshed. A Persian doctor, who was consulted by a Jewess about an eruption on her hand, advised her to plunge her hands into the entrails of a newly-slaughtered dog. She took his advice, and had one of those unhappy street scavengers of the East killed in order to try the cure prescribed to her. Unfortunately she had this done on the very day on which the Mohammedans celebrated the Eidi Kurban (Feast of Sacrifice). The rumour of it soon spread amongst the people; and the slaughtering of the dog was interpreted as an impious mockery of the religious rites of the true believers. The rapacity and murderous instincts of the mob gladly seized this frivolous pretext wherewith to cloak their thirst for the blood of the detested Jew, and their love of pillage. In an instant the Jewish quarter of the city was overrun with a savage rabble, rioting, robbing and murdering. Those that survived the fatal day had their lives spared on condition of abjuring the faith of their fathers and embracing that of their oppressors and persecutors. They yielded to dire necessity, but in their hearts they remained Jews, conforming only in outward appearance, as long as they had to stay in Meshed. Years had passed since, and although the tolerant spirit, which began to prevail under the benign influence of European interference, made the Mohammedans relax somewhat their former rigour, the Jews still deemed it more prudent to pass themselves off in Meshed for Mohammedans.

When I was preparing for the journey to Bokhara, I constantly trembled lest in those regions my disguise of Stambulism should be pierced, and the discovery of my true nationality entail upon me the gravest consequences. Since that time I had been in Bokhara and successfully passed the ordeal of prying eyes and suspicious looks.

I then little dreamt that, in returning from Bokhara, the happy facility with which I could master the most different dialects, would place me in the dilemma of being considered by all my fellow-pilgrims, on account of my speech and costume, as a genuine Bokhariot. No doubt constant practice had made the dialect of Central Asia perfectly easy and natural to me. In vain I repelled the insinuation; in vain I claimed to be a true son of Stambul. I invariably received the reply, accompanied by a knowing twinkle of the eye, "Yes, yes, we know the Bokhariots well; here you would all disguise yourselves for fear of retribution for your cruelties at home. But your trouble is in vain, we see through it all." Luckily such doubts of my statements were of little consequence to me now, I being in a country where at least the semblance of a government existed. But, nevertheless, I could not help being amused at these strange mutations of fortune; to be taken for a Bokhariot in Meshed, for a man from Meshed in Bokhara, and all throughout the journey now for a Turk, now for a Russian, a European and what not! Truly Upper Asia is a land of disguise and incognito, especially in the case of a traveller. How my heart yearned towards the West; how I wished to escape from this world of deceit and dissimulation! I thought, with something akin to ecstasy, of the moment when I should see the beloved West again, the land whose failings, vices and abuses I had learned to forget, and whose superiority over Asia I alone now remembered; the land where lay my native country, the goal of all my efforts and aspirations.

Among the ruins of Tus to the north of Meshed lies, according to the belief of modern Persians, the tomb of one of the greatest of Iran's bards, the tomb of Firdusi.

Before leaving the city I made an excursion to it. It was with feelings of sincere piety and admiration that I approached the modest monument which commemorates the resting-place of one of the greatest national poets of the world. In sixty thousand verses he sang the history of his people, without admitting more than a few foreign, that is Arabic, words into his narration. This wonderful feat will be especially appreciated, if the fact is borne in mind that Persian—which he wrote as well as the modern Persian does—contains four words of Arabic origin to every six words purely Iranian. His generous patriotism rebelled against the thought of employing the language of the oppressors of his country. Not only as a poet, not only as a passionate lover of his country, will Firdusi's memory live for ever, but his exalted private character will always excite the admiration of mankind. He was fearless and independent. As an instance of his high-mindedness, it is told that Sultan Mahmud, the Ghazvenite, sent him on one occasion the remuneration of thirty thousand drachms. This was much less than the sum the Sultan had promised. He happened to be in the bath when the gift was brought, and immediately scornfully directed that the entire sum should be divided among the servants of the bathing establishment. The Sultan, probably repenting of his parsimony, subsequently sent the poet camels laden with treasure, but they came in time only to meet his funeral procession. The gift was sent back to the ungrateful monarch, the poet's proud daughter declining to accept of it. The poet had left a sting in the memory of the Sultan, in a satire which is remembered by the people to this day, which begins with the following verse:

"Oh! Sultan Mahmud, if thou fearest none, yet fear God!"

What an abyss is there between the modern Persians and their great poet! *

Meanwhile I had been preparing at my leisure for the winter journey to Teheran. The means for doing so had been furnished by the govenor of the place, who received me most affably, loaded me with presents and overwhelmed me with marks of distinction. Teheran was still thirty days' journey from Meshed, and so long a ride in winter was by no means a pleasant prospect, yet my heart burned with delight as I rode out of the city gates.

* Amongst the various great poetical compositions of Mohammedan Asia, we may boldly call the poems of Hafiz, Saadi, and Firdusi the household works of every enlightened or rather of every educated Mohammedan. As to the latter one, I have scarcely met with any Persian who was not conversant with the heroes of the great epic called the "Shah-Nameh;" and there is rarely a bath, a caravansary or any other public building, excepting mosques and colleges, which would not be adorned with primitive pictures, representing the heroic feats of Rustem, Zal and Kai Khosrau. The "Shah-Nameh" is the only popular history of the Iranian world, it is the mirror in the resplendent radiance of which the Persian and the Central Asian delight to find the glory of by-gone ages; and really, without having read the "Shah-Nameh," we shall never be able to realize the wonderful spirit of that Asiatic world which was superseded by Islam. A popularization of this masterly epic is therefore a great service done to the knowledge of the East. In Germany Rückert and Schack have tried this task; but owing to the form which they selected, their success was only a partial one, and the large public of the said country possesses but a fragmentary notion of the "Book of Kings."

Quite recently there has come out in England "The Epic of Kings; Stories retold from Firdusi," by *Helen Zimmern* (London: T. Fisher Unwin), which relates in delightfully written prose the chief and most moving stories referring to the great heroes of Iranian antiquity from the Shahs of old to the death of Rustem. Although she has written a paraphrase and not a translation, the author, by uniting a rare poetical gift with a true understanding of the East—has succeeded in rendering the great epic accessible to the large reading public, which can now taste this justly famous poetical production of the East, and which will certainly be thankful to Miss Zimmern for the rare enjoyment.

XXVIII.

FROM MESHED TO TEHERAN.

THE impress of the character of the reigning sovereign leaves its mark on everything in the kingdom of Persia; and so, in a certain limited way, does the character of the governors for the time being of the several provinces of that kingdom determine the comparative safety and comfort of the highways. To travel from Meshed to Teheran is looked upon as an enterprise demanding a staunch spirit, and the bravest man may recoil from the dangers threatening him on that first portion of the road through Khorassan, where Turkomans, Beloochees and Kurds are an object of terror to all men, but more particularly to the cowardly native of Persia. Sultan Murad Mirza, surnamed "The Sword of the Empire," was governor of the province at the time I set out for Teheran. In the flowery language of the country the praise was bestowed on him that a child might with perfect security carry a plateful of ducats upon the highways, without being molested. And, indeed, he was fully deserving of the compliment implied in this high-flown saying, for there was not in the whole kingdom a governor devoting a greater amount of energy and talent than he did to render the public highways safe, and to advance and encourage commerce and safe travelling.

My spirits rose high as I set out on my journey in the company of my Tartar. Two routes from Meshed to Nishapur were open to me—one leading over a mountainous tract, the other through a lower hilly country. I chose the latter. As I passed out of the city, mounted on an active nag, the horse of my Tartar being loaded with everything requisite for the journey, I felt in an exceptionally cheerful humour. It was not merely the pleasurable feeling of returning home which produced this effect. The contrast between the journey now before me, furnished with all the proper equipments, and that which I had made, suffering from all sorts of privations amid the deserts of Turkestan, without doubt greatly added to this feeling. We were continually meeting with caravans either of pilgrims or of merchandise, proceeding towards or returning from the holy city. On such occasions words of greeting are always exchanged. My surprise at recognizing an old acquaintance in the leader of one of these caravans may be easily imagined. He was a Shirazer, in whose society I had two years before visited the ruins of Persepolis, Nakshi Rustam, and that fair city which was the birthplace of the poet Hafiz. To have travelled a long time with a man is in Asia looked upon as a sort of relationship. The gossipping Shirazer was delighted to see me. The caravan was obliged, whether or no, to submit to a quarter of an hour's halt, while we seated ourselves on the sand to enjoy together the friendly *kalian* (Persian pipe). As its fragrant smoke rose before my eyes, vivid pictures of the past, of the majestic monuments of bygone civilizations, arose before my memory. How those recollections animated me! Valerius in his chains, the majestic figure of the proud Shapur, above him floating the form of beneficent Ormuzd, — all those magnificent bas-reliefs whirled kaleidoscope-like past my mind's eye; but their charms were multiplied as I reflected that since I saw them, I had seen, and had left behind me, the classical realms of Bactria and Sogdiana, which had inspired with terror the stout hearts of the Macedonians of Alexander.

I was obliged to assure my Shiraz friend that I would speedily revisit his native country, for it was not until I had soothed him with this sort of promise that he would allow me to part from him. So cheerily did I then go on my way that the first day's journey was not in the least fatiguing to me, and by night we reached the station of *Sherif Abad*. This was the first evening I spent as a well-equipped traveller. In my previous travels in Turkestan I had first of all to gather firewood and collect flour; I had to pronounce prayers and blessings as payment for my night quarters; and I was always liable to be turned out of the house tired and hungry. Now, on the contrary, I was a great man. I rode proudly into the *tchaparkhane* (post-house), and with a loud voice called for lodgings; for although I was still completely Oriental, so far as outward appearances went, the postmaster could easily observe that he had to do with one who had at his command a sufficiency of the sinews of war. And what will not a Persian do for money? My Tartar prepared me an excellent supper; rice, sugar, fat, meat—in a word, everything in abundance. The eyes of my simple Uzbeg sparkled with joy as he thought of his former poverty and looked on the abundance which surrounded him. If the supper which he could prepare was not exactly fit to appear on the table of a Lucullus, it was a very good one for a Persian wayside station.

We had before us as our next day's work, a distance of nine German miles or thirty-six English miles to the next station, *Kademgiah*. Nine fersakhs in Khorassan is a good deal, for there is a saying that in that province the miles are as interminable as the chatter of women, and that he who measured them must have done so with a broken chain. European travellers, without exception, complain of the monotony and wearisome character of the road. But what was that to me who had escaped from the torments of Turkestan? Quite alone with my Tartar, and well armed and well mounted, I now for the first time felt the charms of true travelling. Little know they who coop themselves up amidst the heat of July in close railway carriages, and find, perforce, delight in the dusty, grimy countenance of the guard, what travelling really means. A good saddle is better than all your stuffed cushions. Thereon a man feels himself free and unconstrained. His bridle is his Bradshaw, his sword is his law, his gun is the policeman who protects him, and though he is an outlaw and fair game for all who meet him, so all are fair game for him. When in addition to this, he is familiar with the languages, laws, and customs of the land through which he proceeds, and is independent of dragomans, firmans, and guards, then his journey is truly delightful. Travelling the whole day in the open air, he finds the hour of the midday halt both a pleasure and a necessity. And then the enjoyments of the evening, when having arrived at the spot where he means to rest for the night, his steed pasturing near him, and he himself surrounded by the saddles and baggage, gazing at the crackling fire which is to cook his savoury supper! The rays of the setting sun are not then so bright or cheerful as the glances of the traveller's eyes. No meal is so savoury as his supper, and his slumber under the starry canopy of heaven is a hundred times more refreshing than that of those who sleep on luxurious down in princely chambers.

Kademgiah, the name of my second station, means "footprints," and is a place of religious pilgrimage, where pious faith discovers on a marble stone the print of Ali's foot. Such miraculous footprints are by no means of rare occurrence in the East. Christians, Mohammedans, and Brahmins, all hold them in equal veneration. What especially excited my wonder was the vast size of most of them, suggesting as they did rather the idea of the foot of an unwieldy elephant than that of a man. But religious credulity does not trouble itself about such trifles as logic or the fitness of things. In the mountains near Shiraz, for instance, there is a footprint three feet long; the one in Herat is of the same size, as is also that on Mount Sinai; and even in distant Kothen, in Chinese Tartary, a large footprint is shown, where, as the story goes, the holy Jafer once strolled near Sadik. As I have observed, their monstrous size creates no surprise or doubt in the minds of the pious. Under the auspices of the holy place stand numerous inns for the accommodation of pilgrims. In one of these I had comfortably established myself, and was just engaged in making tea in the shade of the fine poplars, when one of the priests of the place made his appearance, and with a devout look invited me to visit the holy spot. As the only thing the priest seemed to want at the time was a cup of tea, I treated him to one. His further importunities proved him to have more mercenary views; so as the cold marble stone which contains the sacred footprint was of little interest to me, who had seen so many of its kind already, I contrived at the expense of a few krans (francs) to dispense at once with the society of my guest and the performance of a religious duty.

My third day's march took me over a region of low hills into the plain of Nishapur, so celebrated in Persia, and I may add in all Asia. Djolghe-i Nishabur (Plain of Nishapur) is in the eyes of the Persian the *ne plus ultra* of beauty and wealth. For him the air there is purer and more fragrant than elsewhere; its water the sweetest in the world, and its products without rivals in creation. It is difficult adequately to describe the proud joy which is pictured in his countenance as he points out the hills lying towards the north-east, abounding in turquoise mines and precious metals. For myself, I must own that the plain, like the city situated in its midst, produced a pleasing, but by no means the entrancing effect I felt justified in anticipating. Its historical importance would hardly have occurred to me, had it not been that a Persian, who discovered I was a foreigner, joined in conversation with me by the way, and unasked, began to sound with no little exaggeration the praises of his native city. "What is the use of all your talking?" cried I; "look at the ruins strewed round us. Do you call this a flourishing country? Observe this watchtower which guards the herdsman against the predatory raids of the Turkomans. Is that a sign of prosperous circumstances?" But the Persian did not permit himself to be led from his pet theme, and was deaf to all my remarks. In the eyes of an Iranian the prevalence of ruins is an essential feature in a scene of civilization. In spite of all my banter, he continued to descant upon the thousands of agricultural wonders and works of irrigation to be found spread over this plain.

No less inconsiderable did I find the town of Nishapur itself. The bazaar is tolerably well filled with European and Persian wares, but the traveller in vain explores the town for remains of that wealth and architectural beauty which have been so highly lauded by Eastern historians. The only things of note in the town are workshops for grinding and polishing the turquoises found in the neighbourhood. The stones in their unwrought state are of a gray colour, and only acquire their well-known sky-blue hue after repeated polishings. The deeper its colour, the more prominent its shape, and the smoother its surface, so much the more costly is a stone—veins being regarded as flaws. A curious phenomenon observable in these turquoises is that in many specimens the colour fades a few days after being polished. The inexperienced purchaser who is not aware of this circumstance not seldom becomes a victim to Persian fraud; and many pilgrims who have purchased in Nishapur stones of brilliant azure, have no other choice left them on their return home than to throw them away as faded and colourless. At the present day these mines are by no means so profitable as in former times, they being rented altogether for the low sum of two thousand ducats yearly. The commerce in the stones, which was once actively carried on between Persia and Europe, especially with Russia, has also of late years very much fallen off.

Before leaving Nishapur, we must notice two celebrated poets, whose graves confer no small fame on this old city. One of them is Ferid ed din Attar, the great mystic and philosopher, who wrote the interesting work

"Mantik et Teyr" (The Logic of Birds). In this book, all kinds of the feathered creation are introduced, and they contend eagerly, and with great oddity, about the cause of existence and the source of all truth. Eagles vultures, falcons and ravens, turtle-doves and nightingales, are alike interested in the discussion of those important questions. Hudhud, the all-knowing magical bird of Solomon, is introduced as their teacher, and to him they appeal in a curious manner for the much desired information. He conducts himself modestly, lays before them artful riddles, and leads the listening troop on the path by which they may encounter Simurg, the phœnix of the Orientals, and symbol of the highest light. It is easy to understand that the birds symbolize humanity, Hudhud the prophet, and Simurg the Deity. The poem has obtained a great and deserved celebrity by its wealth of gorgeous imagery and its many passages of singular beauty. The second poet whose ashes rest in Nishapur is Khiyam, the very antipode of the first. According to the pious he was an atheist, a profligate reviler of Mohammed and of Islam, who trampled under his sacrilegious feet all that is holiest, fairest, and best, and directed his satirical raillery against the most sacred laws and duties. Yet Khiyam is, for all this, not less read and admired than Ferrid ed din. Persia is in fact just that country in Asia which most clearly shows its Oriental character by representing the most opposite of extremes. Here daring atheism and lowly devotion meet face to face, and, what is more remarkable, without seriously shocking one another. Persia certainly affords the most complete collective picture of the Eastern world.

From Nishapur the road leads to Sebzevar, distant three days' march. The intervening stations have been often described. They do not contain anything of particular note, any more than the last-mentioned itself, which is surrounded by a strong wall, and lies in the midst of a tolerably fertile plain. From Sebzevar the traveller in four days reaches Abbasabad, which is considered one of the most important posts in the country, for here commence the four "stations of terror" of Khorassan. They are Abbasabad, Miyandeshd, Meyame and Shahrud. These four stations can none of them be regarded as places which are inhabited by choice. Their inhabitants are ever confined within their walls, nor do they dare to engage in agriculture. The government maintains them to keep up the roads. Abbasabad is a colony planted for that purpose. Its inhabitants are of Georgian origin, and still retain in their features much of their original Caucasian character; although, as one of them remarked to me, the beauty of the people degenerates continually, inasmuch as they can here no longer drink the Kahiti wine, the Tokay of the Caucasus, No one who has travelled in Persia can have failed to have heard the names of the four "stations of terror," so rich are they in danger and in strange tales of adventure. Whoever amongst the people has the ambition of laying claim to a character for bravery, he never forgets to introduce their names into the story of his adventures. Do you ask why? The answer is very simple. The four stations are posted on the edge of the great plain which extends far away into the steppes of the Turkomans. No river, no mountain, breaks its uniformity, and as those rapacious children of the desert have but little respect for political boundaries, their predatory inroads are frequent, and these four places are just those which are most exposed to their ravages. They seldom fail to profit largely by such incursions, as here runs the principal road towards Khorassan, which is ever full of heavily laden caravans and well-equipped pilgrims. The Persian never tires of dwelling on adventures with the Turkomans. At one of the stations, among much else that was curious, I heard the following story. A Persian general had sent his troops of six thousand men on before him, and was only staying behind for a few minutes to enjoy comfortably the last whiffs of his kalian. He had just finished his pipe and was about to join his soldiers, followed by a few body-servants, when he was pounced upon by a body of Turkomans and carried away on their swift horses. In a few minutes he was robbed and made captive, and a few weeks later was sold as a slave in the market of Khiva for the sum of twenty-five ducats.

On another occasion a pilgrim was captured on his way to the shrine of Imam Riza. Luckily he saw the approaching enemy, and had just time to hide his little store behind a stone ere the plunderers came upon him. After he had been sold as a slave and brought to Khiva, he wrote from thence to his tender spouse as follows : "My dear child, in such and such a place, under such and such a stone, I have hidden forty ducats. Send thirty of them to this place to ransom thy loving husband, and take care of the remainder until I return from the land of the Turkomans, this house of bondage, in which I must now, perforce, perform menial service."

It is true that there is good cause here for fear and caution, but the absurd pusillanimity of the Iranians is the main source of their misfortunes. Their caravans are wont to assemble here in large masses. They are protected by soldiers with drawn swords, and cannons with their matches burning. Often their numbers are very considerable. No sooner, however, do a few desperate desert robbers make their appearance than caravan and escort alike lose their courage and presence of mind, fling away their weapons, offer all their property to the enemy, and putting out their hands to be fettered, allow themselves to be carried away into painful, often lifelong, captivity and slavery. I rode from station to station with my Tartar for my only escort—a journey which no European had ever made before me. Of course I was warned not to do so. But in my Turkoman dress what cared I for Turkoman robbers? As for my Tartar, he looked wistfully around in hope that he might espy a countryman of his. If we had fallen in with some of those Sunnite sons of the desert, travelling as we were in a Shi-ite land, I believe that so far from injuring a mollah of their own faith, they would have rewarded us richly for the fatiha which we would have bestowed on them. For four days I wandered in the steppe; once in the dusk of the evening I lost my way, yet not a single Turkoman crossed my path. I met no one except a few scared Persian travellers. But what annoyed me more than all the terrors of Turkoman cruelty, was the interminable length of the days' marches, especially the last between Meyame and Shahrud. On that occasion I passed sixteen hours in the saddle. It is the longest station in all Persia, and especially wearying both to man and beast.

The reader will easily imagine the eagerness with which the traveller's eyes look out for the gardens which surround Shahrud. As this town is situated at the foot of a mountain, it is visible for miles off on the plain. The wearied horseman thinks he has already reached the end of his day's journey, when it is in reality five German miles distant. The road is as monotonous as can possibly be imagined. It affords nothing whatsoever to attract the eye. In summer, owing to utter want of water, it must be very unpleasant to travel over it. Unfortunately I had mistaken a village which lies in the vicinity of Shahrud for the town itself, which at the point of the road was concealed in a hollow. My anger when I discovered my mistake may be easily conceived. It was in truth no joke to have added to the long day's journey a good half-hour's additional ride. I had mounted my horse before twelve o'clock the night before, and it was already past six o'clock in the evening, when I at last gained the badly paved streets of Shahrud, and dismounted in one of its principal caravansaries. My poor beast was utterly exhausted, and I myself scarcely less so. But as I looked around the square of the caravansary, how great was my astonishment at beholding a son of Britain, yes, actually an unmistakable living Englishman, with a genuine John Bull physiognomy, sitting at the door of one of the cells. An Englishman alone here in Shahrud—that is certainly a rarity, almost a miracle. I rushed towards him. He also, although apparently absorbed in deep thought, regarded me with wondering eyes. My Bokhariot dress, and my evident fatigue had attracted his attention. Who knows what he thought of me then? For myself, in spite of my extreme exhaustion, I hastened as well as I could to this extraordinary *rencontre.* I dragged myself towards him, and staring at him with weary eyes, addressed him with a "How are you, sir?" He appeared not to have understood me, so I repeated my question. At this he sprang from his seat in surprise, the greatest astonishment depicted in his countenance, while he gave vent to his feelings with "Well ! ——. Where have you learned English?" asked he, stammering with emotion: "perhaps in India." I should have liked to have screwed up his curiosity a peg or two higher, and at any other time might have enjoyed a mystification amazingly. But my long ride had so thoroughly tired me out that I had not the spirits required for carrying on the joke. I made a plain confession of what and who I was. His joy was indescribable. To the great astonishment of my Tartar, who until now had always regarded me as a true believer, he embraced me and took me into his quarters. We spent a famous evening together, and I allowed myself to be induced to rest there the whole of next day; for it did the poor fellow no end of good to be able to speak of the West after six months' separation from European society. A few months after our strange meeting he was robbed and murdered on the road. His name was Longfield, and he was agent for a large Lancashire house, for which he had to purchase cotton. He had to carry a great deal of money about him, and unfortunately forgot, as do too many, that Persia is not the civilized land which the glowing representations of its lying agents in Europe would lead us to suppose, and that one cannot place much reliance on passports and royal firmans.

Shahrud is a commercial post of importance between Mazenderan and Irak. The road leading to the former province is miserably kept, although it is not wanting in romantic beauty. It passes through a mountainous ountry, abounding in water, down to the shores of the Caspian Sea. Especially picturesque is the Rudi Shah (King's brook), whose waters run with loud noise bright and clear through the streets of the town. There are several caravansaries here, and in one of the largest is the factory of the Russian commercial company "Kavkaz," which has of late years almost entirely driven English commerce out of Khorassan, by means of its import trade from Astrachan Baku through Astrabad. From the Gulf of Kamtschatka down to Constantinople, throughout all Asia, the influence which the Russians wield is enormous, and there is none other so threatening as that to the rival interests of Great Britain. Inch by inch they gain upon the ground occupied by the British lion, nor is the time far distant when there must ensue a close and bitter contest.

Before reaching Teheran I had a journey of eleven days yet before me. The road is safe. The only point of interest offered along the stations is the observation of the contrast between the manners of the inhabitants of Khorassan and those of Irak. The proximity of Central Asia has left its mark of many rude habits on the people of Khorassan, whilst the polish of Iranian civilization is unmistakable in the inhabitants of Irak. The traveller who is supposed to be possessed of worldly means is always sure here of most polite treatment. Not but that in outward appearance they pretend to a vast amount of guilelessness with not a touch of greediness. The guest is treated as a most welcome personage. He is overwhelmed with the very quintessence of courtly phrases which accompany the presents offered to him. But he had better be careful of his purse if he is uninitiated in the intricacies of Persian politeness. I had become well acquainted with Iranian etiquette during my travels in Southern Persia, and on such occasions I always played the Iranian, meeting compliments with phrases even more complimentary. I accepted, of course, the presents offered me, but never failed with most flowery speeches to invite the giver of the gift to partake of it. It rarely happened that he was proof against my high-flown bombast, and quotations from Saadi and his other favourite poets. Forgetting compliments and courtesy, he would then make a fierce onslaught on the food and fruits he had himself heaped on the *khondja* (wooden table), and tell me with repeated and significant shakes of the head, "Effendi, thou art more Iranian than the Iranians; thou art too polished to be sincere." Nor is it an easy task to impose upon a Persian. Habits and a system of education dating back many ages have trained him to an extraordinary perfection in all the arts of dissimulation and all the niceties of polite intercourse —meaning, of course, the outward appearance of it only. An apparently clownish countryman, a child seemingly as innocent as a new-born babe, will often take in the unwary European. They have a whole arsenal of words, gestures and movements at their disposal, to put the uninitiated stranger off his guard. The European especially, who, proud of his superiority in civilization, despises and undervalues the Oriental, becomes most frequently and most signally the victim of their deceptive arts.

The nearer we approached Teheran the worse became the weather. We were now in the latter part of December. I had felt the cold of the impending winter while still on the plains; but here, in more elevated regions, it was doubly severe. The temperature in Persia is liable to sudden changes, and a journey of a few hours often makes a serious difference. But the weather in the two stations of Goshe and Ahuan was so very severe as to cause me anxiety. These two places are situated on a mountain, and can afford accommodation to but a small number of people. I fared tolerably well at Goshe, where I had the caravansary all to myself and could arrange myself comfortably and cosily, while outside a cruel, bitter cold prevailed. The next day, on my way to Ahuan, I found snow in many parts of the roads.

The biting north wind compelled me often to dismount in order to keep my feet warm with walking. The snow lay already several feet deep when I arrived at Ahuan, and it was frozen so hard as to form along some parts of our road two solid walls. In catching sight of the solitary post-house, I had but one intense longing, to get beneath a roof and to find a good fire by which to warm myself. The eye roving over the hills, white with snow, could not discover within its range anywhere a human habitation or even the wreck of one. We rode into the yard of the tchaparkhane in our usual demonstrative manner in order to attract attention. The postmaster was exceedingly polite, which, in itself, was a good omen, and I was delighted as he led me into a smoky, but withal well-sheltered room; and I paid but little attention to what he was saying, as he expatiated at great length, with an air of great importance, on the expected arrival of the lady of Sipeh Salar, the Persian generalissimo and minister of war, who was on her way back from a pilgrimage to Meshed, and would arrive either that night or the following day with a retinue of from forty to sixty servants. To be overtaken by them in a place affording such meagre accommodations as this post-house did, would of course be far from pleasant. But the likelihood of such an event little disturbed my equanimity; on the contrary I made myself and my weary beast as comfortable as I could. As the fire began to blaze cheerily on the hearth, and the tea to send its steamy flavour through the room, I entirely lost all sense of the cold and discomfort I had so lately endured, and listening to the shrill whistling of rude Boreas without, who seemed to wish to rob me of my slumbers out of spite for having escaped his fury, I gave no thought to the probability of being ousted from my comfortable quarters. After I had taken my tea and felt a pleasant warmth creeping through my whole body I began to undress. I had thrown myself on my couch, my pilar and roast fowl were almost ready, when, about midnight, through the howling of the wind I heard the tramp of a troop of horsemen. I had scarcely time to jump up from my bed when the whole cavalcade dashed into the court with clashing arms, oaths and shouts. In an instant they were at my door, which was of course bolted. "Hallo! who is here? Out with you! The lady of Sipeh Salar, a princess of royal blood, is come; every one must turn out and make room for her." I need not say that there were cogent reasons for not immediately opening the door. The men asked of the postmaster who was the occupier of the room, and upon learning that it was only a hadji, and he too a heretic, a Sunnite, they began to level their swords and the butt ends of their guns at the door, crying out, "Ha, hadji! take thyself off, or wilt thou have us grind thy bones to meal!"

The moment was a very exciting and a very critical one. It is but a sorry jest to be turned out of a warm shelter, where one is perfectly comfortable, and to have to pass a bitterly cold winter's night in the open air. It was not, perhaps, so much the fear of harm from exposure to the cold as the suddenness of the surprise and the shock of the unwelcome disturbance, which suggested to me the bold thought not to yield, but fearlessly to accept the challenge. My Tartar, who was in the room with me, turned pale. I sprang from my seat, seized gun and sword, while I handed my pistols to him, with the order to use them as soon as I gave him a sign to do so. I then took up a position near the door, firmly resolved to fire at the first person who would intrude.

My martial preparations seemed to have been observed by those without, for they began to parley. Indeed I remarked that the elegance of the Persian which I employed in talking with them rather staggered them into a suspicion that they might be mistaken after all in supposing me to be a Bokhariot. "Who art thou, then? Speak, man, it seems thou art no hadji," was now heard from without. "Who talks about hadjis?" I cried; "away with that abusive word! I am neither Bokhariot nor Persian. I have the honour to be a European, and my name is Vambéry Sahib."

Silence followed this speech of mine. My assailants seemed to be utterly dumbfounded. Its effect, however, was even more startling on my Tartar, who now, for the first time, heard from his hadji fellow-traveller's own lips that he whom he had looked upon as a true believer was a European and that his real name was Vambéry. Pale as death, and with eyes glaring wildly, he stared at me. I was in fact placed between two fires. A sharp side-glance from me restored his equanimity. The Persians too changed their tactics. The name of European, that word of terror for Orientals, produced a magic effect. Terms of abuse were followed by expressions of politeness; menaces by entreaties; and as they earnestly besought me to allow two of the principal members of the escort to share my room, while the others would resign themselves to occupy the barn and the stable, I opened the door to the trembling Persians. My features convinced them at once of the truth of my assertions. Our conversation soon became very lively and friendly, and in the course of half an hour my guests were reposing in a corner of the room, completely stupified by over-indulgence in arrack. There they lay snoring like horses. I then applied myself to the task of explaining matters to my Tartar, and found him, to my agreeable surprise, quite willing to appreciate my explanations. Next morning when I left the snow-clad hills, and rode over the cheerful plain of Damgan, the recollection of the adventure came back to me in all its vividness, and I own that on sober second thoughts I was disposed to quake somewhat on contemplating the unnecessary danger my rashness had exposed me to the preceding night.

Damgan is supposed to be the ancient Hecatompylae (city with the hundred gates); a supposition which our archæologists will maintain at every hazard, although the neighbourhood affords no trace of a city to which the hundred gates might have belonged. Of course one must make large deductions from all assertions made by either Greeks or Persians, who rival each other in the noble art of bragging and exaggerating. If we reduce the hundred gates to twenty, it will still remain a matter of considerable difficulty to discover a city of over twenty gates in the obscure spot now called Damgan. The place boasts of scarcely more than a hundred houses, and two miserable caravansaries in the midst of its empty bazaar are sufficient indications that Damgan's reputation for importance in commercial respects is equally unfounded.

Fraser, the English traveller, was puzzled by the inscription of "Tchihl dukhteran" (forty virgins), or "Tchihl seran" (forty heads), to be seen on a monument here, and regretted that nobody was there to explain them to him. Forty is a holy number among the Mohammedans, especially among the Persians, and the "Tchihl ten" (the forty men) whom Moses, according to the Mohammedan legend, first slew and then brought back to life again, are to be found commemorated in many places. What is remarkable here is that the ladies are represented as saints or martyrs, a tradition not so unlikely at Cologne as here at Damgan, whose women do not enjoy the fairest fame.

From Damgan I travelled over two stations to Simnan, celebrated for its cotton, and still more for its tea-cakes. Almost every town in Persia is conspicuous for some speciality, in the production of which it claims to be not only the foremost in Persia, but unrivalled in the whole world. Shiraz, for instance, is famous for lamb, Isfahan for peaches, Nathenz for pears, and so on. The odd thing about it is, that on arriving in any of these towns and looking for the article so much bragged of, the traveller is either greatly disappointed as to its quality, or, more amusing still, he fails to find the article at all. In Meshed I heard the tea-cakes of Simnan talked of, nay even in Herat; but as I had often had occasion to value these exaggerations at their true worth, I did not expect too much. Nevertheless, I went into the bazaar to inquire after tea-cakes. My search, long and painful, was rewarded by a few mouldy specimens. "Simnan," said one, "is justly celebrated for the excellence of this article, but the export is so tremendous that we are left without any." Another said: "It is true that Simnan was once famous for the production of this article, but hard times have caused even the quality of the tea-cakes to deteriorate." Here at any rate people had the grace to invent some excuses, but in most places not even an apology is attempted; and the unblushing fraud of the pretended claim to the production of some excellent article shows itself without any disguise.

From hence the road goes through Lazgird, Dehnemek, and Kishlak, and the celebrated Khavar Pass, to Teheran. This mountain road is supposed to be identical with the ancient Caspiæ Pylæ, and is certainly unique in its way. Cut out through lofty black walls of rock, it is exceedingly romantic, and its sudden turns and frequent windings afford excellent lurking-places for robbers. As was the case in former days so now, the vicinity is infested with brigands. Particular rocks have such names associated with them as suggest the scenes which have taken place near them; for instance, that of Soul-murderer, Parricide, and the like. The powerful echo makes the road still more trying to the traveller's nerves. I saw fear plainly depicted in my Tartar's face. I rode with my weapons ready for use, and met on the way several individuals of suspicious appearance. We escaped unharmed, however, and at length breathed more freely as we rode through the further end of the pass into the broad fertile plain of Veramin. This plain, on the northern extremity of which the city, renowned in ancient history, of Raghes was situated, must at one time have been the scene of busy life in many flourishing cities and villages. But circumstances have sadly changed since; the fertile land having become at various times the resort of ravaging and pillaging hordes, from Tartary, Arabia, and the northern confines of India. Even in the beginning of the Middle Ages Raghes was a coveted prize. Here many of the Seldjukians and Ghuznevites and the Timurides made a halt to rest in their career of war and conquest. Everything is in ruins now; and whilst the European archæologist is ransacking the ground for fallen stones on which he eagerly looks for inscriptions, the Persian regards the plain as a valuable hunting-ground. Indeed, were it not for the numerous underground aqueducts which bear witness to the activity and prosperity of generations belonging to a civilization which has long since faded away, the tales of the former glories of Veramin would be looked upon as idle inventions. The same sensations which overcame me when I arrived in Meshed, I felt now with even greater intensity as I drew near Teheran, the starting-place of my adventurous journey, where I was to meet so many kind friends who, in all probability, had long ago resigned themselves to the thought of my having paid with my life the penalty of my rash enterprise. In order to hasten our march I determined to accomplish the two last stations in one day. I reasoned with myself that though a ride of thirteen hours was very fatiguing, yet that at the last station I should come to I could rest for two months. Thus busying myself with pleasant thoughts, indulging in sweet hopes, I sturdily rode on from early morning until the evening. As the sun was setting beneath the horizon, its departing light fell upon the gleaming cupola of Shah Abdul Asim, and I saw Teheran at a distance. Whether it was the sudden emotion at the sight I had longed for, or the darkness which sets in with extreme rapidity at this season in this latitude, or extreme exhaustion, or the combined effect of all these causes—whatever was the reason, I became confused and bewildered and lost my way. And that in the close vicinity of the Persian capital, near those famous ruins which stand nigh to the rocks on which the Guebres or fire-worshippers were wont to expose their dead to be devoured by birds. For two long hours I scrambled among ditches and swamps, in which my horse once plunged up to the loins in cold water. Then again we became entangled in a maze of gardens and enclosures, until at last, late in the night, we contrived to find our way back to the right road.

But is it not remarkable that no serious accident had marred the success of my journey up to this very moment? Unharmed I had roamed in distant and pathless deserts; I had been able to save my property and above all my manuscripts—the precious prize and reward of all my toils—in spite of most imminent dangers; and yet here, on the very threshold of my abode of rest, at the gates of that spot which my imagination had pictured to me as the land of promise, a most serious mishap befell me. I lost through the immersion one of the manuscripts so highly valued by me. The Oriental is right, after all, in saying that Fate has her caprices, and it is childish to attempt to battle against them. When at last I reached the gates of Teheran they were already closed, and I was compelled to pass the night in one of the caravansaries outside. Next morning, in riding through the crowded bazaar, midst oaths and clamour, I heard many a Persian remark with surprise and indignation, "Is not that an impudent Bokhariot!" I fell in, also, during my progress through the streets, with several Europeans who, owing to my strange costume, did not recognize me at first, but later on received me most cordially. I finally came up to the gate of the Turkish Embassy, and my joy was indescribable at finding myself again near the place of my departure and to the same old friends of whom I had taken leave ten months ago, full of uncertain and fantastic plans which had since assumed shape and reality. Those good friends then thought I was boldly engaging in a venture which was sure to prove fatal to me, and at this very moment they supposed that, in my person, another name had been added to the long list of victims to the ferocity and perfidy of Central Asia.

XXIX.

FROM TEHERAN TO TREBIZOND.

THE Persian capital appeared to me, when I saw it again, as the very abode of civilization and culture, affording to one's heart's content all the pleasures and refinements of European life. Of course, a traveller from the West, on coming to the city for the first time, is bitterly disappointed in seeing the squalid mud hovels and the narrow and crooked streets through which he must make his way. But to one coming from Bokhara the aspect of the city seems entirely changed. A journey of only sixty days separates one city from the other; but in point of fact, there is such a difference in the social condition of Bokhara and Teheran, that centuries might have divided them from one another. My first ride through the bazaar, after my arrival, made me feel like a child again. Almost with the eagerness of my Tartar companion, my delighted eyes were wandering over articles of luxury from Europe, toys, stuffs and cloths which I saw exhibited there. The samples of European taste and ingenuity then struck me with a sort of awe, which, recalled now, seems to me very comical. It was a feeling, however, of which it was difficult to get rid. When a man travels as I did, and when he has as thoroughly and completely adapted himself to the Tartar mode of life, it is no wonder if, in the end, he turns half a Tartar himself. That doublefacedness in which a man lives, thoroughly aware of his real nature in spite of his outward disguise, cannot be maintained very long with impunity. The constant concealment of his real sentiments, the absorbing work of his assimilating to the utmost elements quite foreign, produce their slow and silent but sure effect, in altering the man himself, in course of time, whether he wishes it or no. In vain does the disguised traveller inwardly rebel against the influences and impressions which are wearing away his real self. The impressions of the past lose more and more their hold on him until they fade away, leaving the traveller hopelessly struggling in the toils of his own fiction, and the *rôle* he had assumed soon becomes second nature with him.

I formed no exception to the rule in this particular; the change in my behaviour was the theme of many facetious remarks from my European friends, and drew upon me more than once their good-natured sallies. They made my salutations, my gesticulations, my gait, and above all my mode of viewing things in general, an object of their mirth. Many went so far as to insist upon my having been transformed into a Tartar, to my very features; saying that even my eyes had assumed the oblique shape peculiar to that race. This good-natured "chaff" afforded me great amusement. It in no wise interfered with the extreme pleasure I felt in being restored to European society. Nevertheless, besides the strange sensation of enjoying the rare luxury of undisturbed repose for several weeks, there were many things in the customs and habits of my European friends to which reconciliation caused great difficulty. The close-fitting European dress, especially, seemed to cramp me and to hamper me in my movements. The shaved scalp was ill at ease under the burden of the hair which I allowed to grow. The lively and sometimes violent gestures which accompanied the friendly interchange of views, on the part of the Europeans, looked to me like outbursts of passion, and I often thought that they would be followed by the more energetic argument of rude force. The stiff and measured carriage and walk, peculiar to military people, which I observed in the French officers in the Persian service, seemed to me odd, artificial and stilted. Not but that it afforded me a secret pleasure to have occasion to admire the proud and manly bearing of my fellow Europeans. It presented such a gratifying contrast to the slovenly and slouching gait of the Central Asiatics, amongst whom I had been lately living. It would serve no purpose to point out to my readers, and to multiply, the numerous instances of the strange perversion of views and tastes to which my late experiences among strange Asiatic people had given rise. Those who, from personal observations, are enabled to draw a parallel between life in the East and West, will find no exaggeration in my saying that Teheran compared to Bokhara seemed to be a sort of Paris to me.

The surprise and astonishment of the Persian public at the capital was general when the successful issue of my perilous adventure became known. Ketman (the art of dissimulation allowed by Islam) is a gift well known and diligently cultivated by Orientals; but that a European should have acquired such a degree of excellence in this peculiarly Eastern art as to impose upon the natives themselves seemed to them incomprehensible. Without doubt they would have grudged the successful termination of my journey, had it not been that the joke I had played at the expense of their arch-enemies the Sunnite Turkomans tickled their fancy. The steppes of Turkestan are many ways a *terra incognita* to the inhabitants of Teheran; and although they are situated near the confines of Persia, the strangest and most fanciful ideas prevail amongst the people in regard to them. I was the recipient of a thousand questions from everybody on this subject. I was invited by several ministers to visit them, and had even the distinction conferred upon me of being presented to his Majesty, "the Centre of the World" or "Highly Exalted Ruler of the Universe," as the Persians call him. I had to undergo the wearisome ceremonial of the Persian court, before I was ushered into the august presence of the Shah Nasr-ed-din, in the garden of the Palace, and when there I received from him the condescending compliment of being asked to tell the story of my adventures. I acquitted myself in this with no little vivacity. The ministers who graced the interview with their presence were quite dumbfounded with the easy coolness I exhibited on that occasion, and as I was afterwards told, could scarcely recover from their astonishment at my being able to endure without trembling the looks of a sovereign whose least glance strikes terror into the heart of the boldest mortal. The king himself seemed pleased with my performance, for he afterwards testified to his satisfaction by sending me the Order of the Lion and Sun, and what was more to the purpose, a valuable Persian shawl. The insignia of the Order, consisting of a plain piece of silver, I was permitted to retain, but the rapacity of the minister, so characteristic of the court of Teheran, confiscated the shawl, worth at least fifty ducats, for his own benefit. This conduct is by no means astonishing: his Majesty the King lies and deceives his ministers, and they, in their turn, repay his amiability towards them with usurious interest. Inferior officials cheat the people, and the latter again avail themselves of every opportunity to cheat the officials. Every one in that country lies, cheats and swindles. Nor is such behaviour looked upon as anything immoral or improper; on the contrary, the man who is straightforward and honest in his dealings is sure to be spoken of contemptuously as a fool or madman.

As an instance of this general moral obliquity, I will relate a neat little story of what occurred while I was staying in Teheran. The king, as is well known, is an inveterate sportsman and an excellent shot. He passes about nine months in the year in hunting excursions, to the no small annoyance of the officers of the court, who, on such occasions, are compelled to leave the luxurious comforts of the harem, with its dainty food and soft couches, for the rude life in a tent, the simple fare of the country-people, and the long and fatiguing rides of the chase. The king, on returning from the chase, is wont to send presents of some of the game killed by him to the European ambassadors as a special mark of his favour. This generosity, however, must be paid for in the shape of a liberal *enaam*, or gratuity, to the servant who has brought the roe, partridges and other game laid low by the royal hand. The *Corps Diplomatique* at first submitted patiently to this exaction, but as these royal gifts became more and more frequent, the ministers began to surmise that these repeated acts of distinction did not emanate from the royal household, but were a mere fiction invented by the servants to secure the expected large fees, and that the game brought to them was purchased for the purpose. In order to obviate the recurrence of similar frauds, the Minister of Foreign Affairs was to certify, at the request of the ambassadors, to the *bonâ fide* character of the royal gifts. For a while this proved to be a preventative of the annoyance; but for a short time only, for very soon the presents began to pour in again with an alarming rapidity. Strict inquiries were now instituted, and the astonishing fact was brought to light that his Excellency the Minister connived at the fraud by issuing false certificates, and that he shared in the profits of the disgraceful transaction. The whole thing, when it transpired, was treated as an excellent joke; and the king himself deigned to be highly amused at the account of this singular method of taking in the Frengis.

As I did not intend leaving Teheran before spring, my stay there was prolonged to two months. This time I passed very agreeably in the society of the little European colony. Their joy at my return was sincere, and this they demonstrated not only by cordial and warm congratulations, but by a hundred little acts of politeness and goodwill which rendered my stay with them exceedingly pleasant. The embassies did not fail to acquaint their respective governments with my remarkable adventures. As for myself I was quite astonished at the ado made about my performances; nor could I very well comprehend the extraordinary importance attached to my dervish trick, which presented itself to my imagination, apart from the real dangers, rather in the ludicrous light of a comedy brought to a prosperous end.

I was not a little proud as I left the Persian capital

to find myself provided with letters of recommendation to the principal statesmen of England and France. I was especially touched by the interest shown by a Hungarian countryman of mine, a Mr. Szantó, who plied the trade of a tailor in Teheran. Born on the banks of the Theiss, he left his country to escape conscription, preferring the life of an honest tradesman to that of a soldier. His wanderings took him to Constantinople, and on leaving that city he went through Asia Minor to Arabia, and thence through South Persia to India. This singular man had made all these journeys for the most part on foot. He was about to set out for the capital of China when news reached him of the rising of his people in 1848, in order to achieve independence. Without a moment's hesitation he determined to hasten back and enrol himself in the army of those who were ready to fight and die for their country. But he had calculated without taking into account the immense distance from Asia to Europe and his slender means, which permitted him only the slow locomotion of a pedestrian and conveyance in a sailing vessel. Thus, upon arriving in Stambul he heard of the fatal day at Vilagos, the closing act of the glorious revolutionary drama. In his disappointment he once more seized the wanderer's staff, and, resuming his old trade, reached Teheran by way of Tabreez. The good man spoke a most extraordinary language, jumbling together all the different dialects he had partly picked up in the countries through which he had passed. He did tolerably well at the beginning of a conversation, starting fairly with Hungarian; but no sooner had he become animated with his subject than a perfect farrago, consisting of a conglomeration of Hungarian, German, French, with a still more confusing mass of

Turkish, Arabic, Persian and Hindustani words, would ensue, putting the comprehension of his hearers to a sore trial. His generous heart warmed towards me, his countryman, at whose escape from so many dangers he was overjoyed; and in his simple way, to demonstrate his sympathy, he insisted upon my accepting of him a pair of pantaloons of his own handiwork, although his circumstances were rather straitened. As I could not be induced to accept his gift, he persuaded my Tartar to take it. The inhabitant of Central Asia laughed at what seemed to him a ridiculous garment; but at last curiosity prevailed with him so far as to induce him to put it on, and kind-hearted Szantó was beside himself with delight and pride at having been the first tailor who had put a Tartar into a pair of European trousers.

I must not omit to mention another European I met here, a M. de Blocqueville, who may be justly called one of the most expensive of photographers—at least to the Shah of Persia. In the service of the latter, he had taken part in an expedition against the Turkomans, had the misfortune of being taken prisoner, and was at last released upon payment of the enormous ransom of ten thousand ducats. M. de Blocqueville, a perfect French gentleman, had come to *la belle Perse* in search of adventures. He did not wish to practise as a physician, the orthodox career of a European in the East, but preferred to try his luck with photography, which, being less known in Persia, promised greater success. This amiable young man, as the sequel showed, was right in his calculations, for the king immediately engaged him to be his Court Photographer, and he was attached to the army in the capacity of painter of battle pieces. The king was delighted at having secured an artist who would immortalize on canvas the gallant feats of his heroic army, and his lively imagination conjured up visions of grand pictures in which every one of them would be portrayed as a very Rustem. Unfortunately, fate had willed it otherwise; the twenty-five thousand Rustems were attacked by five thousand Turkomans and shamefully defeated. A large portion of the brave Persian army were taken prisoners, and slaves became such a drug in the market that they could be bought back at the reasonable price of from five to six ducats. M. de Blocqueville, however, on account of his fair complexion and strange cut of features, was suspected of being worth more to his masters, and more, therefore, was asked for his release. Of course the Persians refused to accept other terms, but every new refusal brought on an increase of the ransom, until finally the exorbitant sum of ten thousand ducats had to be paid by the court of Teheran for the freedom of a French subject. Nor would this have been done but for an energetic hint conveyed by the Government of France through their representative, Bellaunay, that if the Persians had not ducats enough to ransom this French subject, they would lend him French bayonets. The gentle warning had its effect, the money was paid, and the young photographer restored to liberty. A year and a half had been spent in these negotiations, and M. de Blocqueville, formerly an officer in a regiment of the Guard, was exposed during all this time to the galling experiences of slavery among the Turkomans. The bitter contrast between the life of a gentleman in the *Champs Elysées* and that of a captive loaded with irons on neck and feet must have often suggested itself to him as he shivered in rags beneath the insufficient shelter of a Turkoman tent, with cutlets of horse-flesh the greatest culinary delicacy within reach.

He had gone through a great deal of suffering, and he all but wept for joy when he safely returned from that terrible country. To a greater degree than any one else he had leisure to study the dreadful realities of life in Central Asia, and I found in him a ready sympathizer with the hardships I had gone through, he being able to appreciate their magnitude.

Now that we are on the subject of the Turkomans, I must not leave unmentioned that several of them, who were at Astrabad on business, hearing of my arrival in Teheran, called on me and asked my *fatiha* (blessing). They assured me that my fatihas had worked wonders, and that the people in the Gomushtepe were often wishing to have me there back again. Although dressed in European clothes, these simple people reverently bowed down before me while I gave each of them a blessing, citing at the same time a few verses from the Koran. They left me apparently much edified, and they were the last people to whom I gave a fatiha, and that was the last occasion on which I performed spiritual functions of the kind. My imagination caught fire at the idea of my religious fame. I picture to myself the possibilities I might achieve among these untutored Children of the Desert, if I had only the will and the courage to dare. Such is usually the way in which Oriental heroes commence their career. They shroud themselves in a mysterious magical obscurity, and crowds follow blindly their lead, and determination alone is wanted to make a man an autocrat whose slightest command is obeyed with slavish and unreasoning submission.

With the very first breath of vernal air I bade farewell to the Persian capital, the seat of Oriental civilization, and took the regular post-road through Tabreez, Erzerum, and Trebizond to the Black Sea.

As on my journey from Meshed to Teheran I had been well supplied with all things requisite for a traveller in the East, so now from Teheran to Trebizond I lacked in nothing to render the journey comfortable. I was provided with even better horses; I had more funds; and the treatment along the road corresponded with my change of fortune. I reached the Persian frontier in the highest spirits, and made merry all along the road, encouraged by the finest imaginable spring weather. The European colony in Tabreez gave me a hearty reception. The clinking of the champagne glasses round the hospitable board of the English Consul gave me a joyful earnest of the social delights to come. The future before me stood out in bright colours, and my busy imagination mapped out, in ever-changing scenes, the successes in store for me. These hopes, dreams and expectations were afterwards more than fulfilled, but, nevertheless, I must own that the anticipation was far sweeter than the proudest triumphs accomplished in after years.

Upon crossing the eastern frontier of Azerbijan, the hilly country which borders on Turkish Kurdistan, I could not refrain from turning round to cast one last look on the soil of Iran. It is a country which will ever attract the attention and invite the genuine interest of the traveller, although its Oriental civilization and culture be disfigured by the inherent drawbacks incident to all Eastern civilizations. The arts of hypocrisy and dissimulation, which are enthroned here in all their glory, odious and contemptible as they are, should not render us blind to some of the finer qualities of the Persians, their polished manners, their courtesy, and their natural mental endowments; for here alone can we find the mental ambition to reach a higher degree of excellence in culture, a laudable feeling inspiring prince and peasant alike. The same rude manners are to be met with in the provinces of the Western border as on the Eastern. There is a vast difference between the Osmanlis and Kurds of Asia Minor and the Persians, the latter having distanced the former in all the arts of civilization; and truly Iran remains, to this day, almost the only seat of ancient Asiatic culture.

Gazing from the Pontic mountain, from whose top the Black Sea is first visible, as I arrived in the neighbourhood of Trebizond, I saw before me the coast upon which I had turned my back with so many strange misgivings two years ago this very month. The harbour, the flag of *Lloyd* fluttering in the breeze—there they were again, as if to salute me on my return. What a wild rush of thoughts were conjured up by those familiar sights, from which my parting had been so bitter!

To reach a harbour, where a ship rode at anchor ready to start, was the same thing as to reach Europe. The comforts of a splendid and commodious cabin on board the Lloyd steamer, the tokens of European life multiplying round us in every imaginable form, may foster the illusion that we are at home again, in spite of the several days' voyage separating us from Europe. I passed two days only in Trebizond, employing my time chiefly in disposing of the larger part of my equipment for Eastern travel, for which I now had no further use, retaining only a few articles as relics and keepsakes of my roamings. In the middle of May I went on board the steamer which bore me back to the scene of my future—Europe.

CHAPTER XXX.

HOMEWARDS.

IF my way from Tabreez to Trebizond resembled an entry in triumph, my journey homewards was the much more marked with signs of acknowledgment by every European I met in Turkey of the great fatigues I had undergone during my travels. On my arrival in Constantinople, I found the Turkish capital not only many times more enchanting than before, comparing the howling wilderness of Central Asia with the natural beauties of the Bosphorus, but I saw in the Turks a totally civilized nation, who are in great advance over their brethren in faith and in nationality who dwell in the interior of Asia; nay, men whose physical features resemble much more the genuine European than the representatives of the Iranian and Turanian race. My first visit was to the Austrian Ambassador of that time, to the learned diplomatist, the late Count Prokesch-Osten, who was always kind to me during my sojourn in the Turkish metropolis, and who received me now with real cordiality. For a moment he gazed upon me, not being able to recognize a former acquaintance in his emaciated and weather-worn visitor; and it was only after I had addressed him in German, that he nearly burst into tears, saying, "For heaven's sake, Vambéry, what have you done; what has become of you?" I gave him a short account of my travels, and of my adventures; and the good old man, moved to the inmost of his noble heart, tried to persuade me before all to stay a few days in his house, in order to recover my strength, and to pursue only after rest my way to Budapest. I declined politely, and listened with great attention to the hints he gave me about the next steps I had to take in Europe. "You do quite right to go straight forward to London," said the Count; "England is the only country full of interest for the geography and ethnography of Inner Asia. You will there have a good reception; but you must not forget to style accordingly the account of your travels. Keep yourself strictly to the narrative of your adventures; be short and concise in the description; and particularly abstain from writing a book mixed with far-fetched argumentations or with philological and historical notes. Philosophic dissertations do not suit the English practical mind; moreover, you can publish these things afterward in a book for strictly scientific purposes. In your English edition you must touch commercial and industrial questions; you must sketch the manners and habits of the countries you went through; and, above all, give the impression of your travels as freshly as possible."

My next visit in Constantinople was to Aali Pasha, the Grand Vizier of that time, to whom I intended to give a report of the political condition of Persia and of Central Asia, he having formerly showed a particular interest in my studies of the Eastern-Turkish language, in which dialect he was pretty well versed, possessing in his library the largest collection extant of *tchagatai* (*i.e.*, Eastern-Turkish) manuscripts. On my way from Pera to Constantinople—I mean to say to the offices of the Porte—I met with many of my previous acquaintances without being recognized by any one. The same happened with me on my passage through the corridor of that large building of the Sublime Porte, and it was only in consequence of my having been announced, that Aali Pasha was able to recognize in me the former Reshid Effendi—my official name in Turkey—the man whom he supported in his linguistic studies by lending him rare manuscripts out of his collection. The Pasha received me in his usual friendly manner, but he could hardly conceal an expression of astonishment which penetrated his urbanity. I thanked him, before all, for the letter of introduction which he gave me to Haidar Effendi, the Turkish Ambassador at Teheran. While I was enumerating all the kind services which this official, who was his particular *protégé*, had rendered to me, his gloomy countenance cheered up a little, and he began to question me about Bokhara and Khiva, of which places he knew a good deal, although his judgment of men and affairs was much influenced by religious prejudice. What struck him most was my account of the Turkomans, and particularly their allegiance to the Sultan, of whom they were anxious to become subjects in order to be safe from the grasp of Russia, already threatening them even then. Aali Pasha next inquired about the social and political conditions of Bokhara and Khiva, and he did not seem much pleased by the dismal picture I showed him of the bigotry and barbarism of the people, as well as of the reigning princes. In relating to him the haughtiness of the Emir of Bokhara, who asked me whether the

Sultan had got such well-disciplined soldiers as himself (soldiers out of whom *fifty* proved afterwards an easy match for *one* Russian!), he showed a bitter smile on his lips, and immediately turned the conversation to the valour of the Turkomans, of whose close affinity to the Osmanlis he had a precise knowledge. His affability made me a little bolder, and I remarked what a pity it was that Turkish statesmen of the past centuries had entirely neglected to keep up an uninterrupted communication with the Sunnite Turks in the distant East, and what an essential political support the Ottoman State would now have in these valiant Sons of the Desert. The timid-looking Grand Vizier answered with his accustomed smile, and very adroitly turned the conversation to the dangers of my adventure by paying compliments for the courage and perseverance I had shown in the whole undertaking. It was with the utmost effort that I suppressed further allusions to the invariably culpable carelessness of the Osmanlis about their brethren in Asia, of whom they scarcely knew anything till quite recently, when Ottoman writers translated sundry English and French books of travels in Asia, and thus gave the Turks in their own language, through the medium of the despised Frengi, the first information of their nearest relatives in the distant East. Yet how different would have been the fate of the Ottoman Empire if, by keeping up a continual intercourse with the Turks in Central Asia, they had cemented that large ethnical body of the Turks into one nation, a nation bound together by one language and by one religion!

Before I took leave of Aali Pasha, he, like Count Prokesch-Osten, insisted upon my staying a few days in Constantinople, but I politely declined, and with the promise that I would always retain in good memory my friends in old Stambul, to whose kindness I am really indebted, I hurried back to the port in order to be in due time for departure of the vessel of the Austrian Lloyd Company bound for Kustendje. On arriving at the port near Fyndykly, I had to fulfil a most unpleasant duty, namely, to dismiss my faithful Tartar, who had accompanied me from Khiva to the shore of the Bosphorus—to say a final good-bye to the sincere and honest young man, who had shared with me all the fatigues and privations of my dangerous journey homewards from the banks of the Oxus, who never showed the slightest sign of discontent, and who really had become like a brother to me. It was an unspeakably painful moment of my life! I handed over to him nearly all my ready cash, keeping only enough to pay for my food until I arrived at Pesth—for the passage was free. I gave him all my dresses, my equipment, &c., made him a long speech as to his behaviour during his further journey to Mecca and concerning his way backward to Khiva; and I had just extended my arms to embrace him, when he burst out in a torrent of tears and said, "Effendi! forgive me, but I cannot separate from you. The sanctity of the holy places is certainly a much beguiling object; to see the tomb of our Prophet is worth a whole life; but I cannot leave you, I cannot go alone! I am ready to renounce all the delights of this and of the future world; I am ready to part even with my home, but I cannot separate from you." The reader may fancy my great astonishment when I heard the *ci-devant* young theological student of Central Asia speaking these words; and I said to him, "My dear friend, do you know that I am going to the country of unbelievers, to Frengistan, where the climate, the water, the language, the manners and customs of the different people will be utterly strange to you, and where you will find yourself speedily at an extraordinary distance from your own home, and will have to remain eventually, without any hope of revisiting again in your life your paternal seat in Khiva? Consider well what you are doing, for repentance will be too late, and I should not like to be the cause of your misfortune!" The poor Tartar stood pale and dejected for a few moments, the great struggle in his soul being noticeable only by the fiery rolling of his eyes; he pressed his lips spasmodically, and then burst out in the following words, "Believer or unbeliever, I care not which, wherever you go I go with you. Good men cannot go to bad places. I have implicit faith in your friendship, and I trust in God that he will take care of us both." Standing thus in the midst of my confusion, I heard the ringing of the bell at the vessel. The time for further consideration and argumentation was gone. I took my luggage and the Tartar on board the steamer, and no sooner had we arrived than the anchors were weighed; and away we steamed through the Bosphorus on the Black Sea to Kustendje.

My journey up the Danube to Pesth in the month of May, 1864, was full of delight and interest. By every step which brought me nearer to the frontier of Hungary, I met new friends and fresh admirers, for the news of my successful travels in Central Asia had already spread throughout Europe, and had in particular roused the attention of my countrymen, with whom the dim lore of their Asiatic descent is not all unknown, and who were now most anxious to get fresh information from the seat of their ancestors, the cradle of the Magyar race. On my arrival in Pesth, I was met first by Baron

Joseph Eötvös, the Vice-President of our Academy, my noble-hearted patron, who had assisted me in my juvenile struggles, who had encouraged me to my travels, and who was now full of joy in seeing me safe, although he was much worn-out by fatigues at home. Baron Eötvös, the greatest literary genius of Hungary of the present century, the author of the brilliant philosophical work "The Reigning Ideas of the Nineteenth Century," did not at all conceal from me the difficulties I should yet have to contend with, by alluding to the scepticism of the world in general, and particularly by calling my attention to the indifference which the result of my travels might meet in various quarters. "Here in Hungary," he said, "it is only the philological, or rather the ethnological part of your investigations, which will find a national interest; these you will have ample time in later years to work out, after having settled down quietly. As to your geographical and ethnological discoveries, you must look for a wider field, for a better market, which you will find only in England, whose far-spreading commercial and political interests justify a deeper and a livelier attention to all that is going on in distant Asia. Go at once to London, and being provided, as you are, with letters of introduction to the leading personalities, you are almost sure of a warm reception, and of a real acknowledgment of your merits." Well, this plan had matured in me since my leaving Teheran, where the late Sir Charles Alison, and particularly Mr. Thompson, the present British Minister at the Persian Court, had likewise given to me similar suggestions. I therefore took the firm decision to go to England as soon as possible—I mean to say as soon as I got the necessary means for the journey. This equipment proved, however, not an easy task, for very few of my countrymen could realize the practical importance of my travels, and more than ten days elapsed before I could procure the necessary fifteen pounds for a journey to the English metropolis. Marks of recognition in the papers, invitations to dinner-parties, &c., were not wanting on my arrival at Pesth; but the funds for my journey to London were not so easily got, and I was obliged to leave my Tartar behind in the care of a friend and to proceed alone to England. It was certainly a great pity not to be able to bring Mollah Ishak—this was the name of the Tartar—to the banks of the Thames, for he would have made a capital figure at Burlington House, before the Royal Geographical Society; but I had to accommodate myself to imperious necessity, and taking with me only my notes and a few Oriental manuscripts, I left Hungary towards the end of May, and proceeded without stopping on the way through Germany and France to England.

CHAPTER XXXI.

IN ENGLAND.

ONLY a couple of weeks having elapsed since I emerged from the depths of Asia to the very centre of Europe, and since I exchanged the life of a travelling dervish for that of a strictly Europeanized man of letters, it may easily be conceived what extraordinary effects this sudden transformation wrought upon me. I shall try to describe some of the prominent features of this change, although I hardly believe that my feeble pen is equal to the task. It was before all the idea of having renounced the life of a wanderer, and of being henceforward unable to change my abode daily, which gave me great trouble. The firm and stable house and its furniture seemed to me like fetters, and filled me with disgust after a few days' stay. Then came the aversion I felt to the European dress, particularly to the necktie and stiff linen, which were quite an ordeal to me, accustomed as for years I had been to the wide and comfortable Asiatic garb, which gives not the slightest restraint whilst its wearer is either sitting or walking. Not even the food, and still less the manner of eating, had any attraction for me, who for years and years had used his fingers as knife and fork, and who had now to observe the European table etiquette with all its rigour. And what should I say about all the multifarious differences between the manners and habits of Europe and those of Asia? I really felt like a child, or like some semi-barbarous inhabitant of Asia or Africa on his first introduction into European society, and I really do not know whether I should laugh at my awkwardness in that time, or whether I should admire the forbearance shown to me by English society during the first weeks of my appearance in London.

With these and similar feelings I spent my first days in the English metropolis. My first care was to hand over the letters of introduction I got in Teheran to those distinguished *savants* and politicians who were connected with Central Asia, and who had a pre-eminent interest in the results of my travels. My first visit was to *Sir Henry Rawlinson*, who was then, and is even now, the greatest living authority on all scientific and political questions associated with Central Asia. He received me in a most affable manner in his house in Berkeley Street, Berkeley Square, where he was living at that time; and although I was able to lead an English conversation, still for the sake of better fluency I preferred Persian, of which Sir Henry, late ambassador of Great Britain in Persia, was a perfect master, and which he really handled with exquisite refinement. The topic of our conversation was of course Bokhara, Khiva, Herat, and Turkestan, places of which the learned decipherer of the cuneiform inscriptions of Behistan had an astounding store of information. My details about the capture of Herat by Dost Mohammed Khan, about the campaign of the Emir of Bokhara against Kokhand in favour of Khudayar Khan, and particularly the rumours I heard about the approach of the Russian detachment under Tchernayeff, were the topics in which he seemed most interested. It was a kind of cross-examination which I had to go through; and after a conversation of nearly an hour's length, I took leave with the full conviction that my first *début* was not an unsuccessful one. The next call I made was upon *Sir Roderick Murchison*, the President of the Royal Geographical Society at that time, whose house, at 16, Belgrave Square, gave me for the first time an idea of the comfort and luxury surrounding an English literary man of distinction. I need scarcely say that Sir Roderick, whose amiability is world-wide known, received me, not like a foreigner introduced to him by his friend, but like a fellow-traveller—as became the good-hearted patron of all those whose efforts were directed towards the furthering of geographical knowledge. He did not care much about the languages, the manners, and the habits of Asiatic people, but rather about orographical and hydrographical facts; and he actually showed some disappointment on hearing from me that I neither brought cartographical sketches nor specimens of the geological formations. Having been asked whether I had brought some drawings with me, I answered not quite to his satisfaction, that I carried only a small pencil not larger than the half of my thumb with me, concealed under the wadding of my dervish dress, and that if people had noticed my making any use of this contrivance, I certainly should not have had the pleasure of my present interview with him. The good old man was unable to realize the great dangers I ran in my disguise, for he always thought on his own journey to the Ural, executed under the princely protection of the

Emperor of Russia—he being provided with ample means from home. The topic which he most decidedly shunned was politics; for whenever I touched the question of the Russian approach to the frontiers of India, and of the very near term of Russian encroachment upon Central Asia, he immediately said smilingly, "Oh you must not believe that; the Russians are a nice people; their Emperor is an enlightened, noble prince, and the Russian plans in Asia cannot mean mischief against the interests of Great Britain." As to the enlightened character of the late Russian Emperor, nobody had any doubt. His esteem and consideration for science had an eloquent symbol in the pair of magnificent malachite vases which were in the house of Sir Roderick Murchison, who was much liked at the Court on the Neva; but, as events have since proved, these were only testimonials of personal feelings, which had no influence whatever upon the course of politics in Asia. Excepting that this single difference of opinion occurred, my first meeting with the President of the Royal Geographical Society succeeded beyond all my expectations. He invited me to lecture before the society at its concluding meeting, and asked me to dinner on an early evening. I confess the kind manner in which this noble-hearted gentleman treated me during my sojourn in London, and the rich hospitality which I so frequently enjoyed in his house, will be ever green in my memory.

The third man upon whom I called was the late Viscount Strangford, the wonderful Oriental linguist and the brilliant writer. I say on purpose wonderful, for I rarely met a man in my life whose almost supernatural ability to speak and to write many European and Asiatic languages caused me so much astonishment. Our conversation began in the Turkish of Constantinople, in that refined idiom, whereof six or eight words out of every ten are certainly either Arab or Persian, only the others belonging to the genuine Turkish stock. To use this language in an elegant way, it is requisite to adapt one's mode of thinking entirely to that of thoroughbred Orientals, to have besides a proficiency in the standard works of Mohammedan literature, and, above all, to have moved a good deal in the so-called Effendi society. It is certainly no exaggeration to say that Lord Strangford, fully adequate to these exigencies, would have been taken by everybody for a downright Effendi, had it not been for the peculiarly Celtic shape of his head, and for the way in which he used to turn it to the right and to the left of his shoulders. Finding that I had come fresh from the East, where for many years I used Turkish as a colloquial and literary language, he was delighted to renew with me all his reminiscences of a long stay on the Bosphorus, and particularly to have somebody who was able to give him oral information about the language and literature of Central Asia, in which he was so much interested. Having flattered myself with the hope that I should become the only authority in Europe on Eastern-Turkish, the reader may fancy my astonishment when I heard from the mouth of an English nobleman the recital of such poems as those of Nevai, which had hitherto escaped my attention, and when he gave me the explanation of words which I had vainly looked for in the Eastern dictionaries. Lord Strangford was quite a riddle to me; for apart from his knowledge in Eastern tongues, he spoke almost all European languages; he was a Sclavonic scholar, he knew Hungarian, nay even the language of the Gipsies; and what struck me most was his vast information concerning the various literatures and histories of these peoples. No wonder, therefore, that I felt from the beginning a particular attraction to the learned Viscount, and that he also, as I afterwards had ample opportunity to learn, took a fancy to me and became my most zealous and disinterested supporter in England. Envy and jealousy had no place in the noble heart of Lord Strangford; he gave himself all possible pains to introduce me everywhere, and to level the ground before me, and the standing I gained in London society was entirely due to his exertions.

Amongst the introductions which I had brought with me from Teheran was one to Mr., now Sir Henry, Layard, another to the late Sir Justin Sheil, formerly Ambassador at Teheran, and recommendations to several men of note connected in some way or other with the interior of Asia. Sir Henry Layard, who was at that time Under Secretary of State for Foreign Affairs, received me in his open, straightforward, British manner. Not many years having elapsed since the politician of high standing was himself a traveller in Asia, he behaved towards me like a colleague and like a former brother in arms. The same I must say in reference to the late Sir Justin Sheil and Lady Sheil; the latter was kind enough to give me the necessary hints as to the complicated laws and social tone of the West End: in one word, all my friends helped together to shape out of the rough material of the *ci-devant* dervish the lion of the London season. No easy task of course, if you consider that the said dervish, although a European by birth, had never before been west of his own country, and that his education and his continual studies were not made to facilitate such a change in his life. But what does not man attempt for the sake of success? Necessity and assistance had soon transformed the lame Mohammedan beggar into an admired lion of the British metropolis; and the man, who but a few months before had to wander about in tatters and to beg his daily bread by chanting hymns and by bestowing blessings upon true believers in Asia, became the wonder of the richest and the most civilized society of the Western world!

It is the details of this extraordinary change that I have to relate to my gentle reader.

The account of my adventures having become known in strictly scientific circles, my friends thought it necessary to bring me before the larger public, and the first forum in which I had to appear was the Royal Geographical Society. There was, however, a rather curious hindrance to the final settlement, an incident which I cannot leave untold. A few days after my arrival in London I noticed that some of my friends began to have a shy look, and that they treated me with a good amount of caution, if not suspicion. Having just finished the career of a dangerous disguise, and being accustomed to the suspicious looks of men, I did not at first feel disconcerted; but the fact nevertheless excited my curiosity, and speaking just then with General Kmethy, my countryman of Kars renown and a popular member of London society at that time, about the strange attitude of people, I was told by the good man, in a half laughing and joking manner, that I was probably unaware of the serious danger in which I found myself in London. I heard then that some, even the best of my friends, on seeing my sun-burned, swarthy face, and on hearing my unmistakably genuine Persian and Turkish conversation, got rather suspicious about me, and took me for some Persian vagabond who had learned English in India, and who, after having succeeded in getting letters of introduction, was now playing a comedy for English scholars and diplomatists. It was only the formal assurance of General Kmethy that I was a countryman of his and a member of the Hungarian Academy, which dissipated the doubts that had arisen. "Is it not strange?" said I to myself. "In Asia they suspected me to be a European, and in Europe to be an Asiatic; languages have really an immense power of fascination!" This difficulty having been removed and an unimpaired confidence having set in, I began to work out a short account of my travels in English, to be read before the Royal Geographical Society—a paper which Mr. Laurence Oliphant, who was acting at that time as foreign secretary of the Society, was kind enough to revise. I must say that it was with a good deal of impatience and anxiety that I looked forward to the evening of my first *début* before a select English audience such as the members of the London Geographical Society have been always, and are even now. My anxiety was the much more justified, as it happened that on the same evening a political question of a far-reaching interest, namely, whether England should side with Denmark in her struggle with Germany, was to be discussed in the House of Parliament, and my friends as well as myself apprehended the presence of a very small audience at our proceedings. The usual dinner at Willis's Rooms which preceded our meeting went off tolerably well. My health was proposed by Sir Roderick Murchison in very kind terms and drunk with much cheering; and, when I returned thanks, I concluded my little speech by conferring a Mohammedan blessing upon the dinner party—reciting the first Surah of the Koran with all the eccentricity of the Arabic guttural accent, and with all the queerness of genuine Moslem gesticulation. I need scarcely say that my mode of recital elicited a good deal of merriment. We left the table and went straight to Burlington House.

Here I found a meeting much larger than I expected, an attendance which I ascribe to the novelty of the whole case. Before all, it was the sight of a European who had wandered about in the interior of Asia in the disguise of a holy beggar without a penny in his pocket, and who had succeeded in penetrating countries hitherto little or not at all known. Secondly, it was the curiosity to hear a foreigner, only a few days in England, address an English meeting in the language of the country; and last, if not least, it was the interest the British public felt at that time in Bokhara, the place of the martyrdom of two heroic sons of Great Britain—I mean of Conolly and Stoddart—and the town from which the Rev. Dr. Joseph Wolff had only returned a few years previously, after his most extraordinary adventures. Suffice it to say that the meeting was most respectable from a quantitative point of view. Sir Roderick opened it with a good humour quite in accord with his jolly and radiant after-dinner face; and whilst Mr. Clements Markham read my paper in his magnificent stentorian voice, I had plenty of leisure to observe the assembly and to prepare for the speech which had to follow. On being asked by the President to come before the public and to give an oral account of what had just been read, I confess that I experienced something of the position in which I stood before the Emir of Bokhara—with the essential difference of course, that in case of a failure the bloody tyrant would have handed me over to the executioner, whilst the indulgent English public would have expressed its displeasure by benignant laughter. I collected, therefore, all my linguistic powers, and, after the utterance of the first ten or fifteen words, the flood of oration went off uninterruptedly. For more than half an hour I spoke with animation of the salient incidents of my adventurous journey to Samarkand. Oh, glorious language of Shakespeare and Milton! I am sure nobody has ever tormented thee so much as I did in those thirty-five minutes; nobody has murdered the Queen's English in such a cruel way as the ex-dervish in Burlington House! And yet the English audience showed itself exceedingly kind towards the reckless foreigner. I was much applauded and cheered; and when, following the summons of Sir Roderick, I gave to the meeting my blessing with the genuine Arabic text, the whole society burst into a fit of laughter, which made the walls nearly tremble. Then followed the long business of hand-shaking and congratulations; and though all the futilities of this world may disappear from me, Lord Strangford's "Well done, dervish!" will never cease to resound in my ear like the sweetest music I ever heard in my life.

From this moment dates the beginning of my career in England. What followed was only the effect of this first successful step. In the report of the next morning's papers I noticed only a few reproaches of my foreign accent; as to the account of my travels there was a unanimous approval and admiration. No wonder, therefore, that a few weeks sufficed to make my name familiar over the whole of the United Kingdom. London society vied in the manifestation of all kinds of acknowledgment. Invitations to dinner-parties and to visit in the country literally poured in upon me, even from persons whom I never saw or met in my life; and it happened frequently that I had to write thirty letters of refusal and acceptance in one day. I got calls from all sorts of persons with well-sounding names, who, provided with a card of one of my friends, came to my humble lodging in Great Portland Street or to the Athenæum Club, where I enjoyed the hospitality of a guest, to shake hands and to have a conversation with me. Infinite was the number of those letters in which I was asked for my likeness or for my autograph.

Surprised by these various kinds of distinction, at the outset I endured the burdens of my reputation with patience, nay with a good amount of satisfaction, but in the end they began to be a little too wearisome—particularly as I had to write the account of my journey and to work up the meagre notes written on small paper scraps with lead pencil, which loose sheets, by having been worn concealed under the wadding of my beggar-dress, were somewhat obliterated and had become hardly legible. Assisted by a happy gift of memory, I succeeded, however, in writing down my adventures; and in three months I had revised the proof-sheets of my first book, entitled "Travels in Central Asia." The task, I frankly own, cost me more trouble and exertion than many of the most trying parts of my travels. Only those who for months and years have moved about freely in the open air, and who have learned to appreciate the charms of a continually wandering life with all its exciting adventures—only those will know with what unspeakable pangs and sufferings a former traveller can shut himself up in a room, from which he sees only a small bit of the sky, and sit down to write consecutively for hours every day for weeks and months! What is the soft chair, what the sumptuous dinner in comparison with the hard saddle and with the simple food, cooked by the traveller's own hand at the open fire on the ground? People may call me exalted or eccentric, but let them try, and I am sure they will say that I am right, and that the traveller whilst roaming about in God's beautiful nature is much happier than the author who has to write down his experiences! I need scarcely say that I breathed more freely after having finished my book, and handed it over to Mr. John Murray, who became my publisher on the recommendation of Lord Strangford, and who behaved towards me in a satisfactory way. The honorarium of five hundred pounds which I got, and of which I spent nearly the half in London, did not make me rich at all. The truth is, my material situation was not very much changed: a dervish in Asia, I remained a *fakir* in Europe; but I gained by my book something more valuable than money, namely, the acknowledgments of the English public, and fame and reputation over the whole European and American Continents.

I remained in London another couple of months after the publication of my book, partly in order to watch the effect produced by it upon the literary world, whose criticisms flowed in slowly; partly, also, because I had not yet decided whether I should settle down definitely in Hungary, or whether I should again take the wanderer's staff and plunge again into fresh adventures. During this time I made several excursions to the Continent. I visited France, Germany and Hungary for the sake of the various editions of my books in different languages, to the preparation of which I was summoned by the leading publishing firms.

Upon the invitation of the friends I had in the meantime made I also went to satisfy the curiosity of leading political men, who were anxious to hear details about the threatening collision between England and Russia in the distant East, of which I threw out only a few hints in the concluding chapter of my book, but which nevertheless had aroused the greatest attention. It was in this way that I came into connection with politics and with the political men of that time. Already, on the occasion of the first meeting of the Royal Geographical Society, the political question had been broached in that strictly scientific circle, and Sir Henry Rawlinson, Lord Strangford and others had pointed to the imminent danger which threatened Great Britain from Russia's approach up the Syr-Darya. The period of "masterly inactivity" being just at its height, the chorus of opponents to all anti-Russian declarations became the much greater, and the worthy President of the Society himself, actuated by his declared Russian sympathies, sided from the beginning with those who styled the Russian advance a blessing for civilization. Their favourite argument was: "There is room enough in Asia for England as well as for Russia; there is no reason for jealousy and no fear of a future collision." This politico-scientific discussion in Burlington House was very soon taken up by the leading papers in London as well as in the provinces, and although apathy, and (I am sorry to say) ignorance, and self-deceit had largely increased the number of the adherents of a policy of unconditional reliance on Russia and of strict neutrality, yet there was also a lively interest shown towards those who were in favour of activity and watchfulness. I came, therefore, very soon in contact with the leading political men of that time, such as Members of Parliament, political writers, retired civilians and military officers of India, and, consequently, got the opportunity of an interview with Lord Palmerstone, to whom I had already been cursorily introduced at a dinner-party in the house of Sir Roderick Murchison. His Lordship received me at his home in Piccadilly, and my visit was therefore of a strictly private character. He did not address me exactly as he did the late Dr. Livingstone, to whom he said, "You had a nice walk across Africa!" But his first remark was, "You must have gone through nice adventures on your way to Bokhara and Samarkand!" And he really listened with greatest attention to all that I said about Dost Mohammed Khan, about the haughtiness of the Emir of Bokhara and about the dangers I ran in the last-named town. On touching the question of the Russian advance towards Tashkend, I took the map out of my book which was on the table, and pointed to Chimkent as the place where the Russians stood at that time; but his Lordship showed, or at least feigned, great incuriosity, trying always to turn the thread of conversation to other insignificant topics. Whenever I thought I had caught his attention he immediately came forward with the question, "And did you not betray your European character?" or "How could you stand that long trial and those privations?" or with similar remarks. It was only after renewed attacks upon his taciturnity that he dropped, in a careless manner, a few allusions either to the barbarous state of affairs in Central Asia or to my over-sanguine opinions of the Russian strength in that quarter of the world. He succeeded in showing outward indifference, but he was far from convincing me of its existence. In my interview with Lord Clarendon I fared much better. It took place late in the Autumn of 1864, when the famous note of Prince Gortschakoff, after the Russian capture of Tashkend, had been made known, and when the public opinion of England seemed to have been roused suddenly from its stupor. His Lordship was frank enough to admit the truth of what I said in the last chapter of my book; but he added at the same time what has since become the standing principle of optimists in England: "Russia's policy in Central Asia is framed in the same way as ours in India; she is compelled to move gradually from the North to the South, just as we were obliged to do in our march from the South to the North. She is doing services to civilization, and we do not care much even if she takes Bokhara."

Here I could not help observing that it was a great fallacy of English statesmen to fancy that Russia would be contented with the three Khanates as the reward of her long, costly and wearisome policy from the Ural to the Oxus. Her goal of desire lies much more to the south; and if it had not been for the utter relapse in which English policy had fallen since the unfortunate Afghan campaign, Russia certainly would not have had the courage to push on with such unrelenting zeal from two sides, namely from the Caucasus and from South Siberia, as she has done during the past two decades. "And do you fancy we could have prevented her from doing so?" asked the Secretary of State for Foreign Affairs. "Yes, my lord, you could have done so," I said; "but now I am afraid it is too late." And here I went on to muster my arguments in the following way. Having pointed at first to the great danger, nay to the impossibility of a conterminous line of frontier on the Suleiman range or on the Hindu Kush, and showing the necessity of a neutral zone or of a geographical buffer—herein his Lordship fully agreed—I continued that this neutral zone would be of real value, if it comprised all the countries between India and the Yaxartes, and that not only ought Afghanistan to be brought under the influence of England, but also the petty Khanates on the left of the Oxus, and particularly Bokhara, Khiva and Kokhand. At the first blush, this would seem a hopeless undertaking, but in reality it is not so. It must be borne in mind that amongst the various nationalities constituting Central

Asia, the Afghans may be properly called the most warlike, the most barbarous and the most treacherous race; a people with whom religious fanaticism is only a means to rouse an innate desire for robbery and murder, and not the result of exalted feeling, as is the case with the Bokhariots. Now if these Afghans, in spite of their hatred towards every foreigner, and notwithstanding their indomitable character, had ultimately given in, and had entered into negotiations with the unbelievers, there was much more likelihood that the Emir of Bokhara might have been much more easily gained over by the English, at a time when he saw himself seriously threatened by Russia, and when he really implored the impracticable assistance of the Sultan of Turkey.

Upon this, Lord Clarendon remarked, that what I suggested had been attempted during the mission of Sir Alexander Burnes; and we all knew the deplorable effect of the first approach of English diplomacy.

"Well," said I, "it is precisely the success of the mission of Burnes which I would quote as an example. He was a good man in the proper place, and the only misfortune is, that the government has made a most unhappy choice in the men who have been entrusted with the subsequent missions to Bokhara; for neither was Conolly, with his pure Christian heart and enterprising character, nor the eccentric Stoddart, the noble-hearted but tight soldier, a fit man to be employed in Bokhara. I fully admit the craziness of the bloodthirsty Emir Nasrullah; but why did he not kill the Russian envoy, Captain Vitkovich, at a time when he had no immediate fear of the chastening hand of Russia? The fact is that the English have always been behind Russia in the use of proper and efficient measures with

Orientals; they have ever been inclined to view men and things in Asia in a light adapted to European matters. That is the chief reason of their failure; for whilst the success of Great Britain in the East is owing to the bravery and to the staunch and persevering character of her sons, we see Russia earning far more substantial benefits, at comparatively much smaller cost in blood and money, through the skilfulness of her diplomacy and the proper employment of the necessary means."

I would have continued my political argumentations, but the servant having announced a new visitor, I left the house of Lord Clarendon fully convinced of the feasibility of my plan. And so I am even now: for I always say to myself, "What a splendid neutral zone would have been made of the steppes north of the Yaxartes, if Bokhara, duly influenced and supported by England and by Turkey, could have got from the South and not from the North the first sparks of European civilization—if her soldiers, who are now drilled by a Russian commander, could have been taught by English officers! The country north of the Yaxartes, which Russia is unable even now to connect by rail with Oxenburg, would not have been so easily made a debatable ground as that of Afghanistan, where—whilst the English would like to fix the Russian frontier on the Oxus, and the Russians themselves are always speaking of the Hindu Kush—a mutual understanding is difficult, if not utterly impossible."

After these interviews with the leading political men of the day, I came frequently in contact with all kinds and all shades of politicians; and whilst the philological and ethnographical results of my travels found an interest with only a very limited number of scholars, the political question had gained daily more and more extension; and wherever I appeared the discussion about the real or feigned dangers which menaced India was immediately entered into. There was no lack of curiosity with the English public at large; but so much the more striking did I find the great popular ignorance not only upon Central Asian, but also upon Asiatic matters in general; and I afterwards put to myself very frequently the question: Is it possible that a nation so superficially informed of the real condition of the East should play such a mighty and influential *rôle* in that part of the world, and can or will that *rôle* be of long continuance? On throwing a flying look over the great mass of commercial and industrial people in England, not excluding even the gentry, one might be inclined to give a negative answer. But the masses are everywhere led; and the leading men in England are thoroughly up in these questions. I do not mean the leading politicians, but I mean the leading men in Eastern matters; and as long as England possesses its Rawlinsons, Strangfords, Layards, Yules, &c, and as long as dogged perseverance, patriotism and undaunted courage form the prominent feature of the character of English traveller, officer, nay private soldier, in Asia, so long will also last the crushing superiority of Englishmen over the native of Asia, in spite of all the deplorable blunders and shortsightedness of the British statesman, and notwithstanding all the afflicting apathy towards politics in the distant East, so frequently met with in English commercial and industrial centres.

CHAPTER XXXII.

IN PARIS.

AFTER being wearied by the endless series of dinner-parties in London—or, as a friend of mine jestingly remarked, after having been properly hunted down as the lion of the season—I felt the great necessity of extricating myself from the splendid, but to me the already tiresome, English hospitality; and I went over to Paris to have a look about in French society. This became the much easier for me—Count Rechberg, the Austrian Minister of Foreign Affairs, having provided me with a letter of introduction to Prince Metternich, who was then accredited to the court of the Emperor Napoleon, and Count Rochechouart, the French Envoy at Teheran, having given me a similar letter to the Count Drouyn de L'huys, the French Minister of Foreign Affairs. I had, moreover, the good fortune to be introduced by my English friends to many other literary men of distinction, such as M. Guizot, M. de Thiers, M. Jules Mohl, and others, all of whom received me very politely—although their first reception impressed me with the feeling that the ground upon which I stood in Paris was quite different to that of London. The French have never indulged a particular foible of geographical discovery; a traveller holds with them an interesting individuality, but is not the great man, as in England, where the successful explorer is somewhat like what the German means when he speaks of "*grosser Gelehrte*," or the Frenchman when he speaks of "*un grand savant*." Whereas the English have a particular consideration for the man who has made himself a name on the field of practical observations, or who has enriched any branch of science with new data collected on the spot, the French, and more particularly the Germans, have always a predilection for the theoretical investigator, for the man who, absorbed in his library, is able to write big books with numerous notes; in one word, in England the spirit of Raleigh, Drake, and Cook is still alive, whilst in France and Germany travellers and explorers have only very recently come into fashion.

Paris society was more impressed with the novelty of my *manner* of travelling—namely, my having assumed the disguise of a dervish—than with the travels themselves; it viewed me in the light of a rather curious adventurer. I was spoken of as a man of restless spirit and of romantic proclivities, and I was gazed upon as some modern Robinson Crusoe. What heightened my reputation most was my happy gift of speaking many European and Asiatic languages. Happening one evening to meet in the *salon* of M. Guizot the representatives of ten different nationalities, and having conversed with them fluently in their mother languages, I was regarded by many as a real miracle. As to the intrinsic value of my reception in France, I noticed in the very beginning that I should remain a stranger there, for Bokhara and Samarkand, Uzbegs and Turkomans are totally unknown, except among a few learned men, in the best French society. Nevertheless, my book, which came out in a French translation under the title "Voyage d'un Faux Derviche," had a pretty good sale.

After having been introduced to some of the best circles, I was told by Prince Metternich that the Emperor would like to give me an audience; having read the English edition of my book, he would like to ask me a few questions. One afternoon the Prince took me to the Tuileries, and we had just entered the gate of the Pavillon d'Horloge, when I saw Napoleon III. on the staircase as he took leave of the Queen of Spain, who had called upon him. On noticing Prince Metternich, with whom the imperial family was on very good terms, the Emperor seized his arm, and beckoning in a friendly manner to me, walked to the interior apartments. The Prince remained behind with the Empress, whom I found surrounded by a stately group of court ladies, in the midst of whom she was decidedly the tallest and the finest. I was led by the Emperor to a room which seemed to be his study; he sat upon an arm-chair, and bade me also to sit before a writing-desk filled with a large quantity of books, papers, maps, &c., not in any particular order. After having fixed me for a while with his whitish-grey eyes, he addressed me in a very slow voice, saying that he congratulated me on the courage I had shown in my perilous undertaking, and that having read my book he was the more astonished on finding that my slight and seemingly weak frame was not at all in proportion to the great hardships I had endured. I remarked upon this, that I was never ill in my life, and that I did not walk in Central Asia upon my legs, but upon my tongue, for it was only my linguistic study which had rescued me out of the clutches of the Central Asian tyrants. "I supposed that that must have been the case," said the Emperor; "but I believe there is also a good deal of dramatic skill in you, for otherwise you would not have played successfully the part of a mendicant dervish." The conversation turned to the ethnical conditions of Central Asia; and the Emperor, who had finished at that time his "Life of Cæsar," said that he was anxious to know whether the Parthians were really the ancestors of the present Turkomans; he was inclined to believe so, but he had been unable hitherto to establish their identity. From the Turkomans we passed over to the ruins of Balkh. I noticed that the imperial author was tolerably versed in the writings of Arrian as well as in Roman antiquities in general; but his knowlege of the modern geography of Asia was sadly deficient. He had only very dim notions about the principal names of towns and rivers, and he had palpably to take particular care not to betray his ignorance. On speaking of the Yaxartes I alluded to the serious political complication which might arise in the near future from the advance of Russia towards India, and although he tried in the beginning to conceal his interest in that question, he nevertheless listened with great attention, and afterwards remarked that he could hardly believe in a collision between England and Russia in that quarter of the world; at least not very soon,—for whereas the English had already got a firm standing in India, as proved by the Sepoy revolution of 1857, Russia was only on the eve of her conquests; besides, as she advanced she left behind her back the broad tract of deserts, inhabited by unruly Nomads, who were a continual danger to the progressing outposts. Upon my saying that the Central Asian diversion is only a lateral movement, and that the real basis of the operations of Russia against India will be the Caucasus, the Emperor remarked smilingly, "I see that besides philology you have taken up also the line of politics;" and diverting our conversation from the Anglo-Russian rivalry, he continued to ask me sundry questions about Persia and Herat, and seemed to be much pleased when I assured him that the Persian people knew a good deal about *Napliun*, as they call Napoleon I., and that they look upon his great-uncle as a national hero, descended from Rustem, and that they laugh at the French, who vindicate him as their countryman. I remained nearly half an hour with the Emperor. I am sorry to say he did not make upon me at all the impression of such a great man as he was then throughout the world supposed to be.

A few days later I called upon M. Drouyn de L'huys, who showed a more eager interest in the Central Asian question than his master. He started by asking me whether it was true that I had given a memorandum to Lord Palmerston on the Central Asian question, and whether I really believed in the imminent danger of collision between the two great European Powers in the distant East. I answered that I had not given, nor was I asked to write any communication to the British Government, and as far as I noticed from my conversation with the Prime Minister of the Queen of England, they had got on the other side of the Channel quite different views from those I held on the question. I then went on to explain to him my reasons for deploring the unavoidable ascendancy of Russia in the interior of Asia; I gave him details about the political conditions of the three Khanates and of Afghanistan; and he really watched with greatest attention all the indications I made upon the large map of Asia lying on his writing-desk.

Besides these two official receptions, I have to mention my interview with the Prince Napoleon, who received me in the Palais Royal, and who, whilst seated under the life-size portrait of his great-uncle, seemed to be watching to discover whether I noticed the likeness said to exist between him and his uncle. Well, I was really struck with the striking similitude existing between the prominent features of both. The two heads resembled each other, however, only in a very external form; and there was a difference in which the Emperor's cousin would never believe, and from this unbelief derived so many disagreeable adventures in his life. I need scarcely say that these official visits did not answer much to my taste. But still less did I like the intruding call of reporters, who interviewed me and published the next day totally false reports of my conversation with them, which I had afterwards to contradict, particularly as some of them announced that I was entrusted by Lord Palmerston with a secret mission to the Tartars, and other similar nonsense. One writer—if I remember well, a Polish prince—went even so far as to write a novel about my travels, in which I was represented as a champion of romantic propensities, with whom a Tartar princess fell in love, and who, having obtained in this way some throne in Asia, was now on a political errand in Europe to secure the friendship of England and France in the contest against Russia. I laughed heartily at these exalted reports; but in the end I got tired of a dubious sort of reputation, and I left France to proceed through Germany to my native country, where I should have to decide whether I should settle down quietly or whether I should plunge again in new adventures and revisit the interior of Asia.

CHAPTER XXXIII.

IN HUNGARY.

I HAVE often been asked how it came about that, after my long and varied career in Asia as well as in Europe, I made up my mind to settle quietly down in Hungary and to look upon the Chair of Oriental Languages at the University of Pesth as a fit reward for my extraordinary struggles in life. People who put that question generally forget what the French say—"*On revient toujours à son premier amour*"—and that the fancy which we have taken in the early part of our life, may well slacken or disappear for a certain time, but it is almost sure to return at a mature age. This is particularly the case if this fancy is congenial to the man in consequence of his natural gifts and personal taste, and if the object of his efforts and aspirations moves in the upper sphere of moral instead of material life. Being addicted to studies from the most tender age, and having tasted the delight of scientific occupations at a time when others were given up to play and amusements, it was but very natural that my feelings were attracted to scientific pursuits with redoubled zeal when

I saw that my travels and my former sufferings had assured me a tolerably good position in life, a position not very bright, but enough to afford a modest subsistence, and to give me leisure for the continuation of my favourite studies. It was during my first audience with the Emperor-King of Austro-Hungary that the kind-hearted monarch asked me whether I intended to remain in the country, and what he could do in my favour. On having alluded to my desire for a professorship at the Hungarian University, his Majesty suggested that such out-of-the-way studies were not much cultivated even at Vienna, how then could I hope to find an audience at Budapest? I remarked upon that, if nobody else would learn, I should learn myself. The Emperor fully understood, and he kindly remarked, "Your sufferings deserve a remuneration, and I shall look into your case." Two or three months had scarcely elapsed, when I got my appointment with the modest salary of one hundred pounds a year, which sum the Hungarian Minister for Public Instruction very soon doubled; and this, together with the income derived from the small sum I got for the English, French and German editions of my book, fully sufficed to cover my expenses—nay to enable me to found a family. When it became public that I intended to marry, people generally said, "What an unhappy idea; and what a pity for that poor girl!" People took it for sure that I must get tired of matrimony in a very short time, and that I should leave home, family, wife and everything, to run again after adventures in the interior of Asia. Well, people were grossly mistaken, for neither was I an adventurer by natural impulse, nor were all the praises bestowed upon me strong enough to drive me again into the wilderness, or to instigate me to renew my wanderings. It is true I was but thirty-two years old when I returned to Europe, and although temporarily worn out by fatigue, I regained my former strength in one year; but already I had spent twenty years in wanderings of all sorts, and the idea of possessing my own room, my own furniture, and my own library, made me exceedingly happy. I revelled in the thought of being able to write down and to publish those of my explorations which interest but a small community, but are of so much more value. First, I burned with desire to publish my linguistic researches in the field of Eastern-Turkish, at that time totally neglected and unknown in Europe; for excepting the studies of Quatremère and of two Russian scholars, this branch of Oriental literature was but rarely touched upon. I published, therefore, my "Căgataische Sprachstudien," in which I gave extracts from those manuscripts which I had collected in the bazaars of Khiva, Bokhara and Meshed, the works of such poets and writers as were entirely new to our Orientalists. I added an Eastern-Turkish glossary in French and in German, of which I am proud to say that it was used not only by our best Turkologists, such as Pavet de Courteille and Zenker, but also by the Russians, who have since conquered those countries, and are still learning the language of the Khanates out of my unpretentious linguistic contribution. Very soon afterwards followed my book on the *Uigur* language, called "Uigurische Sprachmonumente," based upon the unique manuscript in possession of the Imperial Library of Vienna, more than nine hundred years old. The deciphering of this enigmatic work—of which the language was strange and even many letters were unknown, and which was written besides in a most careless handwriting—had given me great trouble. For three years I spent a few hours every day in gazing upon the Sibyline text, until I succeeded in reading and in understanding the greatest part of it. This publication—for material assistance in issuing which I am indebted to the Hungarian Academy —has much weakened my eyesight, but has strengthened my position as an Orientalist. Then followed at short intervals my "Essay towards an Etymological Dictionary of the Turko-Tartar Dialects," my "Primitive Culture of the Turko-Tartar People," and many other papers upon philological topics, published in Germany and Hungary. I tried my pen also in historical work by writing a "History of Bokhara and Transuxania," which, owing to the scarcity of books of reference, and to my being too distant from the collection of Eastern manuscripts, was certainly defective; but it was the first essay in that field of history, and my too severe critics evidently forgot that my chief mistake was that of having carried out my intention in Budapest, instead of in Paris, London and St. Petersburg. As belonging to the line of strictly scientific literature, I must mention my recent work on the "Origin of the Hungarians," which made a great sensation in my native country, and of which the first edition was sold in three days—a rare success considering the controversial nature and the dry scientific contents of the book.

Whilst engaged in these and other strictly scientific inquiries, I could not prevent myself, however, from being carried away from time to time into the field of practical studies. My former connection with journalism in Constantinople, my having written an account of my travels, which has come out in fourteen different languages of Europe and Asia, and, ultimately, my having meddled, very soon after my return to Europe, with the question of Anglo-Russian rivalry—have very naturally led me when tired of dry philological researches to seek a change of occupation in the exciting literature of politics and of ethnography. Other scholars, particularly in Germany, were used to spend their leisure time in social circles, in beer and coffee-houses, or the like. I never knew, nor did I practise, any amusement in life; and when I wanted recreation I sat down to write a leading article on Central Asian politics to some leading paper, or I discussed the question of the day with my distant friends in England. I have been particularly delighted to freshen up the recollection of my wanderings and adventures in the various countries of the Mohammedan world, and to put these sundry sketches of the manners and customs of the various nations in Asia upon paper. In this way I had succeeded in writing a respectably long series of essays in the periodicals of Hungary, Germany and England. Soon I became, without noticing it, one of the most active publicists in Europe. Thanks to my never-failing health, I was able to work from eight to twelve hours daily, and in spite of this extraordinary exertion—for mental work is much harder than manual work—I found my greatest pleasure in this varied occupation of a political and scientific writer. But, alas! roses are seldom without thorns, and the first stings which I got came from a certain class of envious and bilious theoretical writers, who found fault with my doublesidedness and reproached me with the want of solidness and the desire for vainglory. As to the first I can assure my reader that, except during the first years of my appearance before the great public, I did not find a particular pleasure in my popularity; I got rather disgusted on finding my name dragged about at every opportunity, and on seeing that reputation is not always the fruit of honest labour and exertions. There was an impostor, a certain Mr. Davies, who delivered lectures under my name in America, and who coming over to Europe was discovered at Geneva by Professor Charles Vogt, who knew me personally, and who made it necessary for that pseudo-Vambéry to disappear for a time from Switzerland. There were several letters published in Italian and French papers bearing my signature, with the contents of which I did not agree, and which, although repudiated, did me great harm in certain circles. I was cited and quoted in reference to the most varied questions connected with the social and political conditions of the East, in a wrong way, and frequently in the sense contrary to the real meaning of my words. I ask then, Was this a pleasure, and could this degree of renown really offer any charm to a man spending his life in his library? As to the other count of the indictment, namely, the often repeated want of solidness, I fully admit that, as an autodidact, I certainly laboured to a great extent under this reproach, for autodidacts can rarely fill up the gap caused by a defective primary education. But on the other hand, travellers can rarely be shaped out of those students who have spent years at the universities. The exploring traveller is above all a man of practical tendencies, a man of facts; and as such his mode of thinking and his manner of writing must obviously differ from those of his fellow-writer who rarely or never left his room, and who becomes naturally a profound instead of an extensive writer. I could quote many an example to prove how my books, by being read in both hemispheres, have greatly contributed towards the popularization of the knowledge of Mohammedan Asia, and that even my strictly scientific publications, in spite of their defects, are still looked upon as path-openers in their respective branches of science. I repeat therefore that my bilious detractors have no reason to envy me, and still less to bring into discredit the fruit of my labours.

CHAPTER XXXIV.

MY POLITICAL WRITINGS.

HAVING dwelt rather longer than modesty should permit upon the personal details of my career, I must now turn to the question which has hitherto puzzled many people, namely, how I came into connection with English politics, and what were the chief motives of my becoming a zealous defender of British interests in Asia. Being neither an Englishman nor a politician by profession, I have been frequently asked, "What do I care about the future and the present doings of Great Britain in the East? Is there any want in England of authorities and of zealous supporters of my views?" It may be seen from what I have related in the preceding pages, that I am not at all an uncalled-for advocate, and that it was my quality as an eye-witness which brought me into the arena of political contest. The explanations I have to give refer, therefore, rather to the motives which have prompted me to adopt a certain line of policy, and to adhere to it with all the firmness which ripe deliberation and staunch conviction can and must give to the writer. I am neither prejudiced against Russia, nor am

I a blind Anglophile as people are apt to say. I have endeavoured always to be before all a man who, unbiassed by any sympathies or antipathies, is anxious to be of use to his fellow-creatures without any distinction of race or creed, and to whom the sacred cause of humanity in general lies more at heart than the petty quarrels of the various nations. Having come to the East in a tender age, when the man is easily impressed with the scenes around him, and when his feelings are easily engendered with compassion for the misery and misfortune of which he finds himself surrounded, I do not wonder that the unhappy condition, the poverty, the wretchedness, and particularly the despotic rule under which most of the Asiatic nations live, from the beginning deeply moved my heart, and engaged all my faculties upon the possible means of a change for the better. I greatly doubt whether the state of the European peasant in the most dark period of the Middle Ages was so oppressive as that of the present villagers in Turkey, Persia and Central Asia. A hard struggle for existence, poverty and thraldom may have been the equal lot of both; but the European tyranny was mitigated by religion and by the early laws of our social life, whilst in the East tyranny knows no bounds, and the poor victims have neither the understanding nor the courage to shake off the yoke by mutual resistance, or to look about for means of deliverance. Assistance is here unavoidably necessary, and assistance can come only from Europe, where, thanks to the fundamental conditions of our social existence and to the spirit which we have inherited from the old classic world, our civilization has so far progressed that man in full possession of his rights can already turn his eyes to those fellow-creatures of his who, less favoured by circumstances, are inferior to him. For there the duties of humanity obviously demand and fully justify his interference. These are my leading views on the mutual relation existing between the enlightened West and the unhappy East; and under such circumstances it may be easily understood that from the beginning the question, "Which of the European nations is most signally called upon to act as the vanguard of our modern civilization?" has greatly engaged my attention.

In looking upon Europe from this point of view, everybody will agree with me when I say that there are only three nations which deserve duly to be considered as the representatives of our Western civilization in the distant East—namely, France, Russia, and England. As to France, she has begun only quite recently to covet a far-stretching influence in the interior of Asia; but neither by her past nor her national individuality is she much fitted for such a task; excepting the sympathies she has gained among the Catholics in Syria, she has always acted either as a conqueror, or as a power in search of commercial treaties and as a protector of the Catholic missionaries. And besides, it must be openly stated that, with all her good intentions, France has not hitherto shown great ability as a civilizing Power, nor are Frenchmen prone to settle down in distant countries like the Anglo-Saxons. The condition of the Arabs and Berbers in Algeria has very little changed for the better in spite of a half-century of French rule. The Mohammedan children of the large towns are frequently paraded before the foreign visitor as being able to read on the black-board of the school the sentence, "Aimez la France comme votre seconde patrie," if written in big characters; but this forced emanation of patriotism does not extend to the villages, and still less to the desert, where French law is respected only in the immediate neighbourhood of the "Chasseurs d'Afrique." The French, a most amiable and enlightened nation, are, as foreign rulers, always wanting in staunchness of character and in institutions based upon liberty and equality: they cannot reconcile their own national interests with the welfare of the semi-civilized people entrusted to their care, and they will therefore never become teachers fully deserving their remuneration. We have to consider, therefore, as the future arbitrators of the destinies of Mohammedan Asia, either Russia or England, both mighty enough to support their civilizing efforts with the necessary material weight; both apt to leave a deep mark of their influence, but totally different in the effect of their acts. Russia enjoys decidedly the great advantage over England of much more easily assimilating the semi-civilized and barbarous Asiatics to the spirit of the bulk of the Russian people. The difference between the Russian officer, merchant and peasant, and the Sarts, Tadjiks, and Uzbegs of Central Asia, is certainly not so great and not so striking as is the gulf which separates the Englishman from the native of India, be he a Moslem or a Hindu. In spite of the undeniable progress of modern Russia, her sons are nevertheless still much imbued with the true Asiatic spirit. Similarity in modes of thinking and acting, in superstitions and in general views of life, give them an easy approach to the heart of the Oriental. He may hate them as Unbelievers and as conquerors, but he will like them as men and as jolly neighbours, who partake in his meal and will associate with him, using common manners and habits. The English officer who comes fresh from one of the university towns, or from Eton or Harrow to India, who has been brought up in accordance with the stiff rules of English etiquette, whose principles of cleanliness, manliness and dignity are of the most solid kind, and who will naturally get convinced of his superiority over the Asiatic—such an Englishman can hardly be expected to squat down with a Hindu and to partake of a dish of rice swimming in ghee; he will not listen to the Hindu superstitions, he will not vie with the Hindu in mendacity as the Russian does in the company of Sarts, and consequently the Englishman will hardly or never become the intimate of the follower of Vishnu or Mohammed in India. I do not say that this exclusiveness, however justified, is praiseworthy, or an assistance to the civilizing efforts of the English in Asia—as I would not and could not underrate the value of the Russian gift of assimilation. But we have to deal with facts, which prove that the English, in spite of their shortcomings, have succeeded far better than their rivals of the North, and that they have turned up entirely the detestable bog of Oriental vices and abuses, whilst the Russians have hardly succeeded in touching the surface. It must moreover be conceded that the Asiatics entrusted to the care of Russia were alien to the old and genuine civilization of the East, and consequently were much more amenable to modern culture than the Hindu, whose stubbornness is backed by a civilization many thousand years old. Lastly, we may also consider the length of time employed in the work: whereas England has ruled over India for only a hundred years, Russia has been the mistress of Kazan, Astrakhan and of the whole northern Moslem world for more than three centuries. Suffice it to add that the main difference between these two agents of our modern culture in the East can be summed up in the following remark. Russia conquers in order to Russianize and to absorb all the various nationalities in the large body of the Russian people, whilst England conquers in order to civilize, to give the unhappy nations in Asia for a while an education, and to let them afterwards loose, matured in liberal institutions, able to take care of themselves.

These are the leading principles which I have followed in my political writings during the last nineteen years. The greater the opposition which my views met with, the more did I feel the necessity of coming forward with fresh arguments and with new facts. It was certainly no easy task to watch from my quiet studio at Budapest all the diplomatic and military movements relating to Central Asia. In these my efforts, I was assisted first of all by assiduously reading the Russian, English and Persian papers; secondly, by the correspondence of a friend of mine stationed in Samarkand and in Khodjend; and thirdly, by sundry news which I got from Meshed and through Bokhara pilgrims in Constantinople. It is an unpromising source of information, certainly not so costly as that derived from European diplomacy in Asia; but still it has worked well, and it has happened several times that my letters, published in the *Times*, in the *Allgemeine Zeitung*, or in some geographical paper, have raised a question in the Houses of Parliament, or caused a lively discussion in the daily press. I do not exaggerate in saying that the number of the leading articles, letters and paragraphs on Central Asia published by me, anonymously or signed, in different English, German, French and Hungarian papers, amount to several hundreds, not mentioning the larger essays I wrote annually in various periodicals of Europe. The result of this persevering work was my gradually increasing influence in the press on one side, and the great hatred and animosity of my political adversaries on the other side. To the number of the latter belonged, as may be easily imagined, all the Russians, together with the Russophile portion of partly German, partly French publicists, who, either from an ill-digested idea of our civilizing mission in the East, or from an innate antipathy to and jealousy of the English, continually attacked my views, and were always ready to attribute anti-Russian writings either to my so-called national rancour against the Russians, or to my predilection for the English.

I need scarcely say that both suppositions were unfounded and erroneous from every point of view. As a Hungarian, I certainly had no reason whatever to fall in love with Russia, whom I saw in the prime of my life as the oppressor of the national aspirations to liberty and independence of my own country. The Russian campaign in Hungary in 1849 is engraved with indelible characters in the heart of every Magyar; and although the late Emperor Nicholas bitterly repented his brotherly service rendered to Austria, and notwithstanding that every Russian soldier has since torn from his breast the medal bearing the inscription "Vengria (Hungary) 1849," we Hungarians still couple the name of "Muscovite" with wilful tyranny and with all the horrors of despotism and barbarism. But, as I said before, this personal or national feeling of mine has nothing to do with the tendency of my political writings on Asia. Here I do not act as a Hungarian, but as a man in whose eyes free thoughts and liberal institutions constitute the real and only happiness of our existence, and to whom science, wealth, fame and even national greatness is nothing, if he cannot say "I am free!" I may be called an idealist, or a dreamer, but I cannot help it; these are my notions of life, and with these notions I certainly could not become an advocate of Russian supremacy in Asia. I could not join the chorus of those who cried, "Central-Asians are barbarians; the sooner they are brought upon the path of modern civilization the better for the sake of humanity; even the Russian dose of culture is a boon to them." No! I could not agree with these, for I always said, "Yes, the people of Central Asia are wild barbarians, the light of our Western culture is there urgently wanted; but if there is a choice of the torchbearer, I give preference to the English—to the nation which, be it in consequence of its insular home or of any other reason, undoubtedly stands at the top of our civilization. England will certainly do more honour to Europe than the semi-Asiatic Muscovite."

It was in consequence of this judgment of mine that I was held up to reproach as a blind Anglomaniac, who had no eye for the numerous and heavy faults of the English, and who above all did not see that sordid egotism and selfishness by which Great Britain is actuated in her doings abroad, and particularly in her colonial policy. Now upon this question long series of books have been written, and will be written; but, engaged upon studies of men and nations as I was from the early period of my life, I beg to have my own opinion, an opinion based upon autopsy and formed during many years of personal contact, while visiting more than thirty different towns of the United Kingdom. Well, this opinion of mine has taught me that there is a good deal to blame in the individuality as well as in the national character of the Englishman, but in spite of his defects he must still be looked upon as the only perfect representative of all those qualities which have made our Western culture victorious over the East.

The liberal institutions in which the Englishman is brought up have made him straightforward and open-hearted; the damp and foggy air in which he lives has made him stern and reflective; and the continually increasing struggle for existence has strained his nerves to an unexampled activity and to that perseverance called "British clamminess." He is therefore the real embodiment of the European spirit—the rightful civilizer of Asia.

As to the strongly and frequently blamed egotism of English policy in Asia, the belief in which has taken such a deep root in Europe, and the origin of which may be traced to the first decades of the present century, when France tried to denounce her formidable rival, I much doubt whether the inventors of this calumny are *näif* enough to believe in it. I do not except even Macaulay, who out of party spirit, or, what is more probable, from want of accurate information as to the real character of the Asiatics, used his eloquent pen in favour of the oppressed Hindus. Before all, I beg leave to ask, Where in the world is a man or a nation which enters on a perilous undertaking without the hope of, what I call, an honourable benefit for its services? Were the Greeks and Romans better in this regard? Were they not remunerated with the riches of Europe and of Asia for their civilizing work?—which was certainly much inferior to that of Great Britain, who never paraded with long files of captives fettered to the car of her triumphant generals, and whose legions have never trampled upon the liberty of peoples subdued in Asia. You must not read Sir Richard Temple's "India in 1882," but look into the annual reports published by the late Garcin de Tassy on the educational progress in India, on the liberal institutions introduced in the civil administration of the country, and how the ryot, so hardly oppressed by his native ruler, is now raising his head and begins to feel himself a man, replaced in the right which God has given to him! Read these eulogies bestowed by a Frenchman upon England's services to the sacred cause of humanity in the East, and you will not find it extravagant when these services are remunerated by good salaries given to civil and military officers in India; when English commercial houses make good businesses. The exchequer has hardly any profit from it, as the annual estimates of the Indian budget sufficiently prove! I compare the *rôle* of the agents of our Western culture in Asia or in Africa to that of a teacher in a private house; so long as we do not find a teacher who takes an engagement of mere passion and refuses a salary for his troublesome office, so long we have no right to reproach England or any other civilizing power with the material profits gained through the faithful fulfilment of her vocation. This is a just remuneration, and by no means a spoliation dictated by egotism!

If, therefore, my critics will admit the motives here enumerated, I hope that they will modify their opinion with regard to the tendency of my writings. Of those who impute to me base motives, I do not speak at all; my memoirs, which will be published after my death, will show them what allurements have been offered in order to silence my pen; and that there was a time when my publications and my lectures in England did not remain at all unnoticed on the banks of the Neva.

Strange to say, however, it was not only the Russian press in which I was vehemently attacked, and it is not only in Russia where I am looked upon as *Diabolis rotæ;* in England itself I have to meet sometimes with the most passionate antagonism, and am often exposed to a severe and unjust criticism. I have received during late years dozens of anonymous letters in which I am called an insolent intruder, and in which I am advised, not in very flattering terms, "to padddle my own canoe"—to look after the politics of my own country, and not to meddle with the affairs of England, which has no need of my experiences, and which has got authorities better informed and more able to judge on Central Asian matters than I am. I need scarcely say that these warnings came mostly from those persons known as enraged Liberals, who find fault with my staunch adherence to the cause of the Conservative party of Great Britain. If my connection with the said party arose in consequence of my views on the interior politics of England, then my impolite adversaries would be decidedly right, for neither have I got sufficient knowledge in that regard, nor do I feel a particular interest in the home affairs of England. The preference I give to the policy of the Conservatives is mainly based upon the fact that all the steps which have led Great Britain to extend her influence over Asia are more or less owing to the political views of that party, a party which has got a better appreciation of a truly imperial policy, and whose larger views coincide the much more with my own desires, as England is being brought by them in the foremost line of the countries to civilize Asia. The second reason for my adherence to the Conservatives lies in the fundamental principles of Conservative politicians in general, who, according to their motto, "*Festina lente*," have always manifested a particular care not to tumble topsy-turvy institutions sanctioned by old age; with them the necessary changes are gradually worked out, and under their guidance the feeling of the stationary and strictly Conservative Asiatics are less hurt than by the feverish activity of the over-hasty Liberals, who very often chase wild illusions, and naturally run the risk of causing great confusion, as may be seen quite recently by the introduction of the disastrous "Ilbert Bill."

I fully understand that in Europe, and with our thronging and pressing desire for progress, the Conservatives are not always in the proper place; but it is quite different in Asia, where their principles are the best guarantee for success, and where they alone can produce that change so much desired for the sake of humanity, liberty and enlightenment. In order to quote a striking example, I must point to the great difference between the harshly-proceeding Russia and the gradually progressing England. Russia is looked upon in Mohammedan Asia as a destructive and annihilating Power, whilst England has been called until quite recently—until indeed the last Turko-Russian war—a benignant Power which spares and protects, and which will never try to absorb foreign elements into her national body. Everything solid and truthful was connected throughout Turkey, Persia and the north of Africa with the name of England; and if those Liberal Hotspurs had heard and seen what I experienced in my travels, they certainly would have considered twice before they filled their mouths with all kinds of invectives against their "unspeakable Turk;" before they put "The Comedy of Dulcigno" upon the stage; and before they entered into the venturesome affair in Egypt. Considering the valuable services which England can render to the cause of civilization in Asia, it is most desirable that this good reputation of hers should be kept up as long as possible; and since the Conservative statesmen of Great

Britain have been identified with this policy of indulgence and of a slow but sure progress, I have always given preference to their rule, and I shall always side with them in questions relating to the civilizing influence of England in the Mohammedan East.

I may conclude with the saying, "*Dixi et salvavi animam.*" I have exposed to the reader the reasons which have brought me into the arena of political contest; I have shown the motives which have led me hitherto, and which will lead me also in future, in my views on England's mission in the East—a part of our world for which I shall always feel the deepest interest. There is scarcely anything in the world which would shake my conviction with regard to these opinions of mine. Having already behind me a half-century of hard struggles, and being inured and hardened by the continual fight with the most singular freaks of fate, I shall probably maintain my actual position in the defence of my own views to the last moment of my existence. I hope I shall never have to repent the extraordinary fatigues and troubles with which I had to proceed on the thorny path; and if the last rays of the parting sun of my life approaches, I still shall say, "It was a hot, but a fine day, sir!"